The Role and Limits of Government

Essays in Political Economy

Samuel Brittan

TEMPLE SMITH · LONDON

First published in Great Britain in 1983
by Maurice Temple Smith Ltd
Jubilee House, Chapel Road
Hounslow, Middlesex TW3 1TX

© 1983 Samuel Brittan

Brittan, Samuel
    The role and limits of government
    1. Great Britain — Economic conditions — 1945 -
    I. Title
    330.941'0858   HC255.6

ISBN 0-85117-237-7 hbk
ISBN 0-85117-241-5 pbk

Typeset in 11 on 12 point Times by Tellgate Ltd,
Shaftesbury, Dorset
Printed in Great Britain by
The Camelot Press Ltd, Southampton

Contents

CHARTS

TABLES

Acknowledgements and Sources

The following list indicates where the original versions of the essays, most considerably changed for the present book, appeared. I am extremely grateful to the journals concerned for permission to republish.

Chapter 1, *Encounter*, May 1981.
Chapter 2, *Oxford Economic Paper*, November 1983.
Chapter 3, *Encounter*, January 1980.

Part II and some sections of Chapter 8 are based on a 'Hobart Paper', *How to End the Monetarist Controversy*, published by the Institute of Economic Affairs, London, in 1980. I am most grateful to the Institute for permission to make use of as much or as little of the Paper as I liked with as much or as little amendment as seemed appropriate.

Chapter 9, *Foreign Affairs*, special issue 'America and the World', February 1983.
Chapter 10, *Journal of Law and Economics*, Vol. XXI, October 1978.
Chapter 11, *The Washington Quarterly*, Summer 1983.

Preface

This book is a sequel to an earlier collection of essays entitled *The Economic Consequences of Democracy*, which appeared in 1977. The main themes of the earlier volume are carried forward here. The essays are, however, longer and fewer in number; and they have been extensively revised to form a unified whole.

Part I covers some fundamental issues of collective decision and political values, the scope of which extends outside what is conventionally regarded as economic policy. It is in the hope of attracting attention to these essays that I undertook the work required to put this book together.

One theme of Part I is that many people have excessive expectations from government, which prevents government from performing its proper functions as well as it might. The theme is taken up in Part II, 'How to End the Monetarist Controversy', which is basically an essay covering what is usually called, not too happily, 'economic management'. Readers of the original 'Hobart Paper' of that title will find some differences and I hope improvements. On the other hand some of the more detailed material on monetary and fiscal policy has been, as the saying goes, 'crowded out', and interested readers are referred to the original.

Part III applies the main ideas to problems such as the unemployment explosion and the strains and stresses which have developed in the world economy. Part IV considers the case of Britain as one instance of these problems. Some British examples are used in earlier chapters to illustrate problems which affect most countries and the international economy as a whole.

A theme common both to *The Economic Consequences of Democracy* and to the present volume is the strains brought about by the incompatible claims of rival interest groups, which inevitably acquire influence when governments take on ambitious economic functions. Misguided financial policies can aggravate these strains and well-chosen ones alleviate them a little; but no financial policy will remove the underlying problems in which financial crises have their roots. In the earlier volume, I expressed doubts about the future of liberal democracy because of its inability either to tame interest group pressure directly, or to do so indirectly by abandoning the commitment to full employment – inflation being able to buy only a limited amount of time which came to an end some time in the 1970s.[1] If democracy has survived better than some of us feared, it has been because it has after all abandoned full employment. Am I alone, among members of the non-collectivist limited government school, in regarding this as an unsatisfactory and doubtfully desirable basis of survival?

A reader's health warning is in order. The order of presentation starts with the general and moves on to the particular. This seems logical; but it does mean that Parts I and II are somewhat more abstract than the remainder of the book; and some readers might prefer to start with the essays on current problems and policies in Parts III and IV. The most straightforward Chapters in the earlier parts are 1 and 4; and the most complex are 2 and 5.

It is impracticable to list the many people who were kind enough to help me with the original versions of the essays or who discussed them with me afterwards. I must however mention David Willetts who gave me indispensable assistance in revising and recasting the essay on Utilitarianism and indeed on the structure and content of Part I as a whole. Since that part is the keystone of the whole book, it follows that the book could not have appeared without his help. But I must emphasise that he is in no way responsible for, or committed to, any of the judgments on policy questions in any part of the book, all of which are entirely my responsibility.

I must also thank Anne Shotts and Viviene Richards who translated and typed a mass of scribble with which they have somehow learned to cope. In a just world they would have been co-authors.

PART I

Political Expectations

1   The Wenceslas Myth

The confusion; Opportunity cost; The myth in history; The competence factor; Brickbats and blessings; 'Costless' reforms?; Governments and individuals.

The confusion

A celebrated Christmas carol records the good deed of a tenth-century monarch, St Wenceslas, the prince-duke and patron saint of Bohemia. The monarch shared some of his own wealth with a poor man gathering winter fuel. The deed was one of personal generosity, and required no taxes or levies on his subjects. If such acts were repeated on any scale – and the legend hints that the incident was typical – they would have been costly for Wenceslas.

Even the one recorded act involved a personal cost, a march 'through the rude wind's wild lament and the bitter weather'. While his page shared in the physical effort, the brunt was borne by the monarch who marked the initial footsteps in the snow. His gesture was intended as an example to other feudal leaders, of which he was *primus inter pares*, and to lesser lords all the way down the social scale.

> *Therefore, Christian men be sure,*
> *Wealth or rank possessing,*
> *Ye who now will bless the poor,*
> *Shall yourselves find blessing.*

Contrast Wenceslas's gesture with the small bonus (£10 from 1979) which it has become customary for the British Chancellor of the Exchequer to 'give' at Christmas. This involves no personal sacrifice whatever by any minister; it is a pure transfer from other taxpayers and can be given whether the Chancellor is personally generous or stingy. The whole institution started as a temporary measure for injecting spending power in the 1972 recession; but no British government could now go back on the bonus, without a great outcry. A government which increased it would, on the other hand, be praised for that if for nothing else.

It is the discussion of the Chancellor's bonus as if it were the generosity of Good King Wenceslas which epitomises the myth of government that penetrates nearly all political discussion today. According to the myth there exist tiny handfuls of people known as 'governments' who could so act as to increase the supply of satisfactions enjoyed by the population if only they chose to do so, but through malevolence or inefficiency do not.

Most political arguments are between rival groups. They may be economic-interest groups or groups holding different beliefs about Sunday observance or the importance of retaining an historic capital such as Jerusalem. The extraordinary aspect of these conflicts is the way in which people hoodwink themselves into inventing a scapegoat: as a result their disputes are to be conducted vicariously by praising or blaming twenty-odd people around a cabinet table. If everyone blames 'the government', antagonisms between conflicting groups are softened but at the expense of fostering illusions and excessive expectations. The worst sufferers from the illusion are not the extreme partisans who believe that everything depends on their own side being in power, but the *soi disant* cynics, who never tire of decrying the self-serving or incompetent nature of all politicians, and behind whose cry 'They are all a lot of rascals . . .' is the wishful thought '. . . Otherwise they would make us all better off.'

Lurking behind the Wenceslas myth is the true and, indeed, platitudinous statement that at all periods in history human societies have failed to arrange their collective affairs as well as they might. There are ways of improving the rules governing relations between citizens. The position of some groups could be furthered at the expense of other groups. Alternatively – but more rarely – they could be favoured by a more efficient set of policies, which would improve the trade-off between the groups. Such changes may be called 'improvement in government competence'. Proposals for reform contain a mixture of suggestions for improved competence and changes in the distribution of wealth or power. The two elements are usually very difficult to disentangle.

Precisely because many of the subsequent chapters in this book are concerned with government competence and how it can be improved, it is all the more essential not to entertain exaggerated hopes in this direction. The amount of improvement that is possible in a few years through better government policies is often overstated. Easy changes, which involve neither disturbing interest groups nor taking from some to give to others, have usually already been made under normal democratic pressures.

Apart from enforcing rules, governments are responsible for services, like defence, which people believe are better provided collectively from taxation than individually through the market or voluntary effort. Collective or 'public' goods have the technical quality of being either indivisible (such as defence) or difficult to charge separately to each individual user (such as clean air). Certain services such as schooling may appear to be divisible and easy to price; but there are spillover benefits – for instance in widespread literacy – over and above the gains of an individual pupil. Demarcation between public and private goods will always be in part a political issue.

In all modern states, the government also undertakes some redistribution of income. At the very least it accepts some responsibility for the old, the poor and the sick; and it may also take a more comprehensive view of wealth and income distribution. Redistribution is at its most obvious in the tax and social security system; but almost every government service, rule or regulation is redistributive in that it imposes a cost on some people and (sometimes) confers a gain on others.

Opportunity costs

The notion outlined above is nothing more than the economist's concept of opportunity cost – that to have more of one thing you have to have less of other things. If the 'government' – that is citizens acting through a central collective agency – spends more on roads or military hardware it has less available for health services or pensions or cutting taxes. These latter foregone benefits are the cost of the expenditure – money being just a conventional token or measuring rod.

The Wenceslas myth is simply the neglect of this truism which occurs in nearly all debates on public policy. Economists often fall for the myth themselves when they become so excited about what they believe to be the shortcomings in government competence, especially in the overall 'management' of the economy, that they too appear to be presenting costless options.

Reactions to this thesis have varied between dismissal of it as obvious, and vehement denunciation of it for allegedly denying the benefit of any government action in favour of a pitiless *laissez-faire*. Both reactions are misguided. So far from being obvious, hardly anyone involved in public affairs avoids the fallacy in practical instances, as subsequent examples will show. Nor is there anything in the thesis which restricts the sphere of collectively determined actions. The anti-Wenceslas argument is simply that, however collectivist – or market oriented – are our decisions, there will still be an opportunity cost in carrying out any desired objective. Other objectives will have, to some degree, to be sacrificed and some people will be worse off as a result. The government has no resources, but is simply an agency for carrying out those decisions which, rightly or wrongly, are taken collectively rather than left to the market or voluntary action. To ask the 'government' to be 'less mean' towards a particular deserving course is a bad shorthand way of asking for some of our fellow citizens to be 'less mean'. It is *bad* shorthand because it avoids the problem of cost allocation.

Each of us wants the benefit of services while transferring the cost to some other group; but we evade the problem of deciding who should be the losers when we pretend it would vanish if only we had better government. At bottom lies the infantile belief that the government ought to be able to manage the totality of our affairs so that we can *all* have more of something without less of something else. Much of what purports to be criticism of the conduct of the public services is really a cry by particular interest groups for more redistribution towards themselves, enhanced or rationalised by an excessive expectation of what governments can do to boost the national economy so that other identifiable groups do not have to be asked too obviously to pay the cost.

The Wenceslas myth is of course a special case of the fallacy of the 'free lunch'. The invocation of the old Christmas carol further provides some insight into its probable historical origin and its perennial appeal. It is also more accurate than the more popular version: 'There is no Father Christmas.' For King Wenceslas, unlike Father Christmas, really did exist and could well have carried out the actions described in the carol, which would be quite unfeasible for any modern ruler.

The myth in history

In the early days of monarchy, kings disposed of substantial personal resources, and there was no clear division between their own income and wealth and that of the state. If a medieval monarch spent a great deal on the relief of poverty, as King Wenceslas did, it was an act of personal generosity. Luxurious spending, lavish courts, endowments to the church, the relief of poverty or military expeditions were alternative uses of resources. Although most monarchs did all these things, doing one more than another had a cost in terms of alternatives foregone.

The absence of unsuccessful wars and the plunder from successful ones (defined as those in which his own territory was not ravaged) were probably more important to the medieval subject than conspicuous acts of generosity. The whole package of burdens and benefits varied according to the ability of the ruler. Although taxation existed and was a matter of bitter complaint, the ideal was that 'the King should live of his own'. It made sense to speak of 'good kings' and 'bad kings' and to praise or blame them for some small part of the fluctuations of prosperity and adversity experienced by their subjects.

Apart from the hangover from the period of feudal monarchs with substantial personal resources relative to the small populations they ruled, another historical origin lies behind the belief that the government has or should have resources which could 'make us all better off'.

The 'voyages of discovery' in the sixteenth century led to a blossoming of enterprises which had both commercial and governmental aspects. They were often concerned with the development of virgin or colonial territories, or extending trade together with the flag. The best-known example was the East India Company; others were concerned with the development of North American lands for the benefit of the Crown. Definable profit-and-loss criteria applied to their activities. In our own day the New Town Corporations exercise similar activities on a modest scale; and criteria such as the ability to attract industry and population, or rateable value, can be applied.

There are also activities of a purely voluntary kind – such as tennis clubs – which exercise some coercive governmental powers over their members by mutual consent, their final sanction being that of expulsion. The most spectacular examples of organisations with a declared purpose, with their own internal authorities or rules but no ultimate resort to police powers, are the large commercial corporations.

Exaggeration of the similarities between modern government and all these different types of bodies has led to what Michael Oakeshott calls the view of the state as an enterprise association.[1] In the business community there have at times been calls for a '*Great Britain Ltd*' approach, or a '*US Inc.*' Its exponents would like the government to act as the board of a super conglomerate to promote the interests of national companies in competition against foreigners. Such 'corporatists' are fond of talking about the help allegedly given by Japanese and French governments to their industries in contrast to the attitude of Anglo-American governments.

This view is based on a curious travesty of the 'Invisible Hand' doctrine. The striving of rival companies for profit will, under the right institutional environment (and with well-known exceptions), promote the welfare of the community. But to apply the corporate analogy to government involves the fallacy of composition – of supposing that, because it may be sensible for an individual company to maximise profits within a framework of law and against a background of competition, it is sensible for governments to use their powers to maximise the profits of the totality of resident companies by means such as subsidies, import barriers, contract preferences, etc.

Internationally, the strategy has all the wastefulness of wars and armament races. The rival activities of different governments largely cancel out, at great expense to their countrymen. It is a negative sum game from which all lose. Even if there were no retaliation, the strategy makes no sense for the rulers of an individual nation. The competitive striving of rival companies may help to keep business on its toes, but where there is artificial support of the whole corporate sector the element of compulsive transfer destroys the profit motive as a criterion of success in meeting social needs.

The corporate analogy is wrong, root and branch. A company is judged *inter alia* by the dividends and profits it produces: the success of a tennis club may be a little more subjective, but it clearly has something to do with the provision of facilities for playing tennis and perhaps also with the club's record in competitive matches. A nation may have a similar all-out objective during a total war. Just possibly, if a 'moral majority' is interested in a religious crusade (and in imposing a pattern of practice and behaviour to the exclusion of every other consideration) the state can also be considered as one gigantic enterprise. But in most modern countries, most of the time, the citizens have a variety of individual objectives rather than one all-embracing purpose. It is the misplaced desire to subject these conflicting individual purposes to some supposed overall national objective which often lies behind the misplaced patriotism and moralistic exhortation of so many political pronouncements. Citizen welfare is not one single objective; it is an abstract summary of the host of diverse desires and needs of individual human beings.

The competence factor

There is a further force encouraging the myth of omnipotent and omniscient governments – quite apart from the persistence of attitudes appropriate to benevolent medieval monarchs and misapplied corporate analogies. It arises from the deep-seated temptation for modern rulers to make exaggerated claims for the potential contribution of improved governmental competence to the general well-being.

In a democratic system rulers have to respond to a wide range of popular opinions and cannot indulge their personal whims in the way of a medieval monarch, or rule openly in the interests of a small clique of privileged families as in some of the old city states. Yet just when the picture of 'good kings' and 'bad kings' is at its most absurd, the electorate is most prone to classify its rulers as bad kings who ought to be good: that is, it vastly exaggerates the role of governmental competence in personal welfare. Politicians themselves, as part of the vote-bidding process, encourage the public to dodge the inconvenient question of who is to lose from the proposed changes and over-emphasise the competence factor. A promise of improved competence is almost the only way in which politicians can bid for votes without alienating one group or another. Those who lose by the transfer of resources as a result of official policies or the ordinary passage of events will blame government, while those who gain will ascribe this good fortune to their own efforts, or to luck, or will merely take it for granted. Even those who are not at present suffering tend to identify with the losers, perhaps because of the satisfactions of costless altruism or the feeling that 'There, but for the Grace of God, go I.'

The question posed by Lester Thurow[2] – 'If elected, whose income do you and your party plan to cut in the process of solving the economic problems facing us?' – is not merely unwelcome to politicians; it is rarely asked by voters. At bottom they would rather not know that any substantial group will be hurt and insist on the political game being 'positive sum' to a far greater extent than is remotely feasible.

Promises of improved competence may run into a credibility problem, but will not threaten the interests of potential voters. 'Improved competence' can describe a wide variety of projects. It may range from general undertakings to 'cut waste in government' to new ways of running the economy – whether Incomes Policy, or Demand Management, or 'Monetarism' – which are supposed to make *everyone* better off. Even where these theories have validity, they will be prescribed as costless soft options. For instance, 'control of the money supply' was too often presented in the 1970s as a technical device which would stop inflation painlessly. There was little emphasis on the fact that its introduction was likely to mean higher interest rates, limits on government spending, or higher taxes – although a 'reduction in the growth of the money supply' is little more than a rule-of-thumb for assessing what is necessary in a programme of restraint.

Brickbats and blessings

An almost pure example of self-delusion is to be found in the perennial arguments on Child Benefits – transfers of income to families with children from those who have none, i.e. the rest of the population. Such transfers are to be found in the tax and social security systems of most western countries.

Popular discussion of the size of these benefits illustrates the twin aspects of the Wenceslas myth: government as scapegoat, and government as universal provider. However much one supports Child Benefits, there is only one source from which they can come: the tax-paying population. Yet government ministers are attacked for 'meanness' or 'narrow-mindedness' in not making them sufficiently generous, as if the politician concerned had the personal wherewithal to be mean or generous on that scale. Any attacks ought to be on the meanness of our fellow-citizens whose views the government is trying to interpret and implement. It is equally absurd that when Child Benefits are increased (or merely maintained in real terms in the face of inflation) governments are praised for their achievements. If anybody should be praised it is the taxpayers who have made income-transfers to those with children.

Paradoxically, claims to competence tend to exclude genuine reforms, which normally involve a jolt to some group or other, even if only a shock to traditional habits and reactions. The main political reason for economic inefficiency and slow growth in an advanced industrial country is the special privileges claimed and demanded by hordes of special interest groups.

Take the housing market. Any worthwhile reform would bring (at least initially) higher rents for tenants and higher tax payments for owner occupiers. Even though most people would gain from the consequent reduction in basic tax rates, from lower house prices and reduced distortions in the housing market, the immediate impact on the mortgage holder and tenant will attract most attention. It is not surprising that governments run away from such reforms and pledge themselves to maintain tax exemption on mortgage interest and (sometimes) to hold down rents and mortgage interest levels – actions which, however attractive to those looking for costless gifts, make the real problems worse.

Exaggerated hopes from improved government competence play into the hands of groups looking for special privilege for themselves. A subsidy to home owners, financed by taxes on people who are on average worse off, becomes easier to advocate if it is called a 'policy for housing'. Subsidies for unprofitable industries, or new industrial projects with little prospect of paying their way, are more easily maintained if they can be disguised as 'industrial policies' or 'a strategy for advanced technology'.

The most subtle examples of the Wenceslas myth occur when governments are blamed for features of the environment over which they have a deceptive appearance of influence. As a result of North Sea oil, the UK needs fewer non-oil exports to pay its way in the world at any given level of activity. This is an undoubted benefit, as living standards can be higher, but it comes about in part through a higher real exchange rate (i.e. the exchange rate after allowing for international inflation differences), which puts pressure on the profit margins of companies concerned with internationally traded products.

Was there no way in which a British Government could have brought down the real exchange rate and raised non-oil exports to a level uninfluenced by North Sea oil? It could have followed the memorable advice of Sir Michael Edwardes given when chairman of British Leyland: 'Leave the bloody stuff in the ground. . .' Even then funds would probably have moved to London on the strength of the untapped oil reserves. To be absolutely sure of preventing any impact on the real exchange-rate, the government would also have had to take measures to destroy the attractions of the City of London as a financial centre. Needless to say, both actions would have hit living standards. The 'Wenceslas' mistake was to suppose that the government, merely by pulling a few interest and exchange-rate levers, could have achieved results which could not in fact have been achieved without profound and painful policy changes which business lobbyists would have been the first to oppose.

The crowning irony is reached when agencies which themselves share a good deal of responsibility for some social evil lead an agitation to blame government. A typical example is trade-union agitation against high unemployment. If there is one agency which exerts might-and-main to prevent wages from reaching market-clearing levels, where demand for labour balances supply, it is the unions – not only by collective bargaining under the strike threat, but by political support for minimum wages or uniform rates for adults and young people (or between regions), all of which price people out of jobs. At the political level, too, it is precisely those MPs who are most vociferous in support of subsidised housing and rent-control (which discourage workers from moving to where the jobs are) who are usually in the forefront of agitation against high unemployment.

The Wenceslas myth is rampant on the political Right as well as on the Left. One might, of course, expect overblown views on the paternalistic Right about what governments can achieve; but they exist in good measure among politicians who preach a private-enterprise, free-market rhetoric. While the basic mistake of the interventionists is to exaggerate the effects of government action, the mistake of the free-market school is to exaggerate the benefits of government withdrawal. Both Thatcherite British Conservatives and Reaganite American Republicans originally expected miracles of improved growth from marginal reductions in public spending or taxes as a proportion of the national product. They also spread mistaken ideas of the ease with which such spending could be cut. Waste exists largely because it is undiscovered or difficult to dislodge, and despite pledges to cut waste, conservative governments in the event either have to reduce services or go back on their promised tax cuts – usually both.

Many European countries, with real growth-rates much higher than America or Britain, have the same or even higher public spending or tax ratios. The argument for individual families providing their own unsubsidised housing, or making a greater contribution to the costs of education or medical care – and paying less in taxes – relates to freedom of choice, and perhaps to the efficiency of these particular services. It should not be based on highly doubtful speculations about the resulting effect on overall economic performance.

One deceptively dangerous slogan (highly popular among British Conservatives) is: 'Monetarism is not enough.' It could simply be a reminder that a limitation on monetary growth can contain inflation, but cannot solve other economic problems or provide a magic carpet to prosperity. Unfortunately this slogan is invoked most frequently (contrary to the intention of its inventor, Sir Keith Joseph) to suggest that interventionist policies exist which can solve these other economic problems and provide a short-cut to general prosperity. For example, it is often suggested that the proceeds of North Sea oil could be 'invested' in British industry irrespective of the rate of return – in the same way as the state has supported projects like Concorde, British Leyland or British Steel (enterprises, it should be remembered, which had no pejorative or jocular connotations when they were first established).

'Costless' reforms?

One of the worst examples of the Wenceslas myth on the conservative side was that known among US Republicans as 'supply-side economics', with which the Reagan Administration came to office in the USA in 1981, but from which it was eventually forced to retreat. Supply-side economics was the complete opposite of what its name suggested. It was not a careful study of the malfunctioning of particular markets with a view to removing distortions. On the contrary, it was an assertion that large across-the-board cuts in personal tax could be combined with increased defence spending without inflationary consequences or deep cuts elsewhere, because of the productivity miracle it would release. As a practical remedy, it was identical with the demand boosts so beloved by Keynesian economists who accept deficit spending. Yet the Republican 'supply-siders' also argued fervently for the balanced budget which they claimed could paradoxically be achieved by *cutting* taxes.

The whole activity known as 'economic management' will be discussed in later chapters, but it is worth looking here at its general nature. Economic management usually refers to such matters as monetary, fiscal (i.e. budgetary) and exchange-rate policy, by which governments try to stabilise the economy and minimise both inflation and unemployment. At first sight it might seem like a pure search for increased competence whereby the government can provide winners without losers and the Wenceslas myth does not apply. Such free benefits almost disappear, however, on closer examination.

Let us take a decision to provide public works or cut taxes in a very severe recession and support the moves by a policy of monetary ease. Who might suffer? There is first the risk that interest rates will rise because of inflationary fears. Some people may suffer more from higher interest rates than they gain from the overall stimulus. There is also a very good chance that inflation will be worse – even if it only falls less quickly – than if no stimulus is undertaken. There is also the risk that the diagnosis of the unemployment is wrong; that it is not the type which will react to a demand stimulus, or that the stimulus will take effect just as a boom is in any case about to get under way. In either of these cases the gainers are those who benefit directly from the new expenditures or tax cuts; the losers those who suffer when the brakes have to be slammed on again.

The great difference between economic management and other government domestic activity is the enormous amount of uncertainty and risk. There is uncertainty about the identity of the gainers and the losers from taking a risk with either inflation or employment. There is uncertainty about the immediate diagnosis. Most important of all, there is uncertainty about which economic theories of cause and effect apply. Riskless ways of boosting the economy are hardly ever to be found. If they really are known to be riskless they will already have been followed.

On rare occasions it is possible to see with hindsight how sheer intellectual improvement in the management of our affairs could have led to very large gains at very little cost: more of something without too much less of something else. In the early 1930s, the US Government and the Federal Reserve Board *might*, by preventing the destruction of the US money supply, have raised welfare without imposing great costs on anyone. Governments in the 1960s may have also sometimes harmed the public interest (with little to show in return) by hanging on too long to over-valued currency parities.

In later chapters I argue that we have witnessed another such rare occasion in the early 1980s. In this period, many governments, including the British and American, made mistakes in financial policy, which interacted on a world level and made the prevailing recession – the most severe since World War Two – worse than it need have been; and it would have been possible to have avoided some of the loss of output and employment without a reacceleration of inflation.

I am therefore myself in the need of the reminder that occasions when intellectual ingenuity might make it possible for nearly everyone to gain are indeed rare. What should be done on these occasions is seldom obvious at the time and normally remains controversial even to historians. The great mistake is to take such rare periods – when it *might* be possible for nearly everyone to gain, without any clear losers – as the model for public discussion. It is this fallacy which lies behind the media search for 'a new Keynes' who will find some costless technical formula for solving all our problems.

Professional economists are not immune to such delusions. How else can one explain the popularity of gimmicks such as 'tax-imposed prices-and-incomes policies' (TIP) to counter that unfortunate combination of unemployment and inflation known by the ungainly name of 'stagflation'? These technical gimmicks are expressed in the form 'Take away the number you first thought of and divide by X.' They are based on the fallacy that long term stagflation is due to lack of technical ingenuity by governments rather than to the form in which interest group conflicts express themselves under a paper money system.

Spurious technical matters are often raised to avoid the awkward question of who is to pay for proposed policy changes. Those who want the government to be more generous to some special group sometimes argue that the cash should come from a higher government borrowing requirement. The raising of a technical matter like 'public-sector borrowing' assists evasiveness in several ways. Many citizens (who might otherwise have asked themselves whether they were personally prepared to make income transfers) are happy to take refuge in the thought that it is all an argument among experts. Others go further and suppose that they can use the suggestion of the government's technical incompetence to avoid the choice between their personal interests and those of the deserving group (for instance nurses or pensioners) with whom they claim to sympathise.

One should, therefore, be extremely suspicious of sudden discoveries of excessive fiscal stringency at a time of tension or dispute when it would be very useful indeed to conjure up resources from thin air. Should this coincidence occur and a fiscal margin really exist, it is all the more necessary to emphasise that expenditure or tax concession in one direction still has a cost in the shape of alternative benefits to other groups or other kinds of spending which have been foregone. So long as there is some limit, however high, to government borrowing, all fiscal concessions have an opportunity cost.

The myth of government as a group of people who can create something out of nothing increases the strains on democracy. If a succession of governments, led by diverse personalities and under the influence of diverse intellectual fashion, stir up expectations only to disappoint them, there is a risk of the whole system snapping under the strain. The danger is even greater when the commentators, the satirists and those who claim to be drop-outs or apostles of radical alternatives base their condemnation on even more optimistic expectations of what could be achieved if government were rational, uncorrupt or even not there at all. The strains are particularly evident when many countries are passing through a period of economic stress and governments are more likely to fall short of expectation than in the halcyon post-war decades. Occasional lapses from excessive expectations into pessimistic acquiescence in economic depression are no more helpful. Both the more usual state of excessive expectations and the bouts of irrational pessimism neglect the limited but important role that public policy can perform (although not costlessly) in improving the environment and rules under which the economy operates.

There is no need to predict the 'collapse of democracy' to make the case against the myth of 'government-as-King-Wenceslas'. The diversion of human energy into frustrating and futile directions is always sad. Myths about government can lead to tension and conflict, even to acute personal unhappiness (many a steel worker thinks he is out of work unnecessarily, because of a 'stingy' government). It cannot be desirable that nearly all discussion of politics on television, radio and in print should be at the level of such infantile wishful thinking. There are, after all, a great many things which can be done to make the world a better place. The need is to address ourselves to each other rather than to make rival demands on 'government'.

Governments and individuals

One apparent alternative to the myth of omnipotent government is to regard the state as a 'civil association' (Michael Oakeshott's term again) between individuals, each with his or her own set of particular purposes. The main purpose of political activity is then to determine the rules under which individuals can pursue their own interests – which can be altruistic as well as selfish – without getting in each other's way.

The whole idea of civil association, or of a 'rule of law' limiting the action of a temporary majority, is at the opposite pole to the elective dictatorship that has been the reigning political religion in Britain. Some politicians even want to sweep away the last remaining obstacles to an elected government imposing its will (or its latest manifesto) on a country. Followers of Tony Benn would see in the idea of new and specific constitutional constraints a 'Tory plot' to frustrate a future Labour government. Yet Conservative leaders chafe as much at the obstacles which other sources of power (whether local authorities or the civil service) impose against the immediate execution of their will; and they have been hostile to electoral reform, which could be the single most important potential brake on the dictatorial proclivities of any group of people thrown temporarily into a brief period of office following dissatisfaction with a previous government.

The belief that a rule-of-law or civil-association approach would necessarily favour the rich and the powerful is superficial in the extreme. The approach is 'conservative' in the sense that it puts a limitation on the discretionary actions of the government of the day; but this applies to all governments, including those that 'want to put the clock back' or reverse egalitarian measures.

The argument for civil association basically emphasises

general principles (rather than discretionary action), and some limitation on the immediate enactment of the wishes of a temporary majority by rule-of-law and constitutional safeguards such as second chambers, weighted majorities, bills of rights, constitutional courts and so on. Without such institutions, and the inhibitions they embody, the rule of law can degenerate into meaning anything that has been rubber-stamped by the Queen in Parliament. But the devices of constitutional reform are less important than the idea of fundamental principles and working assumptions, to which particular laws and acts are subservient and which change at a different pace to the swing of the electoral pendulum. The demolition job that is required involves destroying the belief that because a government is freely elected it can be as arbitrary as it likes.

A more constitutional approach to government, together with an emphasis on rules rather than executive action, would be desirable in its own right and might ease some of the tensions to which governments are subject. But it would not necessarily eliminate the Wenceslas myth.

If we could ever achieve a 'Government of Laws rather than of Men', the interest-group disputes which now take the form of new claims on government would instead probably become arguments about the fundamental principles and rules governing civil associations. For example, workers in decaying industries might argue that it was a desirable general principle that other more prosperous groups should support them to spare them the costs of adjustment. Other groups would vigorously dispute that principle. Talk of 'observing a tradition' does not help greatly if the tradition offers different intimations to different people.

There is a very thin line between asking government to achieve over-ambitious aims and debating the rival merits of rules or laws from which similar results are expected. Moreover, the instinctive tendency of some conservative writers to insist that political activity should not be concerned with matters such as full employment or social security – or the 'health of the nation' – goes too far. Individual human beings have purposes and aspirations which cannot be ruled out of order *a priori*. Some of them can best be achieved by voluntary cooperation or through market activity. Others require the use of collective coercion; but although coercion is *ipso facto* undesirable it is not the only evil, and not all coercion originates in government. The question is not whether governments or politicians should have purposes – but which purposes can individually best be carried out through the coercive machinery of government rather than by other means.

It is not the search for goals that is the error, but the search for costless options, the supposition that by invoking government we can escape asking at whose expense we want action to be undertaken.

The ultimate therapy for an intellectual malady must itself be intellectual. It would be useful to translate all political demands into statements about individual human beings; or, if that is not possible, into statements about specific personal categories.

Statements about governments, states, or nations should be translated into statements relating to individuals, who alone can feel, suffer or die. The most clear-cut need for such translations is in decisions about war and peace. Were the issues at stake after Sarajevo in 1914, in Viet Nam in 1964-72, in the Falklands in 1982, worth the death, mutilation, and degradation of so many lives?

Reference to individuals is also necessary in the more mundane case of income transfers to help those suffering from an adverse turn in the market. Such a translation should be made with some rigour. Aid for most specific occupational groups within the terms of particular disputes is likely to cost less than one percentage point on the basic rate of income tax. It is easy to be in favour of each special case taken in isolation. The criterion of 'really meaning it' is met when a voter accepts the totality of transfers from himself for all cases of comparable priority over a specified period.

A shift from the abstraction of 'the government' to the level of the individual is also necessary in another sense. Political demands would be less liable to frustration if those who made them had some idea of the specific actions they required of their elected representatives.

Members of a cabinet are supposed to differ from the rest of us in being able to make decisions which can have the force of orders. Yet you only have to dip into the latest ex-cabinet-minister's memoirs to see how little this power is worth in practice. It is not merely that ministers are hemmed in by colleagues, officials, past laws, subordinate authorities, inertia, and so on. Much more fundamentally, often no set of decisions exists which can satisfy what some people are urging without creating at least equal dissatisfaction on the part of others.

If anybody supposes that this chapter is a plea for a more respectful and less critical attitude to government, he or she has wholly misunderstood it.

On the contrary, an attitude of superficial hostility combined with potential reverence for government comes from expecting vast benefits which it is not in a position to provide. Indeed, if we no longer look at government as a Good King Wenceslas or a Father Christmas, its real role as head of a coercive apparatus – a necessary evil, but an evil – will come more sharply into focus. Then we will be far closer to seeing the true sources of the abuse of power and the kinds of vigilance we need to exert.

2 Two Cheers for Utilitarianism

The appeal of utilitarianism; The two levels; Distribution; A weighting system; Welfare, choice and freedom; Illiberal preferences; Changes of taste; Personal rights; Appendix: The Falklands example.

The appeal of utilitarianism

It is quite impossible to make decisions on public policy, or in any other sphere of human affairs, without some general principles of evaluation. This applies equally to the appraisal of the rules of a civil association mentioned in the last chapter and the specific policy decisions of conventional politics. It is impossible to take decisions entirely 'on their merits' or 'on the facts', because without some principles of evaluation we do not know what their merits are or where the facts point. It is just the self-styled pragmatists whose principles of evaluation are most likely to change with the fashions or pressures of the moment and whose decisions are least likely to be related to 'the facts' in any stable or predictable way.

On the other hand virtually all the substantive principles of evaluation suggested by moral and political philosophers have been found on closer examination to be highly unsatisfactory. They are either ambiguous or internally contradictory in important instances; or they lead to conclusions which people find they cannot in practice accept. Thus we are unable to do without doctrine, yet should be on the lookout for snags in any doctrines we adopt. It is best to bring out in the open – rather than to suppress or keep implicit – the doctrines we cannot help using, but to appreciate that they are no more than broad presumptions in continual need of reformulation.

Controversial as it still is, utilitarianism is one of the most strongly established of the suggested systems of evaluation. Although it is in principle applicable to all human conduct, it has always been regarded as having special application to public policy. It has provided most economists with their policy yardsticks, although the more down-to-earth 'applied' practitioners have not always been conscious of the fact. It is the starting point for much of current theorising on 'ought' questions, even on the part of those who reject it or wish to modify it drastically. Above all it has had a great attraction for thinkers of a 'liberal' variety, who have, like John Stuart Mill, agonised and puzzled over it but found it difficult to reject or replace.

To understand both the appeal and the problems of utilitarianism, it is helpful to go back to the formulation of one of its best known fathers, the British jurist and political theorist, Jeremy Bentham:

> By the principle of utility is meant that principle which approves or disapproves of every action whatsoever, according to the tendency which it appears to have to augment or diminish the happiness of the party whose interest is in question . . . if that party be the community in general, then the happiness of the community: if a particular individual, then the happiness of that individual. . . .
>
> The interest of the community then is, what? – the sum of the interest of the several members who compose it.

These sentences from the opening of the *Introduction to the Principles of Morals and Legislation*[1] show that utilitarianism was from its early days, and still remains, a challenging assertion, rather than the grey or platitudinous doctrine which it is often popularly supposed to be.*

Since Bentham's time a vast literature has developed and there are almost as many varieties of utilitarianism as there are writers. This chapter will have to be very selective, concentrating on a few points which I think *ought* to be of interest to the non-specialist or where I have something

---

* An ambiguity in the word 'utilitarian' has fostered this misunderstanding, for it has a common-or-garden meaning of 'narrowly functional'. If a building or article of furniture is described as strictly utilitarian, we will expect it to be adequate for its purpose but without any attempt to make it attractive or pleasing. The wartime 'utility scheme' was designed to save resources by concentrating on a minimum number of functional designs. Thus it becomes all too easy to present utilitarians as opposed to all colour, variety or fun – whereas a true utilitarian values everything that makes people satisfied, no matter how frivolous or 'inessential' it may appear to the man in Whitehall. Bentham himself became aware how unattractive and misleading the label could be, and in the 1822 edition of the *Principles* canvassed the substitution of a term such as 'the greatest happiness' or 'greatest felicity'.

special to say. (An example of the kind of omission is whether utilitarianism is best stated as the promotion of pleasure or the prevention of pain, or whether the two can be assimilated in a common formulation.) Nor will there be any discussion of the vast mathematical literature on the measurement, comparison and assessment of utility levels produced mainly by economists of an abstract bent. More seriously, it will not be possible within the space available to discuss metaethics – the logic of moral judgments and the logical status of utilitarianism or other normative systems.

Utilitarianism is compatible with many different metaethical views and utilitarians come from many different philosophical stables. In my view, the principle of utility is most convincingly regarded as neither a mysterious intuition nor a deduction from some theory about the nature of moral discourse, but as a *proposed standard* for judging actions. It is thus not capable of strict proof; but it can be supported by asking people to reflect on their basic judgments.* Consider for instance: 'International aggression should always be punished.' Many people who assert such propositions have never reflected on whether this is a basic judgment, beyond which no argument is possible, or whether it is part of a vaguely articulated view of world politics in which unopposed aggression is deemed likely to lead to greater long-term suffering than the effort to resist. If it is the latter, it is necessary to ask about the cost of either any particular act of resistance or such resistance in general, and its likely benefits. If people are prepared to assess these costs and benefits by their effects on individual – not necessarily identifiable – human beings, their 'principles of foreign policy' stand revealed as subordinate to the principle of utility, to which direct reference may have to be made in case of difficulty.

Prima facie, utilitarianism should be a highly humane doctrine. It accepts the need to deter wrong-doers who could bring misery on society; but punishment – as the infliction of suffering on human beings – is always an evil, even if a necessary one. In the words of an early utilitarian jurist,

---

* As one philosopher has put it: 'I propose to rely on my *own* moral consciousness and to appeal to your moral consciousness and to forget about what people ordinarily say.' J.C. Smart, 'Extreme and Restricted Form of Utilitarianism', *Philosophical Quarterly*, Vol. 6, 1956. Reprinted in *Theories of Ethics* (ed. Philippa Foot), OUP, 1967.

Beccaria, punishment must be 'public, prompt, necessary, *the least possible in the given circumstances*, proportionate to the crimes, dictated by the laws' (my italics).[2]

But not only is it humanitarian, it is also, as the quotation from Bentham brings out, highly individualist in its methodology. Statements about nations or about large abstractions such as the 'morale of the country' or 'the health of the economy' must be translatable into statements about individual human beings and their well-being before a judgment can be made.

It is easy to fall into tautology when attempting such translation. Professor Harry Johnson once argued – one hopes tongue in cheek – that although policies of economic nationalism adopted by new nations caused material loss, they also brought psychical satisfaction to individuals in these countries by gratifying their taste for nationalism. 'The psychic enjoyment that the mass of the population derives from the collective consumption aspects of nationalism suffices to compensate them for the loss of material income imposed on them by nationalist economic policies, so that nationalistic policies arrive at a quite acceptable result from the standpoint of maximising satisfaction.'[3] In like manner, costly wars involving much human suffering and little tangible reward can be rationalised by saying that the psychic satisfaction – say from the thought of a certain disputed area being administered by people of one's own ethnic group – outweighs all the miseries involved. If such assertions are made *as a matter of definition*, then utilitarianism degenerates into blank endorsement of whatever is happening: revolution, counter-revolution, war, peace or whatever.

We do not, however, have to proceed in this way. The translation of policies into effects on individual satisfactions can lead us to pose such useful questions as: 'How much suffering is justified by the gratification of my feelings of national pride? How much less take-home pay is my psychic satisfaction in Ruritanian ownership of Ruritanian resources worth?' Analysis along these lines would be likely to make people more self-conscious than they would otherwise be. It might even lead to a weakening of unreflective willingness to 'die for one's country' and to a waning of nationalist and ideological enthusiasm in general.

Nevertheless I shall argue later that recent utilitarian writers have too often tried to assimilate together two fundamentally different goals – the maximisation of personal choice and of personal satisfaction. Utilitarian writers have often also been attracted by a third goal – the enlargement of the area of freedom in the good, old negative sense of 'absence of coercion'. These are all worthy but *different* aims; and there can be conflicts between them.

The original utilitarian doctrine can be analysed into three components:[4]

1 Consequentialism – judging actions or policies in terms of their consequences for individual human beings;
2 Welfare – judging states of affairs or policies in terms of the level of satisfaction achieved, which is identified with utility;
3 Sum-ranking – the technical term for the summation of everyone's satisfaction to give a global utility total.

Thus utilitarianism is a member of the family of moral doctrines which judge actions neither by their motives nor their intrinsic qualities, but by their consequences. It is a form of what used to be called teleological ethics and is occasionally known today by the ungainly term 'consequentialism'. The contrast is with 'deontological' systems which judge actions exclusively by their conformity to some law or rule. It is possible to accept the consequential aspects of utilitarianism without accepting, or accepting in a very qualified form, the other two aspects.

Many people have instinctive deontological views and are shocked by consequentialist morality of any kind. An age-old objection to utilitarianism is that it runs counter to common ideas of good behaviour embodied in maxims such as 'Do not punish the innocent', 'Keep promises', 'Do not break treaties' or 'Do not invade another country's territory'.

In one sense this criticism is unfair, and was already rebutted in John Stuart Mill's *Utilitarianism* (first published in 1861). Utilitarians are not so foolish as to imagine that they have either the knowledge or the disinterestedness to assess directly the utility consequences of alternative courses in either private or public life. The maxims of commonsense morality embody the accumulated (if imperfect) wisdom of generations; and their observance may do more to promote utility than any attempt to pursue it directly.

The two levels

Professor Richard Hare of Oxford has thrown light on the role of normal rules of behaviour in a utilitarian system by drawing attention to two different levels of thinking, the first or 'intuitive' level and the second or 'critical' level.[5] At the intuitive level we take for granted the maxims of popular morality and their public policy counterparts. *Prima facie* rules are necessary, as it is quite impractical to make a direct calculation of the utility effects of every decision; and the attempt to do so would probably be clouded by self-interest and prejudice as well as insufficient knowledge. John Stuart Mill long ago pointed out that utilitarianism was not only consistent with, but required, the 'intermediate generalisations' of popular morality.

The second 'critical' level of thinking is required (a) when the generally accepted principles appear to conflict (e.g. truth-telling versus preventing suffering); (b) in determining exceptional cases when there seems to be an argument for waiving the rules; and above all (c) in the critical reflection required for the choice of the first level *prima facie* rules, their elaboration and development.

It is the failure to move to this second critical level, when it is clearly required, which makes so many policy arguments merely a heated exchange of slogans. If debate on an issue such as the 1982 Argentine invasion of the Falklands remains stuck at the level of 'They have invaded our territory!', 'Britain has been knocked around enough' – or on the other side 'Do nothing without the UN', 'You will alienate world opinion', no rational discussion is possible.

Because of the emphasis on *prima facie* everyday rules of behaviour at the first or intuitive level, Mill and Hare may be regarded as rule utilitarians (in one sense of that rather ambivalent term).*

---

* Rule utilitarianism was invented to try to reduce the clash between the Principle of Utility and the rules of ordinary morality. It comes in many forms, but it is worth distinguishing two important types, 'Primitive rule utilitarianism' and 'Ideal rule utilitarianism'.

According to the primitive variety 'An act is right if, and only if, it conforms to a set of rules, conformity to which would maximise utility.' In other words if, weighing up the evidence and trying to allow for his own prejudices, someone is convinced that breaking a rule of conduct

In considering whether to disregard some rule of everyday morality in an exceptional case, a utilitarian of this type will not stop at the direct effects of observance and non-observance. He will have to ask about the effect of his actions in weakening valuable rules and institutions. He is never on this interpretation content just to ask: 'Will telling a lie to save the feelings of a terminally ill patient' or 'Will breaking a treaty to avoid a bloody war' cause more happiness or pain in this particular situation? He must also ask whether the comfort of the patient or the avoidance of bloodshed will outweigh the cost in future human suffering of the marginal weakening of the practices of truth-telling and treaty-keeping, which do in general promote human well-being and thus have a high acceptance utility. Even if he can act secretly, he has to consider the effect of his breach of the rule on his own future dispositions and character.

Distribution

Whose satisfaction should be promoted when the interests of different people and groups come into conflict?

For purposes of public policy it is necessary to assume that an evil affecting two million people is worse than a comparable evil affecting one million (e.g. a missile attack on a smaller or larger city). A benefit of given size for two million people has to be regarded as better than the same benefit for only one. These are judgments on which most people can agree even though they are unlikely to agree on the reasons for them, if 'reasons' be required at all.

Sometimes it is necessary to go further. If the amount of harm likely to be suffered by a representative member of the one million community is clearly far far greater than that suffered by a representative member of the two million one, most people would want to reverse their initial decision as

would promote more utility or less disutility than observing it, the rule should be broken.

Under 'ideal rule utilitarianism' on the other hand 'An act is right if, and only if, it confirms to a set of rules *general acceptance of which* would maximise utility.'

As David Lyons, from whom these definitions are taken, has shown, primitive rule utilitarianism is theoretically equivalent to act utilitarianism (*Forms and Limits of Utilitarianism* Oxford, 1965). The everyday rules are simply practical aids (which may differ very much from one society to another). 'Ideal rule utilitarianism' would however sometimes prescribe a different conduct to that of act utilitarianism. Where the two systems diverge, however, the ideal rule utilitarian would be knowingly departing from the principle of utility.

Hare fully accepts that his form of rule utilitarianism is not ultimately distinguishable from act utilitarianism. The distinctions between the two levels of thinking and the respect paid to popular morality are best regarded, not as a new kind of utilitarianism, but as a prudential way of applying the old kind.

they would regard the suffering of the larger community as the lesser evil. However vague and imprecise the comparisons, they cannot be avoided; and the necessary estimates typically involve units such as real income, casualty numbers, accident risks and so on. Some kinds of decision (e.g. military expenditure versus social services or take-home pay) can only be rationalised if there is some way of converting these units into each other.

It is tempting therefore to think in terms of units of utility and say that we are maximising either total utility or, more sensibly, utility per head. This does no harm as a piece of mathematical shorthand, so long as we are clear that we are dealing with a fictitious entity which corresponds to nothing which actually exists.

The mistake of many utilitarians has been to conceive of something called 'total utility' as one great total of which each individual's utility is a part. The concept can be likened to a 'national petroleum tank' representing the total stock of petroleum to which each individual petrol tank contributes. It is known technically as 'sum-ranking', the third of the components of utilitarianism mentioned above.

The concept of one huge utility tank, if it makes any sense at all, suggests a giant collective consciousness of which each individual consciousness is part. If the object of moral conduct is to maximise some utility total, then each individual is important only as a utility carrier contributing to the total stock.

This seems to me not only objectionable, but factually wrong. Two patients in hospital may each be suffering to roughly the same degree, which we may call x. But two patients, each suffering x, are by no means equivalent to one patient suffering 2x. Utility or satisfaction belongs to individuals. Satisfaction, or pain, can be compared;* but I can

---

* The objections given here to the tank concept of total utility are entirely different from those usually advanced by those economists (such as Lionel Robbins in the 1930s) who 'denied the validity' of interpersonal comparisons. This seems to me misconceived. We can and do say 'A is slightly better off than B but much worse off than C.' Such statements cannot be made with great precision and are prone to error. But they are neither meaningless nor pure value judgments, as they have a factual component.

Doubts expressed about the legitimacy of interpersonal comparisons of satisfaction probably represent the intrusion of the epistemological doubts about the 'existence of other mind' into a sphere where they do not belong. For when we engage in discussion on ethics, political philosophy or economic policy, we necessarily have to assume that other minds exist. The best discussion of the topic is still to be found in Chapter 4 of I.M.D. Little's *Critique of Welfare Economics* (Oxford University Press, revised edition 1957).

attach no meaning to the aggregate of everyone's satisfaction and pain. Who is supposed to experience it? It is either obfuscatory metaphysics, or it presupposes some giant Hegelian collective consciousness of which each consciousness is but a subordinate part. Total utility may be a computational convenience, but it is not something which actually exists, like the joy of one human being or the suffering of another.

Utilitarians need a principle of distribution which they cannot derive from their own system. Many utilitarian economists have tried to derive egalitarian conclusions from the principle of diminishing marginal utility, which asserts that each additional unit of income or wealth leads to a continually diminishing increment of satisfaction. Thus, other things being equal, an extra pound or dollar is worth more to a poor man than to a rich one.

This reasoning has led many utilitarian economists to a qualified egalitarianism. A typical formulation, still held by many mainstream economists, is that equalisation should be pushed to the point where further redistribution would reduce total utility by its effects on incentives. Its application should, of course, take into account other qualifications such as Hume's observation that 'It would be greater cruelty to dispossess a man of anything than not to give it to him.'

Even from the point of view of traditional utilitarian ethics the benefit of redistribution is entirely the gain to the less well off. The discomfiture of the rich is always an evil, if a lesser one, never to be welcomed for its own sake.

More fundamentally, to build a justification for redistribution on the principle of diminishing marginal utility involves extremely questionable value judgments. For many policy purposes people have to be treated in broad categories. Policy-makers can reasonably assume that a representative individual earning £5,000 per annum will value an additional pound more than a representative person earning £100,000. (The rich are different. They have more money.) But once we have knowledge of individual cases, it would be no surprise at all to find a particular poor man so physically handicapped or dispirited, and with so little power of enjoyment, that his welfare is little affected by changes in income over a considerable range. A particular rich man may be, on the other hand, a riotous liver with a huge unsatisfied capacity for enjoyment. Do we then make a reverse transfer from poor to rich?

Almost certainly not. Most people, whether egalitarians or not, who are concerned with the level of the poorest and most disadvantaged, would not find, even after critical reflection, that their concern is derived from some beliefs about the shape of the individual utility curve. We would not be in favour of taxing the poor and handicapped to benefit the rich and healthy, even if some utility meter showed that 'total utility' had thereby been increased.

The conclusion to which I am leading is that the common practice of analysing utilitarianism largely in terms of its distributional implications has shunted discussion on the wrong track. Utilitarians have often been attacked by radicals for being insufficiently egalitarian, and occasionally by conservatives for being too much so; and they have been tempted to reply. In my view the principle of utility does not have much to contribute to the distributional question, one way or the other. The main utilitarian contribution is the assertion that actions should be guided by their effects on the welfare of individual persons. Anyone who thinks this trite or obvious need only reflect on the variety of reasons for which wars have been fought and punishment inflicted. It is much less use as a guide to whose welfare should be raised where there is a choice. Thus the discussion of policies towards the distribution of income in particular political communities can be postponed to the next chapter.

A weighting system

There is one question which cannot, however, be avoided; and its implications particularly affect matters of war and peace and foreign policy. Utilitarians, along with many other moral philosophers, endorse a general impartiality towards all our fellow human beings. How do we square this requirement with the greater sympathy which most people instinctively feel towards their family, friends and fellow countrymen compared with the unknown millions of the Third World?

Utilitarian moralists are not so foolish as to condemn these very natural human feelings. They tend, however, to regard them as being no more than useful rule of thumb maxims at the first or intuitive level. Richard Hare defends them as being in practice the best way to promote the interests of all the inhabitants of the world. For instance, if mothers were expected to care equally for all children, and not just their own, then children in general would almost certainly be less well provided for than they are now. Loyalty to country is a virtue only to the extent that it happens to promote the interests of all human beings.

Let us look a little further. Take the case of the person who consciously attaches more weight to his family and friends than to unknown millions in the Third World or even to the mass of his fellow countrymen, and insists that this is a perfectly moral course. He may say that this is how he believes everyone else in the world ought to behave too (subject, perhaps, to certain exceptions statable in general terms – e.g. unless he is working as a minister, official, judge or recruitment officer).

On the other hand he may reply that these are the standards he expects from the people with whom he is likely to come into contact, but that he is either completely indifferent to, or cares much less about, how people in the forests of the Amazon do or should behave.* The reader should also ask whether on critical reflection he really does give equal weight to the interests of creatures with partially human characteristics who may be found on other planets. Or to animals on this planet? Or to some link in the evolutionary chain between primordial ape and man who might one day be discovered still existing in some corner of the world?

An impartially benevolent utilitarian will try to justify giving more weight to family and friends than to unknown millions in the Third World, by saying that we can do more for them. But this is not self-evident. It is conceivable that we could do more to promote human satisfaction ('we' being

---

* If asked whether he would be prepared to accept this *dictum* if he lived in the Amazon basin himself, he can reply without making a logical mistake, that he is not prescribing for the inhabitants of Amazonia, but only for the more restricted groups with which he can identify, and that he is not worried if one school of academics chooses to label him as 'amoral'. As some readers will see, I am trying to avoid discussing the thesis that all moral judgments are necessarily universal as well as prescriptive. If, as usually maintained, universalism is a logical thesis about the use of the moral terms, then nothing follows about how much weight we ought to give the interests of the different inhabitants of the world.

those above a certain level in the world income scale) if we gave every minute of our non-working time to Oxfam.

Too many moralists have paid lip service to the idea of the whole human race counting equally (sometimes including generations yet unborn) and then gone on to concentrate on policies affecting exclusively their own communities. Ordinary people are then presented with the false choice of either giving equal value to every inhabitant of the earth or giving no value at all to those outside their immediate circle or country. The result of paying lip service to impartial benevolence is too often in practice the total neglect of those outside our own group.

There would have been no way of persuading many of the most pacific Englishmen or Israelis in two recent conflicts that an Argentine or Lebanese life was of equal value to that of an Englishman or an Israeli. But he would, one hopes, have accepted that they were of *some* value. If I may quote from an essay I wrote in the aftermath of the Suez Crisis, a weighting system under which different people counted in different degrees 'designed to fit these successive circles of feelings of obligation (which people actually have) might appear to some less exalted than an equal concern for all human beings; but surely it would be preferable to a narrow nationalism which arbitrarily rules out the small but existent sympathies that most people have for their fellow men of different nationalities?'[6]

The weights are measures of relative concern in the minds of the individuals making the assessment. Utilitarianism cannot supply the weights. The weights are a precondition of applying utilitarian-type principles.

Welfare, choice and freedom

It is now time to turn to the second component of utilitarianism – the promotion of satisfaction (a less question-begging term than Bentham's happiness, but it contains the gist of what he meant to convey). For a liberal (in the traditional English sense of the word) the promotion of satisfaction is not the only goal.[7] A person who is attracted by the general concept of freedom is likely to be attracted by negative freedom (from coercion) and by the enlargement of choice; but the two objectives can sometimes conflict with each other and both may conflict with utility in the simple sense of satisfaction.*

Freedom, choice and satisfaction will sometimes point in the same direction and sometimes conflict; and I know of no overriding principle to choose between them except that of the diminishing marginal rate of substitution. That is, when there is plenty of freedom and choice, but little satisfaction of wants, it is worth sacrificing some freedom and choice to gain a little want satisfaction. When there is plenty of satisfaction, but little choice or freedom, then it might be worth sacrificing some satisfaction for the sake of greater freedom or greater choice. Beyond this, the actual trade-offs remain subjective.

The tension between different components of the liberal idea has been obscured by a shift in utilitarian doctrines since Bentham's time. The shift has been towards interpreting satisfaction or happiness in terms of the opportunity to satisfy desires. These desires have in turn been assessed by observing people's actual choices as revealed in the market place and elsewhere – known as 'revealed preference'. This shift of emphasis was originally the work of economists looking for a way of making the doctrine operational, but a number of philosophers have also taken this path. The resulting doctrine may be conveniently labelled 'choice utilitarianism'.

The key role assigned to the individual and his choice in this doctrine seems to offer an attractive combination of welfare and freedom. For policies are chosen which give people the maximum of opportunities and the minimum of restriction in making use of them. Opportunities depend on real income and wealth defined quite subtly to take account of leisure, the quality of the working environment and the satisfaction gained from it; but they also depend on people's health, the physical environment and other amenities of a public goods kind. Restrictions on the exercise of choice are condemned, except when this exercise has harmful effects on other people. Thus if people prefer push-pin to poetry that is their business. People are treated *as if* they are the best judge of their own satisfaction. Thus 'choice utilitarianism' will often help the

---

* Even the division of liberal objectives into satisfaction, choice-fulfilment and negative freedom is a gross oversimplification. There are many interpretations of all these three and many finer classifications exist. But without oversimplification no reasonably brief discussion is possible, and we are left with the *dictat* of the self-styled pragmatist.

campaigner against restrictions on personal freedom ranging from the Scottish sabbath to compulsory military service and censorship.

Thus the doctrine *looks* like one of giving as much opportunity as possible to satisfy their choices to as many people as possible. It would seem at the opposite pole from authoritarian or paternalistic systems which either attempt to tell us our own good or subordinate individual freedom and happiness to some higher collective or metaphysical goal.

The choice utilitarian goal lends itself to representation in economists' jargon as putting each person on the highest possible indifference curve. (An indifference curve represents combinations of goods and services with which a person is equally content, e.g. five oranges and five bananas, two oranges and eight bananas). Improvements which make at least one person better off and no one worse off are known as 'Pareto improvements' and are unequivocally to be welcomed. (Gains in welfare deriving purely from what I called in the last chapter 'improvements in government competence' are of this nature.) If, as is usually the case, some people gain and some lose, a distributional judgment has to be applied outside the utilitarian scheme. But even then it is still a helpful first step in judgment to ask if a change is a potential Pareto improvement – i.e. if the gainers could compensate the losers and still be better off. As can be imagined, a vast academic industry has arisen to develop the mathematics of all this with the name of Welfare Economics – most of it far too rarified to be of help to any practical economist concerned with actual welfare issues.

In positive economic theory 'it is customary to postulate that an individual seeks to maximise something subject to some constraints. All that counts is that we can assign numbers to entities or conditions which a person can strive to realise.' Thus individual utility maximisation is made true by definition. Everyone tries to maximise utility; and utility is whatever he or she is trying to maximise.[8] This is not as silly as it sounds as a working axiom, provided it is used in conjunction with empirical information to produce results that are not tautological.

An economist can use the utility-maximising assumption without any commitment to any particular normative doctrine. He is only a 'choice utilitarian' if he insists that people should have every chance of satisfying as many of their preferences as possible to the maximum feasible extent and wishes to see social institutions which will further these aims. The 'choice utilitarianism' of the economists has however ceased to be utilitarianism as originally understood. People can make choices which turn out to provide them with sorrow rather than satisfaction. The act of choice, at certain times for certain people and beyond a certain limit, may be painful. Sometimes, too, people will knowingly sacrifice their own well-being, for altruistic reasons or in pursuit of honour or revenge. A utilitarian may of course treat 'revealed preferences' as an index of satisfaction to be used for lack of anything better. In that case, however, his attachment to choice is but an expedient, and he cannot challenge Aldous Huxley's Brave New World in which a happiness-inducing drug, 'soma', is administered to the population. Alternatively, he may attach importance to choice itself, in which case he is no longer a utilitarian in Bentham's sense.

An example of the distinctions between freedom from coercion, maximising satisfaction and maximising choice is provided by Amy Gutman in a recent book on utilitarianism.[9] She discusses the case of the Old Order Amish in the USA who are denied secondary education by their parents for religious reasons. Should the wishes of the parents be overriden? From the point of view of *satisfaction* or welfare the argument may go either way. Amish children might well feel better off brought up in an Amish way and integrated into their own communities. But one cannot rule out the possibility that their level of satisfaction will rise as a result of a modern education and the career opportunities it provides. The answer is likely to vary from child to child. Assuming that the children do not dissent, even in retrospect, from the views of their parents, the argument for *freedom* on the one hand suggests that they be left alone. But if providing *choice* is the objective, then surely Miss Gutman is right to argue for compulsion 'as education will expand the opportunities of the children for rational choice in the future'.

Illiberal preferences

But of course, it is always possible that however much

translation into more basic statements about individual wants or choices is accomplished, and however precisely the relevant questions are posed, people may at times derive psychic satisfaction from the humiliation of their enemies. This conclusion brings us to the basic weakness of utilitarianism whether in its 'happiness' or its 'choice' variety. It arises from the fact that people have desires of a hostile or restrictive kind, for others as well as for themselves.

Amartya Sen is well known for his demonstration that free choice in personal matters can easily conflict with utilitarian principles.[10] His best known illustration is that of two people 'Prude' and 'Lewd', deciding who should read *Lady Chatterley's Lover*. Clearly the liberal solution is for Lewd to read it and Prude not to. But it so happens Prude would rather read it himself, however reluctantly, than allow Lewd to indulge his 'depraved tastes'. Lewd on the other hand, given that only one of them can, would like it even more if Prude were forced to read it to shake him out of his stuffiness. Thus Prude reading *Lady Chatterley* has a higher utility ranking for both men and would be said in the jargon to be 'Pareto optimal', in contrast to the libertarian solution of allowing Lewd to get on with his reading himself.

The Sen paradox is but one example of many potential conflicts. A fully fledged utilitarian would take into account the desires of some mature citizens for compulsory haircuts for long-haired youths (desires reflected in police practice in Singapore). He would also take account of the desires of other citizens for restrictions on the number of overseas villas or yachts the wealthy can possess. (This is not a question of the distribution of income and wealth but of the freedom of people to spend whatever wealth they have.) These linkages of one person's well-being to the behaviour of others, whether reflecting envy or aesthetic or 'moral' views, are labelled 'interdependence effects' in the economic literature, and it is their recognition which can make utilitarianism an illiberal doctrine. If negative interdependence effects are taken into account in public policy, people will be penalised for carrying out private personal acts which affect others only through thinking making it so.

Anyone with liberal value judgments will therefore have to qualify his utilitarianism by the exclusion of some interdependence effects. Wants arising from non-benign interdependence effects are a disguised form of coercion which arise from a desire to regulate the way other people spend their lives or from envy of their well-being or success. Many utilitarian writers are willing to make this qualification. According to one typical formulation 'All clearly antisocial preferences, such as sadism, envy, resentment and malice should be excluded from the social utility function.'[11]

Once such qualification are made it is admitted that other principles are being used to qualify utilitarianism, which thus loses its status as a single ultimate guide to moral conduct in favour of a tacit pluralism. Critics have remarked on the amount of 'doctoring or idealisation' of choice-based preferences in which utilitarian writers indulge.[12]

Utilitarians often go too far in their attempts to demonstrate that it is only the principle of utility that is being used. Professor Hare considers cases where total utility might, it seems, be increased by allowing a sadist his way, or a Nazi to free himself of the presence of Jews. He dismisses these cases as 'fantastic' examples, factually highly unlikely. But why is it important to show that perverse results would not occur? Either the expositor is using some yardstick other than utility with which to evaluate utilitarianism, or he is saying that current 'humanitarian' rules happen to be justified as a practical application of the principle of utility, but if they proved not to be so, they should be abandoned. We should not be ashamed of using some other notion, such as that of human dignity, to supplement the principle of utility and not attempt to govern our behaviour by one principle, whether utilitarian or otherwise. Utility can remain important in a pluralist set of values.

Changes of taste

Another difficult problem for the utilitarian relates to the effects of changes in tastes. Even a spontaneous change of tastes may be welfare-reducing on a strict utilitarian view. If demand for commodity X is replaced by demand for a novel commodity Y, capital used to produce X becomes obsolescent. New investment which could have been used to produce more of X and raise living standards has to be diverted to the production of Y merely to maintain the existing level of satisfaction. *A fortiori*, activity designed to make people dissatisfied with their lot so that they try out new products, services or ways of life, risks being utility-destroying.

This applies not only to advertising (which has always attracted the ire of utilitarian economists) but to political propaganda, imaginative literature, the dissemination of new technical knowledge and most cultural activity. The result of social innovation on the level of well-being is in fact indeterminate. If total capacity of satisfaction has increased, because human imagination has been stimulated, then a person may be better off with a smaller proportion of his new desires satisfied than with a larger proportion of his old. On the other hand cultural change and exposure to new habits and methods may make a person restless and disturbed, and less satisfied than if he had been left alone.

Let us consider a stylised historical example. Suppose that for a certain group of workers the changes brought about by the Industrial Revolution are, from the standpoint of their initial tastes and preferences, changes for the worse. Nevertheless as a result of the Industrial Revolution these workers may acquire a greater desire for manufactured goods, become more tolerant of factory conditions and less prepared to put up with their earlier rural privations. So they would be worse off still if they returned to their old life. Their attitude can be characterised by the saying: 'We were happier before we got these fancy new things, although we would now be miserable without them.'[13] But why should we not assert that the loss of satisfaction is offset by the increase in choices or opportunities resulting from industrialisation?

The difficulties arise partly because the shift of utilitarianism from a doctrine about happiness to one about maximum satisfaction of revealed preferences has taken place imperceptibly without the implications being sufficiently analysed.

The more liberal view would regard the enlargement of opportunities as good in itself (or at least not so bad as to be prevented by state action). So long as people are allowed to do the best for themselves (as they interpret best at any particular time) the liberal will not busy himself with sorrowful comparisons about how much better off people might have felt themselves if culture, circumstances and tastes had not changed. But to think of the satisfaction of wants purely in terms of people's existing range of choice, however determined – without too much worry about the increment of happiness or welfare over time – is a big departure from traditional utilitarianism.

Personal rights

The preceding argument suggests that any utilitarian system, which could both serve as a practical guide to action and respect individual liberty and autonomy, has to be heavily circumscribed and heavily supplemented. Utilitarianism, despite its claim to the contrary, needs distributional criteria which it cannot itself provide. The desires it aims to satisfy must be people's desires for themselves, not their wishes for others, especially when the latter are affected by envy, malice or disapproval. Comparisons of satisfaction should moreover be made with extreme caution over a period when tastes have changed in important ways, partly as a result of utilitarian policies and institutions.

Is there another system which will provide more directly the goals of a qualified utilitarianism without the need for such a large protective belt of explanations, exceptions and disclaimers? The main alternatives on offer, likely to win liberal converts from utilitarianism, are some modern versions of individual rights theory.

The main characteristics of rights-based theories are (a) that some preferences or choices are treated much more favourably than others and (b) the concentration is on the opportunities open to people rather than the use they make of these opportunities and their resulting psychic states.

Many systems of rights have their origin in 'contractarianism' (or 'contractualism'). A contractualist regards an action as wrong if it would be disallowed by any system of regulation 'which no one could reasonably reject as basis for informed, unforced general agreement.'[14] Contractarianism is, however, only a method of assessing principles of conduct. There is no guarantee that it will lead to one unique system. Indeed some writers argue that a form of utilitarianism would arise from a contractualist process of reasoning.

Conversely not all personal rights theories are based on contractualist reasoning. The most widely discussed non-contractarian theory of personal rights is that of Robert Nozick's 'entitlement' system.[15] This maintains that property holdings are just if they have been justly transferred by gifts or free exchange or if they have been justly acquired in the first place. The only legitimate state in his scheme is the night watchman version, confined to protection of the person and property and to the enforcement of contracts. The community has no right to interfere with property rights in even as general a way as redistributive taxation to help the very poorest.

Nozick has not in fact even claimed to have given us a theory of 'just acquisition'. His ingenious and illuminating treatise is mainly preoccupied with deriving the implications of such rights, assuming that a justification will eventually be forthcoming, and with exhibiting the drawbacks of the 'end-state view' of some other writers. Nozick gives no reason for the prohibition of state-enforced transfers which will persuade those who do not accept his minimal state at the outset.[16] We badly need a conception of liberty and individual rights which will provide protection against the proclivities of a temporary majority for trampling over the rights and liberties of the rest of us in the name of a debased kind of act utilitarianism. Unfortunately all the well known variations of libertarianism and limited state conservatism – Nozick, Hayek, Oakeshott *et al* – lack a theory of legitimate property rights, without which they are powerless to provide a comprehensive theoretical defence against collectivism, and we have to fall back on vaguer notions of a sufficiently large 'protected area' for the individual.

The leading fully developed 'contractualist' theory of personal rights is still that embodied in John Rawls's system of 'justice as fairness'.[17] These – to risk summarising a summary – are

1 each person to have equal right 'to the most extensive scheme of equal basis liberties compatible with a similar scheme of liberties for all.
2 social and economic inequalities must (a) work to the benefit of the least advantaged and (b) be attached to offices open to all.

Principle (1) has priority over (2) and (2b) over (2a). As is well known, these principles are supposed to derive from a social contract to which people would agree under a 'veil of ignorance', i.e. when they are ignorant of their own position in society and thus likely to deliberate impartially.

The discussions since the publication of *A Theory of Justice* have thrown extreme doubt about whether these or any other 'end state' principles necessarily follow from the 'veil of ignorance' assumption. Like Hare, Rawls expects too determinate a result from a few very general postulates and stylised facts.

Nevertheless 'justice as fairness' has independent appeal, irrespective of its derivation. In a later contribution[18] Rawls makes comparatively little use of the veil of ignorance and argues directly in terms of the conditions for personal self-respect. He wants people to pursue their own differing concepts of 'the good', and he opposes utilitarianism for its recognition of only one good: happiness or welfare.

Equal liberties and opportunities, and a distribution of income and wealth geared to the interest of the least well off, are regarded by Rawls as 'primary goods'; that is not as independent objectives, but as necessary conditions for the fulfilment of a wide range of human ends.

The Rawlsian principles are subject to widely varying interpretations. Rawls has been attacked for being everything from a Gladstonian free-market liberal to a ruthless egalitarian – and both extremes of criticism find sustenance. 'Equal liberties' can mean different things according to whether the emphasis is on 'liberties' or on 'equal'. The system is also much less collectivist if it is regarded as a guide to basic institutions than to current government policy.

Rawls's criterion for distributive justice will be discussed in the next chapter. Meanwhile it is worth remarking that the 'liberties' postulated in systems such as Rawls's (and emphasised by many less formal theorists of democracy for over a century) consist partly of good old negative freedom best defined in Berlin's words 'I am normally said to be free to the degree to which no man or body of men interferes with my activity'.[19] But they also contain certain 'participatory rights' – the right to vote, to stand for office on the same terms as other citizens, to be consulted on decisions, and in many formulations, to receive education enabling one to play a full role as a citizen. These rights, however valuable, have to do with ideals of participatory democracy. They may and often do enlarge choice, but it only confuses the issue to associate them with freedom, which is a different value.

Leaving aside the distributional principle (2a), a great deal of further elaboration is required of principles (1) and (2b) about equal rights and liberties, and offices open to all. One worry is that certain devices such as representative democracy, which are convenient ways of changing governments peacefully and indicating where the shoe pinches for particular societies at a particular time, are given a universal status they do not deserve. We are all aware of the sentiment: 'You've got to be an active, informed citizen or else.' Rawls himself nowhere says it; but many enthusiasts for participatory democracy give this impression.

It may be that the Rawlsian primary goods could be stated in a way which did not attract such worries. Even then they would still have a much more limited domain of application than the principle of utility. There are many issues – war and peace, foreign policy, crime and punishment, even the 'management of the economy' – which have a moral dimension and where principles of the Rawlsian type shed little light, but where utilitarianism has something to contribute.

There are thus attractions in trying to combine a system of personal rights or primary goods and the principle of utility in a hierarchy. An improved Rawlsian system of personal rights based on contractarian reasoning might be most suitable for the basic constitutional and structural features of a society and utilitarianism may be a better basis for everyday policy. Such a synthesis would require an operational method of separating structural and constitutional changes from everyday policy, which would be far from easy to establish.

No synthesis yet exists; and it is extremely doubtful whether there will ever be any organised hierarchy of principles which will not occasionally come into conflict with some moral judgments not incorporated in them and which after the most extensive critical reasoning we are still not willing to drop.* It is indeed possible to improve on utilitarianism; but it is also possible to fall short of it. My own suspicion is that in the majority of cases where we fail to take a utilitarian stance, it is because we fall short of it rather than because we improve upon it. Hence I should like to offer 'Two cheers for utilitarianism'.

Appendix: The Falklands example

A powerful neo-utilitarian critique can be made of much conventional policy thinking without introducing an unconvincing universal impartiality. A good instance was the British military expedition to retake the Falklands after the Argentinian invasion in the Spring of 1982. Many of the arguments used in favour were entirely invalid on any utilitarian approach. One example was the personification of nations. The most frequent argument I met from the supporters of the war took the form 'If someone takes your property, should you allow him to get away with it?' The treatment of the Argentine as a person who had behaved badly to another person, the UK, is inappropriate – because it is only a metaphor and a highly misleading one. Nations are composed of individuals, and what mattered most was the effects on British citizens of reconquest of the Islands, compared with alternative courses of action. According to the previous argument, the effects on Argentinians should not have been ignored, but could not have been expected to have the same weight.

Faced with the cry that national honour was at stake, a utilitarian would have asked with Falstaff:

> Can honor set to a leg? No. Or an arm? No. Or take away the grief of a wound? No. Honor hath no skill in surgery then? No. What is honor? A word. What is in that word honor? What is that honor? Air – a trim reckoning. Who hath it? He that died a Wednesday. Doth he feel it? No.

---

* Amartya Sen presents a simple but forceful example. Ann has the opportunity to prevent Bill from making a surprise attack on Charles this evening by breaking into David's room. But she knows that David is secretive and would not permit it, even in so good a cause, even though it would enable her to find Charles and warn him of the planned assault. On certain not implausible assumptions about the utilities of the respective individuals, a utilitarian calculation would not allow Ann to break into David's room. Nor would a Rawlsian interpretation of utility do, in which she tries to maximise the minimum utility (which is Bill's who is depressed and unhappy). An emphasis on rights or negative freedom would not help, as the rights in question are David's. ('A Positive Concept of Negative Freedom' in *Ethics, Proceedings of the 5th International Wittgenstein Symposium*, Holder-Pichler-Tenpsky, Vienna, 1981.)

Doth he hear it? No. 'Tis insensible then? Yea, to the dead.
But will it not live with the living? No. Why? Detraction
will not suffer it. Therefore I'll none of it. Honor is a mere
scutcheon – and so ends my catechism. *(Henry IV, Part 1.)*

On very simple 'act utilitarian' calculations, there was surely
no justification for fighting. There were at least a thousand
deaths – a quarter of them British – and several times that
many wounded; and there was a clear risk of far larger
casualties. These deaths and injuries – not to speak of the cost
of the war and the continuing cost of a large British garrison –
were incurred for the benefit of 1,750 Falkland Islanders.
There was no suggestion that their lives were at stake – nor
even their material welfare. For a fraction of the cost of the
war they could have had the option of being resettled
anywhere they liked and at a far higher standard of living than
they could previously have expected to enjoy.

Some people argued that it was immoral to worry about
deaths, suffering and casualties, when principles were at
stake. They failed to reflect that the avoidance of unnecessary
suffering is itself a moral principle – if not the moral principle
– from which most of the others follow.

The one potentially cogent utilitarian argument for the war
was the need to protect certain principles of international
good behaviour such as resistance to aggression, while being
ready to negotiate over disputes. The weakening of these
principles could weaken international stability and encourage
wars in future years. The suffering thereby caused would have
to be added to the immediate British interest at stake. The
true moral argument was between those who thought that the
reinforcement of the international order was worth the
casualties and those who did not.

Mere evocation of the principle of resisting aggression does
not settle the argument. One first has to ask 'How firmly is the
principle established?' and 'How far would a fudged
compromise with the Argentine have weakened it?' The
principle of not settling territorial disputes by force is in fact
more honoured in the breach than in the observance. It was
never recognised before the twentieth century (much of the
British Empire was acquired by raids similar to General
Galtieri's). It has applied in practice mainly to East-West

relations in the Western Europe and NATO areas, where the risk and cost of nuclear escalation is so obviously high. Elsewhere it is struggling for a toehold. It did not stop the Russians from invading Afghanistan, nor pulling the strings in Poland. For most of the postwar period, there have been armed conflicts over territory in one or other part of the world.

Then there is the question of whether the British action really could be expected to strengthen the international order. It was obvious to the world that the motives of most of the British public in supporting the war had nothing to do with safeguarding international law; the struggle was a symbolic one over hurt national pride.

These doubts about the true nature of the operation may have severely weakened any exemplary effects of its 'success' in promoting international order. After the failure of the international community to act in Goa, Afghanistan or Vietnam-Cambodia, was the lesson of the British recapture of the Falklands that 'Aggression does not pay after all' or that 'Even middle-sized countries such as Britain and the Argentine have armed forces to be reckoned with'?

Will the world be a safer place if the Falklands become a new Berlin in the South Atlantic, deflecting NATO forces from their primary tasks? Or if Britain and the Argentine – and other countries in imitation – start piling up both conventional and nuclear arms to be better prepared next time?

It is also worth a closer look at the exact international rules of behaviour which the war was supposed to reinforce. In most human institutions (e.g. schools, armies, clubs) punitive measures which might be acceptable against the infringement of rules taken seriously by authority are not nearly as acceptable when the injunctions seem to have fallen into disuse. The impression, given by the Foreign Office to the Argentine over many years, that the Falklands were not a vital British interest – hence the genuine astonishment in Buenos Aires at the London reaction – weakened the *moral* case for warlike retaliation at the level of *prima facie* rules of accepted behaviour.

A final reflection. The consequences of alternative courses were, as usual, highly uncertain; and emotions were heavily engaged. Moreover, on the argument of international order, the British action was a highly altruistic one, the benefits of which would spill over to many other countries. There was surely a case for giving very heavy weight to the attitudes of other allied governments, able to take a more detached view. The fact that Britain's allies (with the exception of France) were urging restraint (despite a show of formal support) should make one reflect again over the validity of the international order justification.

It is possible for a utilitarian to go too far in his attempt to take seriously the *prima facie* rules of conventional behaviour which are in the last resort only aids, and to make his approach too sophisticated. Before embarking on a course which is certain to lead to death, injury and bereavement to many people on both sides of the conflict, it is best to ascertain whether those who are able to take a more detached and less emotionally charged view really think that warfare is the lesser evil. The true utilitarian will think many times before he accepts the visible and tangible suffering of people here and now for some problematic future benefit.

3 Hayek, Freedom and Interest Groups

Why Hayek? The radical right; Evolution and liberty; Towards a critique; Libertarianism; Market signals; Rule of law; The myth of just reward; Redistribution and reassignment; Redistribution and equality; The interest-group threat.

Why Hayek?

As we have seen in the previous chapter, it is hazardous to attempt to assess directly the effects of any proposed action on people's satisfaction or any other objective. It is wise to make use of *prima facie* rules or presumptions which embody more experience and knowledge than any one person (or committee of people) can hope to have.

One reason for using the works of Friedrich Hayek as a starting point for this chapter is that he, almost more than any other late twentieth-century thinker, has reflected on the nature and derivation of such rules in the sphere of public policy.

A second reason is that individual freedom – in the negative sense of absence of coercion – is at the centre of much of Hayek's work. As we have seen, this is not a subject on which utilitarianism provides a very clear focus.

Thirdly, despite Hayek's postwar absorption in political theory and philosophy, he has never ceased to think as an economist; and some of his work will provide an entry into the policy problems which will occupy the remaining parts of this book.

Fourthly, there are links – as well as differences – between Hayek's ideas and radical right movements in several countries, above all the USA and Britain. By 'radical right' I mean the more thoughtful sympathisers with the *domestic* policies of governments such as President Reagan's in the

USA and Mrs Thatcher's in Britain. (I am defining 'radical right' to exclude movements of a 'moral majority' kind, but to include conservatives who stress a reduced role for government and more reliance on the market.) There is a danger, however, that if we become too preoccupied with this political aspect, we will miss the most interesting features, both good and bad, of Hayek's thought. For since the publication of his *Road to Serfdom* in 1944, Fredrich Hayek has been cursed by sneerers, who dismiss everything he has to say without giving it a hearing, and even more by admirers, who agree with it before they have studied it, and regard it mainly as a highbrow stick with which to beat the left.

In fact there is a great deal to be learned from Hayek's teachings, even by – or especially by – people who do not consider themselves either Hayekians or members of the radical right. Hayek himself has not made it any easier for them by explicit assumption in writings over many years that something called 'socialism', which includes the doctrines of social democrats, is the intellectual and political enemy. If Hayek believes, as he does, that socialists and their pale pink imitators in other parties are guilty of 'scientific error' (he never doubts their moral goodwill) and liable to usher in an age of barbarism, it has been his duty to say so and not to shelter, as so many academics do, behind a bogus impartiality. Nevertheless, in my own view, 'collectivism' would be a more accurate name than socialism for the evils which Hayek has diagnosed and would indicate more clearly that its practitioners extend throughout the political spectrum.

The radical right

We cannot, however, quite leave the more emotive subject of the radical right and the extent to which Hayek provides it with intellectual sustenance. The radical right places a good deal of emphasis, alien to many market economists, on a return to 'the old values'. The less clearly one tries to define the phrase 'old values' the more accurate one will be; but it clearly covers a belief in patriotism, authority of the traditional kind centering round the family, the school, the business manager and, above all, the police and army. These are felt to be legitimate, in contrast to bureaucrats and tax inspectors, who are regarded as *ersatz* authority figures, all too ready to act as subversives themselves. It has always been an intellectual paradox that the non-Muscovite left favours freedom in everything but economics, while the right is sympathetic to freedom only in the economic sphere. The evolution of the new left and the new right has not dissolved the paradox created by their old parents.*

Where apparently contrasting attributes are found among practising politicians, or bodies of electors, one can do little but note the paradox and pass on. A vast number of different permutations of beliefs on different subjects have at one time or another been grouped together. Among some ascetic religious sects 'plain living' has been linked, with apparent logic, to an abhorrence of technical progress. Among others such progress has been highly prized, for apparently equally cogent reasons. Nor is it surprising that middle-class Conservative voters should favour market forces for pay differentials, but advocate state support to reduce the cost of home mortgages. It is always possible to create a distinction between such cases and thus rationalise an apparent anomaly, if only one thinks hard enough.

Evolution and liberty

Yet when Hayek himself combines libertarian economic beliefs with authoritarian inclinations in other directions, it is time to sit up and take notice. I may claim to have contributed in a mild way to the revival of interest in Hayek with my own *Capitalism and the Permissive Society*[1], which came out in favour of *both* of the concepts in the title.

The first page of the first chapter of Hayek's own *Constitution of Liberty*[2] starts with the sentence:

> We are concerned in this book with that condition of men in which coercion of some by others is reduced as much as possible.

He contrasts his idea of freedom with Ignatius Loyola's ideal of the Jesuit who should be 'as soft wax' in the hands of his

---

* How far Conservatives are from any general dislike of coercion was brought out clearly by the presence of *not one* Conservative Member on the list of MPs voting in 1976 for leave to bring in a Bill to ban corporal punishment in schools. This convinced me after earlier hesitations that the Conservative Party was decidedly not where I wished to be.

superior, putting all his fervour into 'executing zealously and exactly what he is ordered'.

Yet familiarity with Hayek's work makes it clear that he himself could not possibly regard a title endorsing the 'permissive society' as anything but a distortion of his message. Indeed the Epilogue of the final volume of his last major work, *Law, Legislation and Liberty*[3] includes a fierce denunciation of permissiveness in general and educational permissiveness in particular. 'Permissive education' has become a cant slogan covering a wide range of different practices. Yet it is remarkable that someone who wishes to reduce the role of coercion in human affairs should express unqualified hostility to those who wish to reduce the role of coercion in the bringing-up of young people.

Nor is this a unique example from a late phase of Hayek's writing. In *The Constitution of Liberty* itself there are passages endorsing peacetime conscription – in striking contrast to Milton Friedman's personal lobbying against the US draft. Indeed, in a much earlier essay, *Individualism and Economic Order,*[4] Hayek praises the conformism of the inter-war British public school student, in contrast to the personal diversities cultivated by their continental counterparts.

The most revealing part of *Law, Legislation and Liberty* is the Epilogue already mentioned entitled 'The Three Sources of Human Values'. The source which Hayek wants to emphasise is evolved social institutions. Not every part of behaviour is either hereditary or the result of deliberate intention. It can also result from traditions, rules, and institutions, which are the product of a social rather than a biological evolution, and are thus the result of human action, but not of conscious human intention.

In contrast to libertarians, such as Milton Friedman, who take liberty as an absolute value, Hayek is quite ruthless in saying that the test of evolutionary rules is the simple one of success, identified, in turn, with progress. Resistance to the commercialisation and repressions of modern civilisation, whether from the romantic right or the libertarian left, arises from our tribal inheritance and impossible longings to get back. Hence Hayek's deep-seated opposition to the teachings of Freud and their attempt to bring into the open instinctive or unconscious longings and desires.

To those of us brought up on Hayek's definition of freedom as the absence of coercion, his condemnation of permissiveness came as a shock. What he really dislikes about educational or social permissiveness, and has frequently condemned in the Bloomsbury of Keynes's day, is the notion that rules which cannot be rationally explained do not have to be observed; or that people of any age should 'reason why' before accepting rules – conventional as well as legal.

Thus while Hayek's ultimate values are those of the radical apostle of human progress, his ethical philosophy is highly conservative. He faces the question of how rules should change; and maintains that we break them at our peril. Innovators may experiment with new rules or practices, but always at their own risk. The test is whether they can get away with them.* Moreover, the pioneer of new rules can proceed on only one or two fronts at a time. The condition of his success is his acceptance of the great bulk of other rules which, like his fellows, he follows blindly.

This looks like pretty standard conservative philosophy with which Edmund Burke would have felt at home. But there are important ways in which Hayekian social biology is very different from old conservatism. First, he actually welcomes the disturbance and change of the last two centuries. These have, he believes, been brought about by individual effort and initiative within a known framework of rules. Gradual changes in the rules themselves will, Hayek believes, further progress so long as they are spontaneous. But frequent deliberate tampering with the rules by over-ambitious reformers will, he fears, put an end to the whole development that began with the Renaissance and received a new lease of life from the Industrial Revolution.

The interesting question about this blend of radical evolutionary fervour and conservative insistence on rule observance is why someone holding it should regard himself as a libertarian, which Hayek undoubtedly does.

The libertarian element is injected into Hayek's philosophy by the assertion that rules which have evolved through custom or common law will in practice allow a large amount of

---

* His system has some resemblances to rule utilitarianism, but in contrast to the type of rule utilitarianism considered in the last chapter, the emphasis is very heavily on the rules; and the criterion for possible breaches lacks the moral evaluation common to all forms of utilitarianism.

individual freedom. Certain courses of action and behaviour will be forbidden; but, apart from those, people will really be free to 'do their own thing'. It is not clear whether this assertion about the linkage between freedom and evolved law is meant to be empirical or to follow necessarily from Hayek's definitions of 'law' and 'freedom'. Granted the premise (unfortunately rather dubious) that evolution is towards libertarian rules, then all the arguments about not seeking to impose a conscious, artificial pattern on our inheritance point in a libertarian direction. Nevertheless, in Hayek's last analysis, liberty is an instrumental value in the service not of happiness or welfare (as in utilitarianism), but of progress – material and intellectual – seen as an end in itself.

Towards a critique

How acceptable is the outlook? Hayek's ultimate criterion is open to serious question. By 'progress' he means movement and increase of complexity (in the biological sense). This is not a self-evident ethical yardstick. There are more important things (e.g. happiness) than the 'evolution of the human race', even assuming that we can identify the latter when we see it. Advance may be for the bad; and it is not a sufficient condemnation of intervention in the rules, even of a highly liberal society, to say that it may 'hold up progress'.

But it is not merely the outside critic who has difficulties with Hayek's rule-bound evolutionism. Hayek has difficulty himself. If there is an inbred wisdom, not apparent to the naked eye, in the evolution of common law or common custom, why deny this hidden wisdom to more interventionist or authoritarian structures? After all, institutions such as rent control, price control, a large nationalised sector, and heavy progressive taxation have existed in many countries for generations and have often evolved gradually. Might they not contain their own wisdom, not obvious to Hayek when writing as an economist? And will not, say, the abolition of rent control in Britain – let alone the reintroduction of capitalism, or free elections, in the Soviet Union – set in train all sorts of events not foreseeable by the simple-minded democrat or free-market economist who looks only at immediate consequences? Indeed are not Hayek's own economic arguments for free markets as superior ways of disseminating information and coordinating activity put into jeopardy by Hayek's philosophical insistence on our invincible ignorance of longer-term consequences? The introduction of a free market – say in the transmission of television programmes – can have remote effects on values, tastes, and behaviour never suspected by the economist who thinks in terms of satisfying existing consumer preferences.

Indeed, nothing could smack more of social engineering and be less respectful of slowly emerging rules and practices than Hayek's two most notable policy suggestions in his later writings. One is for the competitive circulation of rival privately-issued currencies. The other is for two parliamentary assemblies, elected in highly novel ways; the first concerned with the passing of laws and the second with supervising the policy and administration of the government of the day.

These contradictions can be resolved in a formal way by saying that, normally, spontaneous social evolution is the best way to change society. But occasionally social organisms, like natural ones, develop diseases, and drastic surgery may then be necessary. The problem then is to say who is to be entrusted with the diagnosis. (It is rather similar to the problem with the Marxist system, under which human beliefs are determined entirely by class status, but Marx and his disciples have somehow managed to escape from this class determination so that they alone are able to analyse society 'objectively'.)

It is more fruitful to avoid such artificial reconciliations and to accept that Hayek is attracted to two different political philosophies: classical liberalism (based on limited government, free markets, and the rule of law) and a conservative philosophy which stresses tradition and the hidden wisdom of existing institutions. When in some golden age – say Gladstonian England, as seen through nostalgic spectacles – the prevailing tradition was itself that of classical liberalism the two systems of Hayek might seem in harmony. When prevailing conditions are authoritarian or collectivist, there is tension between the two ideals.

Libertarianism

What are the main alternatives for those who find the Hayekian outlook, so far from displaying the anarchism of which it is accused by ignorant critics, too authoritarian in many elements?

Some libertarians (including Milton Friedman's son, David) call themselves 'anarcho-capitalists' and believe that personal safety and property can be secured by private armies and police forces; and that the way to choose between rival rules of law is competition, including competition between courts, in which the better system will gain adherents and be enforced in private bargains.[5] The arguments used are often ingenious and subtle. But the reality which corresponds to such proposals is too much like the warring private armies of Renaissance Italy, or the feuding factions of the Mafia and the Red Brigade in the Italy of today. These are potentially even more oppressive than many authoritarian governments – and hardly a model for reformers.

Those libertarians who wisely retain the idea of state authority would confine it to 'night watchman' activities, mainly law and order, and defence. Such writers are far more clear-cut in their policy views than Hayek. But they achieve this clarity by advocating thorough-going *laissez-faire*. There would certainly be no conscription, no anti-drugs legislation, and no interference in private sexual behaviour. But there would also be no social security – not even the provision of the barest minimum – and nothing remotely resembling a health service. There would be no place for town-and-country planning rules. Attempts to limit the spillover effect of one man's use of space on his neighbours would be confined to what could be achieved by a suitable framework of property rights with a wider concept of damages than exists at present.

The libertarians are not necessarily lacking in personal compassion; but their system is. Redistribution in any democratic society depends on altruism or solidarity on the part of the more fortunate citizens. But whether one thinks of the relief of poverty or (more ambitiously) of income redistribution, personal charity is not enough – for reasons of economic logic. Redistribution is, like defence, a 'public good'. This means that there is little incentive for the individual to provide it. I might be – indeed would be – willing to pay a voluntary contribution to transfer some of my income to the poor as part of a compact with millions of others. But it would not be rational for me to do so, to the same extent, on my own. The benefit to the income of the poor would be negligible, and the loss of my own income and welfare substantial. (These very elementary considerations are discussed in contemporary economic literature in highly technical articles about 'Pareto-optimal redistribution'.)

Similar arguments about public goods apply to support for the arts. There is a great deal of contemporary music which I, along with many other concert-goers and record-buyers, am quite unable to appreciate; but I accept the arguments for supporting it, and I will pay my share if other taxpayers will do the same; passing round the hat is not a substitute. There will be other activities which I would be unwilling to support on a club basis, but other taxpayers would be. Some state activity can be understood as a network of implicit contracts, which it would be prohibitively expensive to negotiate explicitly, both because of transaction costs and because of the incentive to act as a free rider and leave others to finance the activities of which one privately approves.

My doubts about the treatment of liberty by free market economists go deeper than misgivings about the treatment of redistribution or public goods by particular writers. The mistake of classical liberals and, even more, of radical right conservatives, is to equate *all* authority with *state* authority. Oppression in an old people's or children's home, or even in the family, can be just as great.

As John Stuart Mill pointed out, conformism and the intolerance of individual divergence in small communities can in practice be the greatest obstacles to individual liberty. The option of 'voting with one's feet' and finding elsewhere a community to one's own taste, on which many modern free market writers base their preference for local over central government, exists mainly for prime-age adult males, who make up a minority of the total population. Hayek's ideal of abstract impersonal law is more likely to be applied – admittedly, at some bureaucratic cost – in centrally administered federal or national services than at a local government or community level. The trouble there is that everybody knows everyone else; and although it is easier to take account of particular circumstances, it also becomes easier to bend general principles in favour of those who matter locally and against those considered a nuisance.

Libertarian doctrine applies most convincingly either to

'ageless' isolated individuals or adult heads-of-family. It is much less convincing for the many people who are too young, or too old, or too dependent, or too muddled to 'stand on their own feet', and to take out their own insurance against the vicissitudes of life.

The difficulty of the modern libertarian is to find a way of combining the Christian-socialist awareness that we are most of us very vulnerable and terribly dependent on the help and sympathy of others, with the equally important insight that the attempt to coerce someone into being a tool or instrument of another is a great evil.

Mill's distinction between 'self-regarding' and 'other-regarding' action is an essential protection against public interference with private behaviour among consenting adults, but by itself it is insufficient. Almost anything that anyone does is liable to 'affect others' unless in an enclosed space behind curtains. Is liberty to make offensive gestures to others in the streets, or to fornicate in public, or to be smelly or unsightly in crowded places, a basic human right? Do I have to enlist to fight for these things because I find the military sadism shown in *Chips with Everything*, the public-school horrors of *If*, or the use of the closed shop to bar people from a chosen profession, offensive?

A disposition towards personal freedom, both as an end in itself and as a means to other ends, does not imply that it should be the only political value any more than the pursuit of satisfaction or happiness, urged by utilitarians, should be the only goal. There may at times have to be a trade-off between freedom and other goals. The heavy (and arbitrarily enforced) penalties on all soft drugs in most countries, when people are rightly allowed to drink and smoke at their own risk, reflect mainly intolerance and prejudice; but a recognition of this does not commit one to legalising heroin nor to adopting a completely *a priori* attitude towards the law which would treat all research findings with disdain.

It is time, however, to pass from criticism of the whole Hayekian system, and of the 'libertarians' who have taken his ideas much further, to discuss a few of the more illuminating features of Hayek's writings. These have shed light on fundamental issues, where we have been badly misled by the intellectual mainstream.

Market signals

The first contribution of Hayek that I want to stress is his treatment of economics as a social science rather than as an exercise in the optimum allocation of resources. For a long time he was almost alone among market economists in being concerned with the effect of the market system on the evolution and stability of society. Whereas most 'macro' economists, whether of the left or of the right, concentrate on mathematical exercises (sometimes verbal mathematics), trying to work out 'solutions' in given conditions, or spend their time on forecasting exercises, Hayek has been interested in markets as examples of human institutions, like language or law, which have evolved without any conscious plan on anyone's part.

For instance, even before the fashion for forecasting models had fully developed, Hayek wrote a shrewd critique of bogus quantification based on the complexity of the phenomena studied.[6] His essential point is that we cannot count on the good fortune of being able to discover by direct observation simple quantitative regularities between economic variables – but it is still possible and worthwhile to formulate general rules. For instance, economic theory can tell us that we cannot maintain a fixed rate of exchange and at the same time maintain an independent financial policy with a national price level objective; but this does not mean that we can predict where the exchange rate will go if the latter option is chosen.

The breakdown of one supposed numerical relationship after another in macroeconomics in the last decade has made this view far less eccentric than it appeared in the heyday of econometric predictions. Keynesian type relations between consumption and income, and monetarist predictions of 'the demand for money' have alike failed to give even rough enough approximations to be useful for policy. Writers, themselves reared in the quantitative tradition, have recently begun to stress that the relationships in their equations ('parameters', to use this word for once in its correct sense) are not stable, and depend on such forces as the climate of expectations and the policies that the authorities are believed to be following. Much of the discredit into which economics has fallen would fail to surprise readers of Hayek's methodological papers of the late 1950s and early 1960s.

For several decades, Hayek has stressed that markets are means of disseminating information diffused among millions of human beings (who will not be conscious of all the information they possess). This information is transmitted in the form of signals – price changes in flexible markets, but also shortages and surpluses where price changes are delayed by habit or law.* They also provide an incentive to meet unsatisfied needs and to move resources from where they are no longer required. Wants, techniques, and resources are not given, but are constantly changing – in part due to the activities of entrepreneurs who suggest possibilities (whether digital recordings or cheap stand-by transatlantic flights) which people did not know existed before. The market system is a 'discovery technique' rather than a way of allocating known resources among known wants with known techniques. The latter problem could, in principle at least, be solved by computers on the entirely libertarian principle that people's preferences should be satisfied to the maximum possible extent for any given distribution of income. No computer can predict, however, the emergence of new knowledge, original ideas, or commercial innovations – and people's reactions to them.

Over and above this, the market provides a method of coordinating the activities of millions of people and of solving problems without a vast apparatus of political decision and of governmental enforcement. The very existence of this self-regulating system is quite unsuspected by ninety-nine per cent of the population, who (to the extent that they think about these matters at all) assume that we must have a national or international 'policy' for energy, jobs, productivity, or whatever other problem hits the newspaper headlines.

This view of markets as a discovery procedure and coordinating mechanism is now common property to many economists, especially in the United States (away from the eastern seaboard). But it is still 'double Dutch' to large numbers of Oxbridge graduates who have been brought up to suppose that they have only to diagnose a departure from

* The 'but also' is my own, not Hayek's, gloss. The case is stronger if this concession is made.

some theoretical optimum (so-called perfect competition) in a market to believe they have made a case for government intervention – without asking whether the human beings who will have to carry out that intervention have the knowledge or the motivation actually to improve matters. Too often the defects of real world markets are compared with the hypothetical action of a benevolent and omniscient dictator (as frequently – in the more technical writings – for reasons of mathematical convenience as from any deeply-held convictions).

Here, as elsewhere, the Hayekian approach opens up rather than solves problems. Hayek sees the market network as a gradually evolving social system rather than as a mathematical solution to the problem of resource allocation on the basis of known, certain, and unchanging information. But just like language and law – those other products of social evolution with which Hayek makes explicit comparison – the transmission and incentive mechanisms of the market can be improved. So shifting attention from the static allocation of resources to 'the market as a discovery procedure' does not remove the issue of intervention.

Unfortunately, much of recent government intervention does not make any sort of sense in terms of improving the market, either in the textbook sense as an instrument of allocation, or in the Hayckian sense of a signalling system. The roots of such intervention lie in the defects of the political system. The economic rationalisations given make no sense at all, and they seem to come from people who, far from wanting to improve markets, have never even heard that they exist, and feel they must rush in with a physical and collectivist 'solution' to any 'problem'.

Examples range from the supposed importance of exports to the assumed necessity for an energy policy. Included in the list would be the postwar cult of boasting about how many houses governments of differing political parties 'built', the encouragement of home ownership, and indeed the need for a housing policy at all. It would encompass 'the Importance of the Farmer', so dear even to the most free-market of Tory Governments.

The list of conventional policies to be condemned can be made to sound heretical, far-out, or downright bizarre, but it is based on very elementary textbook economics as interpreted by iconoclasts who prefer to turn their iconoclasm against the world rather than the textbooks. One does not in the least have to be on the radical right to accept such a critique. This critique would be compatible with support for a much higher degree of redistribution of income and wealth than we now have, which could only be at the expense of the large mass of voters in the middle. It would also be compatible with much collective action to provide genuine public goods or to discourage anti-social spillovers. (Examples range from the protection of city centres and spending on the arts, to improvements of the Health Service, and better state-financed technical training.)

It is instructive to contrast the knee-jerk hostility to markets of many western reformers with the Communist economic reformers who are thoroughly disillusioned with 'central planning' and are trying to bring in price and profit incentives. Tempting though it is to say that Communist economists in Hungary have a better understanding of market forces than some paternalist British Conservatives or 'liberal Republicans' one should go slowly at this point. To publish a set of rules asking the managers of state enterprises to behave *as if* they were profit-maximising entrepreneurs in competitive private industry ignores the actual personal motivations faced by these men; and this approach became badly unstuck in the British nationalised industries. You do not make a donkey into a zebra merely by painting stripes on its back.

Hayek long ago pointed out that 'market socialism' among state enterprises might provide a few mechanical rules such as 'Invest where the expected return exceeds a market rate of interest plus a risk premium.' But it would not tell us whether to believe the estimates of return made by state managers. Nor would it help to decide who should be allowed to bid for the available funds, or how new entrants with completely different ideas about techniques, products, and return were to be accommodated. The benefits of the market system can be combined with a considerable state sector and a good deal of redistribution; but they cannot be as easily divorced from 'capitalism' as some academics (who do not want to arouse the hostility provoked by this word) would like. Above all, one should avoid the trap of supposing that the copying of a few western textbook rules (such as marginal cost pricing) would eliminate the Gulag Archipelago. By all means, encourage Communist countries to try to make their economic systems more efficient and humane. But there is a limit to what can be achieved by economic liberalisation alone; and I suspect that many eastern European economists would be shouting this from the housetops were they but free to do so.

The frequent fallacy of, for instance, radical playwrights in the west is not that they expose the hypocrisy, shallowness, and double standards of society. It is that they jump from the demonstration that many things are wrong to the inference that evils are due to 'capitalism' rather than to authority in general. To decide whether the capitalist elements increase the abuse of authority or act as a check on it requires considerable penetration of economic issues. Writers who are avowedly bored by economic analysis should not be encouraged to pronounce on them. Their attempt to do so discredits the exposure of evils which are very real, though wrongly attributed to 'capitalism'.

Unfortunately, many 'left of centre' politicians have reacted to recent strains in their mixed economies by retreating towards an anti-intellectual interventionism. The Bad Godesberg programme, under which the German Social Democrats (in 1959) formally dropped the demand for a centrally-directed economy, has become less and less typical of the approach of socialists (even in Germany). As a result economists wanting to make intelligent use of the market place are likely to find their most sympathetic audiences on the radical right.

This should put them particularly on the look-out for underlying divergencies. Professional economists who favour market forces put the emphasis on the price mechanism and on the profitability test (which is also valid for state industry or workers' co-ops). By contrast radical right politicians put the emphasis on reduced taxes and government spending cuts, without too many fine nuances about their exact effects.

We might note that a belief in marketplace economics conflicts much less with conservative political values when it places its emphasis on the-carrot-and-the-stick (especially the latter) than when it is founded primarily on a belief in individual freedom and the realisation that there is a strong affinity between 'capitalism' and 'the permissive society'. The carrot-and-stick man will be quite happy to talk of 'the punishment fitting the crime'. The permissive free-market economist feels uneasy about talk of responsibility and punishment; he prefers to say that people should pay for the social costs of their actions, and he would design institutions and laws to that end. These may seem differences of language, but language is important. On crucial, unforeseeable occasions the differences between Conservative Gradgrindism and the more libertarian marketeer will come to the surface.

Rule of law

Contrary to popular belief Friedrich Hayek has not provided any easily recognisable economic criteria for recognising state intervention of the harmful type. Some commentators suppose that he thinks the slightest move from *laissez-faire* will take us irrevocably along the road to serfdom, while others find that he is, if anything, too pragmatic.

The free market arguments in *The Road to Serfdom* were based on the incompatibility of central planning with personal liberty. In subsequent years Hayek has approached the issue indirectly. He has argued, especially in *The Constitution of Liberty* (probably his magnum opus), that the main condition for a free society is what he calls 'the rule of law'. He certainly does not mean by that that the mere observance by rulers of constitutionally enacted laws is enough. On the contrary he would condemn many perfectly valid legislative acts for being arbitrary, discriminatory, and giving far too much discretion to politicians and officials. It is less misleading if we translate 'the rule of law' to mean a presumption in favour of general rules and against discretionary power. Hayek attempts to derive not only the fundamental political and legal basis, but also the economic policies, of a free society from this conception.

'The rule of law' may not, however, rule out everything that Hayek would like it to rule out. Many of the economic doctrines flow better simply from assertions that, if one believes in free personal choice, the direction of economic activity must be decided by the consumer, saver, investor, and worker. This is a straightforward economic deduction, made in *The Road to Serfdom* but accepted – with qualifications about imperfections and externalities – by many mainstream economists.

Nevertheless, Hayek has performed a very great service by bringing back on to the agenda of discussion the idea of the rule of impartial general laws, as something different from the mere constitutional enactment of the policies of elected leaders. The latter has been aptly named 'elective dictatorship'[7] and is at the opposite pole to the civil association discussed near the end of the first chapter.

Unfortunately neither Hayek nor anyone else has been able to give a statement of the doctrine of the rule of general laws which will make clear what it implies in particular cases. To say that 'laws must not single out named individuals' would not be controversial even among collectivists, and would not be enough to protect us against a great deal of arbitrary legislation. On the other hand general rules must mention categories: traffic laws deal with motor-cars, sales taxes make traders liable and so on. Once this is admitted, it is very difficult to see how rules can be prevented from singling out occupations or industries, nor is it necessarily always desirable that they should be prevented from so doing. But once we have gone along this road a supposedly general law may well pick out for especially severe treatment a group or even a single individual.

A further restriction is required, but is extremely difficult to formulate. Hayek's proposal – that a general rule should be acceptable to a majority of both those whom it benefits and those whom it harms – is much too strong. For it gives a veto to any minority in any circumstances – for instance, to the Mafia in a proposal for a new law against banditry. His illustration of progressive taxation as contrary to the rule of law, because it is not acceptable to high rate payers, hardly helps his case. There are many arguments against high marginal tax rates; but the objections of those who pay them are hardly conclusive.

The quest for a foolproof definition of just general rules is most unlikely to succeed. This is not an argument for throwing out the notion. The basic concepts of mathematics, formal logic, and even physics are far from easy to define, but this does not make them useless. ('What is electricity?' said the examiner to the hopeless pupil. 'I don't know' was the reply. 'Good,' said the examiner, 'that makes two of us. You pass with honours.') The Rawls veil of ignorance does supply a criterion of disinterestedness, and helps to narrow down the alternative possibilities.

Once the ideal of just general rules has been outlined, however hazily, we know well enough that many of the items of the criminal code are as close to impersonal general rules as we can hope to get, just as the Star Chamber and the Press Gang are at the other extreme. We know too, if we are frank, that a piece of legislation which defines an illegal monopoly or restrictive practice, even if only in *prima facie* terms, is closer to the ideal than one which leaves everything to the discretion of the minister or some official commission.

General rules are desirable for their own sake. The limitations of the law are more akin to the constraints imposed by nature than are the unpredictable discretionary orders and prohibitions of public officials, and as such are more acceptable to anyone with self-respect.

There is, of course, no hard and fast dividing line between general rules and discretionary power, but a spectrum between them. Rules require interpretation; and discretion is rarely unlimited. One of the best practical tests is probably not administrative or legal, but that of predictability. If a citizen can predict what he will be permitted to do without knowing the identity of those making the decisions, general rules apply. If a great deal depends on the reaction of a particular politician, official or judge, or the bargaining skills of the interested parties, we are nearer a regime of administrative discretion.[8]

Hayek is right to emphasise that general rules are an important protection – perhaps the most important single protection – for freedom. However, he often argues as if general laws are a *sufficient* condition for a free society; and this is mistaken. Many policies involving a high degree of coercion can be imposed by general rules – not only the Scottish Sabbath conceded by Hayek, but for instance a ban on foreign travel (to which the exceptions, such as business and official travel, could be stated quite impersonally). There is no one philosopher's stone for minimising coercion in society. We should applaud Hayek's resurrection of the ideal of 'a government of laws rather than men' without expecting that it will always be unambiguous or a sufficient guarantee against oppression.

The myth of just reward

The most radical of Hayek's contributions is the denial that it is possible to assess a just reward for people's services and pay them accordingly. This strikes at the most cherished illusions on the right as well as on the left. Not merely does Hayek deny that there are ethical or scientific principles of determining, say, a socially just 'incomes policy': he also denies that there is any moral merit attaching to the rewards people can obtain in the market-place. Many conservatives, including some who regard themselves as Hayekians, say that the market price for a person's services reflects their marginal value to society and is, therefore, just.

But Hayek is right to insist that, although the first proposition may be true, the inference does not follow. It is *expedient* that pay relativities should reflect market valuations in order to steer resources towards where they are most needed. To attempt to override market relativities in the name of 'reward according to merit' presupposes that some outside authority can assess how much pain and effort a task has cost (which will, in any case, vary enormously between individuals in the same occupation), and whether people have made as much of their opportunities as they should, and 'how much of their achievement is due to circumstances'. This is an impossible undertaking, and the attempt to undertake it involves *hubris* of a frightening extent.

Nor is the aim sensible. As Hayek writes, it is more rational for people 'to achieve a minimum of pain and sacrifice and therefore a minimum of merit'. Perhaps the single most attractive feature of a reasonably free market economy is that a person's livelihood does not depend on persuading a public official, or a trade union, or a workers' cooperative of his merit. It is sufficient that he should be able to perform some service for which his fellow-men express a demand, irrespective of whether they like him or not. It is, incidentally, worth observing that 'reward according to merit' is quite incompatible with egalitarianism, and is indeed a completely contrary idea.

All this is a far cry from saying that the rich, the poor, and the in-between deserve their respective places in society, or would do so even if hereditary wealth were eliminated and opportunities more evenly distributed. It is expedient to relate relative pay to market demand and supply; to attempt to substitute a different scale of relative importance would produce extremely damaging results for reasons touched on later in this book. Nevertheless, actual rewards will depend on an unpredictable mixture of effort, ability, and luck. The ability to sing the *Liebestod*, having a nose for commercial opportunities or sporting an attractive appearance, are matters of luck not merit. Nor is it a demerit to have trained for an occupation for which the supply has increased (such as academic teaching) or the demand fallen off (such as steel workers).

This aspect of Hayek's teaching is the most difficult for many of his conservative supporters to accept. Irving Kristol, for instance, complains in a well-known critique[9] that there are deep-seated yearnings for a moral or theological justification of differences in well-being or position; and that the rational arguments for accepting a system which does not even claim to bring a just distribution of rewards are too abstract to accept. This may be true psychologically. But Hayek is still abundantly justified in warning that a defence of the market system on the grounds that it offers just rewards is bound to fail.

A true Hayekian has no more sympathy than any member of the far-out left with the white-collar worker who dislikes being overtaken by blue-collar workers, or with professional men who complain that truck drivers are now earning more than they are. (A reader of Adam Smith's teachings on 'equality of net advantages' among people of comparable abilities and opportunities would expect something like this to happen sooner or later.)

Hayek's denial of the doctrine of just reward is especially attractive because it undermines so much conventional wisdom. It is the complete opposite of what most Conservative and Republican politicians and most middle-class voters wish to believe. These all feel much better if they can suppose that their relative affluence of former years and any advantages they still retain have been and are rewards for conspicuous merit.

But, characteristically, Hayek spoils a splendid and heretical contribution to understanding by extending the denial of just occupational reward to the much more sweeping assertion that there is no such thing as 'social justice'. The value, or otherwise, of distinguishing a special kind of justice from justice in general is not the issue; and it is a semantic problem whether people's ethical views on the distribution of wealth and income should come under 'justice' or under some other heading. The substantive point is that Hayek (in striking contrast to John Rawls) insists that *any* public policy towards the distribution of income and property (beyond the provision of a basic social-security minimum) is incompatible with a free society and the rule of law. (I have already mentioned his objection to progressive taxation.) In this he performs a disservice to market economists, who have tried for generations to convey to uncomprehending politicians that it is quite possible to change the distribution of wealth without interfering with market relativities. A combined progressive and negative income tax reduces absolute rewards at the top and increases them at the bottom, *without* attempting to evaluate jobs or merit and without interfering with market rankings.

An ideal shape of an income or property distribution can be expressed in perfectly general mathematical terms without any mention of merit, occupation, or individuals. Its instruments can be taxes, positive and negative, or the law of property and inheritance.

Redistribution and reassignment

Hayek's hostility towards redistribution would have been better directed towards another process which may be termed 'reassignment'. The distinction has been the subject of an important book by a Canadian economist, Dan Usher.[10] Redistribution means narrowing the gap between the rich and poor ends of the existing income scale. Reassignment means changing people's *order* on that scale. The degree of political assignment is shown by the proportion of a representative person's position, income or wealth which depends on who runs the government and what politicians and officials decide.

Professor Usher uses a well-known result in the theory of games to demonstrate that there is no stable method of deciding on the allocation of income by majority voting. It might seem that if manna came down from heaven a community might agree on an equal division. In fact any group of slightly more than fifty per cent would have an incentive to despoil the minority. Further, such majority rule would be unstable as well as unjust; for it would normally pay a few members of the minority to make offers to part of the majority to form a new coalition. Alternatively the minority would ultimately refuse to be bound by majority vote. Thus endless strife could be expected and the community would become 'ungovernable'.

Nor does this result depend on unlimited greed. The mere knowledge that such spoiling coalitions are possible will induce even the meekest citizen to join in the game. In the course of the battle any link such as race, language, religion or regional association which can help to form winning coalitions is eagerly seized upon. Questions such as the tribe of the president, the number of French speakers in the Canadian Government or the religious composition of the Northern Ireland authorities become far more sharply divisive when a citizen's livelihood, job and housing depend on the answers.

Professor Usher has no difficulty in showing that state socialism would not be able to provide for a non-political determination of rewards and positions or even of business decisions. Most of the apparently precise decision rules, such as applying a discounted cash flow rate of return, leave an enormous amount to individual judgment. Any kind of state-run economy based on centralised planning and large public undertakings would in practice throw the key decisions about which industries to expand and in which regions, and which appointment to make, into the political arena.

The *non-political assignment of income*, which Professor Usher believes to be the great advantage of market systems, has to be balanced against another principle, which he calls 'acceptability'. Market assignment of income will be acceptable if a majority of voters believe themselves 'better off in the long run than under any alternative method'.

The majority of citizens have to be persuaded that the

contradictions between their equality as voters and the inequality of their economic status is worth accepting for the sake of other benefits. Unlike Hayek, Usher believes that redistribution to reduce income disparities is both desirable and necessary to secure the acceptability of capitalism. Redistribution is exemplified by the progressive income tax and social security payments.

Unlike redistribution, a reassignment which changes people's order on the rich-poor scale, and does so at the discretion of government, has no obvious resting place. Once it occurs on a large scale 'every regional, ethnic or industrial interest group is at once at war with every other group . . . every bond becomes a nucleus around which people may coalesce in the scramble for private access to public funds.' This phenomenon was long ago labelled the 'problem of faction'.

Examples of reassignment are new tariffs, industrial subsidies and price supports such as those in the Common Agricultural Policy. An extreme example of reassignment occurred in a Bengal famine when the Indian Government used its limited supplies of grain to feed the urban poor, while letting landless agricultural labourers starve because they were too dispersed to be dangerous.

Less lurid examples abound of the damage done by reassignment policies. An 'industrial strategy' might seem harmless enough – until it is remembered that if it is to have any meaning, profitability becomes dependent on official decisions, and resources are diverted from production to lobbying. The criteria for industrial assistance are typically so vague that the economy is moved from market towards political assignment, thus increasing the scope for patronage. One man prospers because his firm is subsidised at a critical moment while another goes bankrupt because he fails to persuade officials that his management is 'enlightened' enough.

It is the shift to political assignment that makes wage and price controls so harmful. The controller has to decide whether profits of textile firms are appropriate, whether professors should be paid more or less than civil servants and so on. Brief episodes of pay or price control based on a simple norm can work on the basis of past relativities; but once changes in relativities are required, we have moved a long way to political assignment where the strike threat, party allegiance or simple bribery come to have a progressively larger role to play. Eventually the removal of some key controls (e.g. rent controls) itself becomes a political act, which would harm a major group.

The pragmatic politicians – who look only at the immediate effects of a tariff here or a subsidy there to favour a vocal interest group, or impose wage and price controls in order to be seen to be 'doing something' about inflation or unemployment – may seem to be doing only moderate harm from the point of view of prosperity and income distribution. But they are doing immense harm by increasing the *political assignment of incomes*.

Redistribution and equality

Having accepted the legitimacy of redistribution, the next questions are: 'What sort of redistribution should there be?' and 'How far should it go?' Redistribution towards the least well off is a generous notion so long as we avoid the King Wenceslas myth and realise that the great majority of citizens will have to provide the wherewithal and that it cannot be provided at zero cost to the majority by squeezing the rich or by some magic change in government financial policy.

Many people who talk about equality are mainly concerned with transfers to the poor. But, strictly speaking, the goal of equality means, as already mentioned, that it is desirable to reduce the wellbeing of the better off for its own sake – even if no one else benefits. The existence of a submerged twenty per cent getting far less than the average income can lead to the same 'coefficient of inequality' as a situation in which no such pockets of poverty exist but where there are a number of high incomes among the top five or ten per cent. Yet the second situation would seem to most of us far more satisfactory than the first. Indeed Puerto Rico and Italy emerged from one investigation[11] with lower coefficients of inequality – and thus as supposedly more equal societies – than Sweden, Denmark and the Netherlands; and India had the same coefficient as West Germany.

An interest in reducing the wellbeing of the better off, even if no one else benefits, is nothing but envy. The word 'envy' is of course pejorative. Academic writers have tried to make it respectable by talking about 'relative deprivation' or 'interdependent utilities', and politicians by saying that certain rewards are 'socially unacceptable'. But a desire for equality for its own sake, even if no one at all benefits, is envy, however dressed up the sentiment.

One more attractive notion is that of maximising the welfare of the representative (i.e. median) voter. As Dan Usher remarks, 'It has a natural stopping place. For as more and more income is transfered from rich to poor, the marginal tax rates required rise, and total output is diminished until a point is reached when the median voter has more to lose from the adverse effect on total output than he has from redistribution.'

This notion may be much better than crude envy, but it is far removed from justice, as it does nothing to safeguard really poor, oppressed or handicapped groups who may be a minority among the electorate. Nor is it a recipe for stability, as those who lose out, whether at the top or the bottom, will have every interest in forming coalitions with other groups, or in calling for reassignment, to redress the balance.

The most promising way out of the impasse is still along the lines suggested by John Rawls, in *A Theory of Justice*. This book, which has already been mentioned in the previous chapter, is probably the most influential book on moral or political philosophy since John Stuart Mill.

His method, it will be recalled, is to carry out a mental experiment. He asks which principles people would be likely to accept if they were working out the rules of society from beneath a 'veil of ignorance'. This is a device for ensuring impartiality. The idea is to work out the principles on which free and rational people concerned to further their own interests would desire their community to be run if they did not know their own social or economic place, the market value of their own talents, and many other key features of their real situation. A wealthy man might like to establish principles which minimised taxes for welfare purposes; a poor man might espouse principles of an opposite kind. If one excludes knowledge of one's own actual position, there is some chance of working out the principles on a disinterested basis.

Rawls attempts to derive some fairly precise principles from the veil of ignorance, in particular the principle that social and economic inequalities are to be justified only if they benefit the least advantaged representative person. These principles, summarised on page 41, are a good deal more questionable than the method itself. The veil of ignorance is a very useful device for narrowing the range of disagreement, despite the imaginative leap required; but it cannot eliminate differences in subjective preferences and thus cannot lead to a unique result which all people of goodwill will accept.

Rawls would like his reader to suppose in some formulations that he or she is ignorant not merely of his own personal position in society but even of the society or century to which he belongs. The use of the veil of ignorance requires a large imaginative effort, even in its less rigorous conception. Moreover, the vast literature generated by John Rawls's work suggests that it is not enough to provide determinate substantive conclusions on which all who accept the basic idea would agree. Personal attitudes towards risk (e.g. the risk of being one of the unlucky ones) and the value attached to the small chance of a large prize will affect a person's attitude to the distribution of property rights, taxes and transfers. To deprive someone of one attribute after another in quest of the veil of ignorance is to come near to asking him to imagine himself divested of all qualities, in which case he would hardly be a person able to engage in discourse on just rules.

But even if we reject his precise principles, the Rawls social contract can help to narrow differences on the subject of distribution. To the extent that we can make the imaginative leap, it is a way of removing obvious bias, although not of removing all differences of opinion.

My own first desire under the veil of ignorance would be to make sure that everyone had a basic minimum, defined not in absolute terms but in relation to the wealth of my society. This would be a safeguard in case I drew the unfortunate cards and found myself at the bottom of the pack. Secondly, I would want to ensure a large area of personal freedom where I could make my own decisions, and to ensure political, social, cultural and economic opportunities which could not be literally 'equal' all round, but could be free of barriers of privilege and irrelevant entry qualifications.

Would I carry redistribution beyond the idea of a basic minimum? I would be tempted to turn round Rawls's principle 2(a) and say that *redistribution* is only justified if it improved the position of the least well off, instead of saying that *inequalities* are so justified. The inversion shifts the onus of proof where knowledge is imperfect and leaves at least a shadow of the entitlement principle, by giving the benefit of the doubt to the incomes or holdings which people have acquired through their own efforts or from gifts and bequests. (Even then the principle is plausible only in conjunction with Rawls's more detailed presumptions – for instance his 'lexical principle' that something which benefits the least well off is likely to benefit those one degree higher, and so on up the scale, so that the welfare of the bulk of the community is not ignored in policy determination.)

The interest-group threat

The distinction between generalised redistribution, on which some partial consensus might be possible, and the reassignment of income and property rights among pressure groups, over which struggle is likely to be endless, lends force to an important theme in Hayek's later writings. Hayek's most recent warnings have no longer been about the overambitious centralised planning castigated in *The Road to Serfdom* (closely paralleled, incidentally, by George Orwell's *1984*), but about the threat posed by the combination of rival interest groups. This can lead, not to a single centralised tyranny, but to shifting pockets of anarchy and petty dictatorship, occurring simultaneously in different areas. The relative stability of expectations about the political and economic framework – which allows individuals to make long-term plans with some stability of expectations about the social rules – is under threat.

The main theme of Hayek's latest work is that democracy has degenerated into an unprincipled auction to satisfy rival organised groups who can never in the long run be appeased, because their demands are mutually incompatible. His main contribution to the discussion of contemporary 'stagflation' (the combination of high inflation and high unemployment) is through his analysis of interest-group politics. This is not to underrate his reopening of key issues in monetary theory glossed over by most monetarists,[12] but to agree with him that the obstacles to appropriate monetary policies for containing inflation and to labour market policies for containing unemployment lie in the political sphere.

Hayek endorses in a descriptive sense the American-inspired economic theory of politics, which analyses the political market in terms of competitive bidding for the citizen's vote, just as commercial businesses compete for the citizen's pound or dollar. But, unlike these theorists, he regards unprincipled vote competition and competitive lobbying as not merely defective – in the way that commercial markets can be, only more so – but inherently objectionable because they have nothing to do with justice. He sees them as simply the sharing-out of spoils which people take from their fellow-citizens.

Thus in a sense Hayek takes further the discussion of interest groups and the 'Wenceslas Myth' in Chapter 1. There I argued that a great deal of political and economic debate is essentially about rival claims on scarce resources, and that while government can reallocate resources, it can only with the greatest difficulty increase the total. I argued that political life would be healthier if it were realised that the main governmental functions were concerned with formulating laws and rules and deciding which services should be financed collectively from taxation rather than individually through the market – remembering that both methods of provision have to be paid for by the citizens themselves, governments having nothing to give.

Hayek (and Usher) then raise a further question: What are the proper limits on a government's power to reallocate either through the fiscal system or through collective provision of services? They question the view that government should just be content to record the results of – or itself initiate – a haggle among interest groups to divide the spoils according to the balance of pressures prevailing at any particular time.

Many political theorists, including the American pluralists, have long taken it for granted that politics is and can only be about the accommodation of rival interest-groups, and that if a fair compromise is reached between them we have nothing to worry about. It has been natural for people brought up on this false common sense to claim that what we need is to extend the process further into economic policy. They advocate institutions such as 'a national pay forum' in which employers meet trade unionists and government representatives, to a point where there can be real horse-trading.

Here I can give only a rough sketch of why horse-trading between groups is unlikely to produce a satisfactory economic result. Each party to the bargain is likely to be given some concession which is only mildly damaging to the rest of the community. One group may be granted a tariff on foreign imports; another a protection from the threat of new domestic entrants; a third a delay in the introduction of new methods or deliberate overmanning (called 'work sharing') to keep up employment. One group may receive an injection of public money to finance a wage increase unavailable in the market; another large section will receive rent controls and subsidies, thus leading to permanent housing shortage; and another large group 'mortgage concessions' leading to overinvestment in dwellings. But the harm done by the sum total of these restrictive practices and special deals is very far from mild. Each of us suffers from the concession to the groups to which we do not belong. We would all be better off in the not-so-long term if we could achieve the only horse-trading worth doing, i.e. an agreement by every group to relinquish its special privileges on the understanding that other groups did the same.

It should be stressed that the appointment of spokesmen for wide-ranging groups such as consumers or home-owners makes matters worse rather than better. Such spokesmen are all too inclined to press for policies such as 'price controls' or 'mortgage-rate subsidies' which are in the end detrimental to the welfare of the community and thus to the people they claim to represent. The best way to promote the consumer interest is to encourage competition to serve it in the market place, aided perhaps by generalised policies not aimed at favouring interest groups (for instance subsidising consumer information services, or making sure that people are legally liable for adverse spillovers such as dumping noxious substances in rivers).

Of course politics have always had a large element of 'pork barrel' and 'feeding trough' about them. This was especially true in the USA where 'pluralist' (i.e. interest-group) political theory and free-market economics developed, side by side, in splendid isolation. The 'pork barrel' in fact does little harm when government activities and aspirations and popular expectations of their results are modest. The defects of politics viewed as an accommodation of interest-groups are thus not probed until it is too late.

Hayek sees the source of interest-group domination in what he calls majoritarian or unlimited democracy. This is known more popularly as 'the mandate doctrine' – the belief that a government elected by a majority of voters (usually a plurality) should be able to enact what it likes without any check. These excessive pretensions can only destroy the real value of democracy as the best way we know of changing the government without force and making rulers accountable to their citizens.

'Majoritarian democracy' is not the only source of interest-group pressure. Such pressure is experienced in communist Europe, although the interest-groups may be different. But the great expansion of the political sphere (and the crumbling of restraints and inhibitions on what governments may attempt) has increased both the pressures by organised interests on governments and the responsiveness of political leaders to these pressures.

We face a real, not a bogus dilemma. There is a crucial connection between personal and political freedom, on the one hand, and economic freedom on the other, as *The Road to Serfdom* clearly established. In the decades since it appeared there has not been a single example of a fully collectivist economy retaining basic freedoms. Yet the only societies which seem able to protect a market economy from erosion by interest-groups are certain Pacific Basin countries in which either political freedom or democracy, or both, are absent.

If, as I believe, this authoritarian cure is worse than the disease, what reforms are possible in liberal democracy itself? The dilemma is that we need authority to prevent people tearing each other to pieces and to safeguard at least some personal liberty; but how can we prevent this authority from becoming a source of oppression itself?

Hayek does not analyse the question of how legislatures

should tackle entrenched interest-group powers without undermining liberal principles by the methods used. His proposals are related to the other problem: the protection of the legislative body from interest-group pressure. He proposes two entirely different parliamentary bodies, elected in entirely different ways: one concerned with 'the general rules of just conduct' – the legislature in the true sense – and the other a governmental assembly concerned with supervising the managerial decisions of the executive, who would be acting within the framework of basic law developed by the legislative assembly.

This is not as strange as it sounds. The distinction has roots in both political theory and practice; and it is very similar to the distinction which Michael Oakeshott makes between *politics* (which is discussion about the framework of law in which individuals should pursue their aims) and *ruling* (the activity of people who occupy certain offices). Politics is even more to be distinguished from the management of an enterprise association, such as a company or a church or club, which has agreed common purposes. Oakeshott's 'civil association' (described in Chapter 1) has no purposes. It provides the rules under which individuals seek to fulfil their own aims.[13]

Oakeshott is too fastidious to recommend anything. He is ostensibly just discussing what 'civil association' really is, although his own convictions do slip out when he remarks that 'caring for the condition of a civil association . . . calls for so exact a focus of attention and so uncommon a self-restraint that one is not astonished to find this mode of human relationship to be as rare as it is excellent'.

Hayek, unlike Oakeshott, tries to find some artificial means for restoring the conditions of civil association, although he has no illusions that his ideas stand a chance until there has been a great change in the climate of opinion.

However sceptical we are about the mechanics of Hayek's own proposals, they are at least a response to clear and present dangers. Political auctioneering, interest-group pressure, and the combination of excessive expectations from collective action with excessive contempt for governmental and legal institutions, are a threat not merely to some pure imaginary *laissez-faire* dream, but also to a functioning 'mixed' or 'corrected' market economy – and for that reason a threat to individual freedom and popular government. If we are ever to reconstruct our politics, some of the key Hayekian doctrines – such as preference for rules over discretionary authority; the non-divine right of a temporary majority; the connection between markets and freedom; the realisation that rewards in this world neither can nor should reflect merit; and that a healthy political system is not a horse-trough at which interest-groups drink – will have to come into their own.

Conservatives may pay lip-service to some of these ideas; and even follow a few of them partially and erratically. It is progressives and radicals, now looking for new directions, who have most to learn from them – if only they could shed a few prejudices and illusions.

PART II

How to End the Monetarist Controversy

4 The Argument Summarised

A confusion of issues; The demise of the postwar wisdom; The 'Misery Index' rises; The 'monetarist' counter-attack; No long term trade-off; The postwar dollar standard; Nominal versus real; 'Monetarist' victory turns sour; A provisional strategy; Does lower inflation bring more jobs?; Is the economy self-stabilising?; Policy Goals.

This Part of the book is devoted to macroeconomic policy: in other words the ways in which output, jobs and prices can be affected by such matters as the government's budgetary stance, money supply and interest rates or, in some cases, exchange rate movements. The handling of these aspects of policy is sometimes known (not all that happily) as 'economic management' or 'demand management'.

The change of topic from the previous Part is less drastic than it may seem. For the political auctioneering and interest group pressures with which the last chapter ended will soon, unfortunately, reappear among the forces impairing the performance of a modern economy and among the obstacles to any government 'economic management' designed to improve matters.

A confusion of issues

Unfortunately, public discussion of macroeconomic questions has been bedevilled by the political symbolism acquired by that accursed word 'monetarism' and by the professional difficulty economists (like all other specialists) experience in distinguishing the wood from the trees. The campaign of vilification has been at times so successful that many educated citizens have believed the principal tenet of 'monetarism' to be support for Latin American dictatorships employing torture. Those of a more charitable disposition have supposed it to be a label for hardships deliberately imposed on peoples by governments to punish them for laziness or poor productivity.

Nor has understanding been helped by official explanations of economic policy. Questions of broad principle, about which every interested citizen has a right to be informed, have been hopelessly mixed up with highly technical questions of strictly specialist interest. At times it has even looked as if the choice of which political party to support, and which wing within that party to adhere to, has depended on the quirks of banking figures understood only by a handful of financial experts, if by them.

The preoccupation with technical means rather than basic objectives can perhaps be explained by the way in which the 'monetarist' counterrevolution came to both the USA and Britain. Until the late 1960s demand management had been seen in both countries largely in terms of fiscal policy. A minority of economists had always thought this a mistaken emphasis and maintained that the neglect of monetary policy was a grave error. These contentions achieved headline status as a result of two events. In the USA a tax increase, won from Congress by President Johnson to offset the inflationary forces set off by the Vietnam War, took effect in 1968, and there was a large swing out of deficit in the Federal Budget. The fiscal tightening failed, however, to have its expected restraining effect until the Federal Reserve Board responded by sharply reducing the rate of monetary expansion at the end of the year.

The second event was in the UK when, despite a highly restrictive fiscal policy, the 1967 devaluation proved slow to work and domestic consumption rose more than forecast. Partly on IMF insistence, monetary policy was tightened and the last year and a half of the Chancellorship of Roy Jenkins saw a firmer conscious control of monetary magnitudes than in any period of British history before or since. The balance of payments soon swung round into surplus and inflation dropped slightly in 1970.

Subsequently concern with monetary magnitudes first came back to Britain in the latter part of the reign of Mr Denis Healey (who was Labour Chancellor from 1974-1979) and even more under the Thatcher Government which took office in 1979. But the most interesting test was in the USA in 1980-

82, when a tight monetary policy pursued by the Fed under Paul Volcker coincided with national and international alarm over rapidly escalating budget deficits. In crude terms, the monetary forces once again 'beat' the fiscal ones. For the US experienced all the effects – both severe recession and a sharp fall in inflation – normally associated with a large contraction in the growth of demand.

Nevertheless these later experiences were not all that satisfactory for the more technical sort of monetarist. Put simply, the contraction in demand growth in both countries in the early 1980s was greater than intended and far greater than would have been expected from the rather moderate decline in the growth of the money supply as officially measured.

The demise of the postwar wisdom

There was nothing in the switch of emphasis from fiscal to monetary instruments which necessitated the abandonment of postwar full employment policies. The essence of postwar wisdom, often known as 'Keynesian demand management', was the attempt by governments and central banks to achieve full employment through actions to regulate demand. These actions took the form of variations in the budget balance or in the ease or tightness of money (and occasionally in the exchange rate). It will always remain an open question how far such policies and the doctrines behind them truly reflected the teachings of John Maynard Keynes, a great economist of subtle and frequently changing views, who died in 1946. But we are stuck with the label 'Keynesian' (or 'orthodox Keynesian', to hint at this doubt) as we are with 'monetarist'.

The key orthodox Keynesian belief was that increases in total spending – whether brought about by monetary or fiscal policy, or occurring spontaneously – had their main effects on output and employment, at least until unemployment reached extremely low levels. If unemployment was forecast to rise above the target, demand was supposed to be boosted by tax cuts, higher spending, credit relaxations, and so on. That such boosts tended to take a budgetary form, with the money supply responding passively, was a secondary matter. The same underlying philosophy could just as well have been allied with planned changes in the money supply if that had been thought the appropriate weapon. The belief was that a sufficient boost to demand would raise output and reduce unemployment until the target was reached. If unemployment threatened to fall too low ('overfull employment') the government would restrain demand; but it usually required a sterling crisis before it would restrain it in a major way.

Despite the official doctrines, British governments did not always boost demand when unemployment rose above the chosen target; and they sometimes took restrictive measures even when recession loomed and unemployment was expected to rise. The alibi was invariably the threat of an overseas payments deficit or a run on the pound. Thus it came to look as if the fixed exchange rate for sterling was the main constraint on the growth of output. It was rarely suggested, even by the 'sound money men' of the time, that there were any obstacles, apart from the balance of payments, to achieving chosen output and employment levels. Together the main industrial countries in pre-OPEC days were in current payments balance or surplus. Thus it seemed, according to this philosophy, that if they expanded together they could spend themselves into chosen levels of economic activity.

The big blank in orthodox Keynesian doctrine was that it said very little about the price level. Many Keynesian economists, especially of the older generation, believed that domestic prices were mainly determined by wage costs, which were themselves dependent on largely non-economic institutional forces such as the attitudes of union leaders. Inflation was sometimes, according to this view, aggravated by import prices; but an individual industrial country had little control over these and fluctuations in commodity prices were in both directions over a period of years. The main weapon proposed for combating inflation was incomes policy. This meant either wage and price controls or a government deal (misleadingly known as a 'social contract') with union leaders.[1]

Not all 'orthodox Keynesians' washed their professional hands of wages and prices to that extent. Some believed there was a trade-off, known as the 'Phillips curve', between unemployment and inflation, with more of one bringing less of the other.

According to the first or purely institutional version of the traditional Keynesian doctrine, governments could more or less ignore inflation in their attempts to raise demand to full-employment levels. Inflation, if it was a problem, had to be tackled by non-financial means. The second version accepted that a price might have to be paid for full employment in terms of *some* inflation; but in neither version was there any suggestion that demand management aiming at full employment might be *entirely* dissipated in higher prices.

The 'Misery Index' rises

After two decades of apparent success, orthodox Keynesian economics demonstrated an increasing failure to deliver the advertised benefits. Not only did inflation begin to rise to alarming proportions but so also did unemployment – a combination of events which completely contradicted the notion of a simple trade-off between them. Trouble was apparent in the late 1960s when the 'Misery Index' (the sum of the inflation and unemployment rates) began rising in country after country. Internationally, the deterioration was reflected in the growing difficulty of maintaining the postwar Bretton Woods system of fixed exchange rates against the dollar and the fixed dollar price for gold. The system finally broke down in 1971 when President Nixon formally suspended the last remaining vestiges of dollar convertibility.

The next turn of the screw for all industrial countries was the fourfold increase in world oil prices at the end of 1973. Although the Yom Kippur War of that year set off the oil price explosion, an important underlying influence was the world-wide inflation resulting from the synchronised attempts of industrial countries to spend their way out of an earlier recession.

Since 1973 unemployment has been on a strongly rising trend throughout the industrialised world. The increase has gone on remorselessly both when inflation soared and when it began to decline. Until the late 1960s, '500,000 unemployed' (or less than 2½ per cent of the working population) was a crisis level in the UK leading to policy reversals and the sacking of cabinet ministers. In the early 1970s, the alarm bells rang at one million; in the late 1970s, at one and a half million. In the early 1980s, the burning question was how

much above three million (or 12½ per cent) the
unemployment total would go. The deterioration in Britain
was but an extreme example of a trend in evidence
throughout the industrialised world. Unemployment in the
main industrial countries which make up the Organisation for
Economic Co-Operation and Development (OECD) rose
from ten million in 1970 to nearly thirty-five million in 1983.

After the 1973 oil crisis some countries, including the UK,
did try for a time to spend their way back to prosperity, but
their efforts collapsed amidst currency crises and IMF
rescues. The USA made a similar attempt under President
Carter in 1977-8; but he too had to put on the brakes sharply
and reverse course when the dollar plunged; and the last part
of his presidency was marked by the ascendency of Paul
Volcker, the Fed chairman who adopted a monetary policy
geared to reducing inflation.

After the second (1979-80) oil price explosion no major
country attempted to expand its way out of recession. The
French Socialist Party under François Mitterand and the
British Labour Party were in principle committed to massive
demand boosting. But the Mitterand Government, elected in
1981, called a halt to steps in that direction and introduced
severe restrictive packages following the franc devaluations
of 1982 and 1983.

In Britain the total stimulus required in the early 1980s to
restore postwar levels of full employment would, on the
traditional Keynesian arithmetic, have amounted to well over
10 per cent of the national income or over £30 billion in public
expenditure increases and tax cuts plus a very aggressive
cheap money policy to try to prevent interest rates from rising
as a result. There was no chance of any government
successfully administering a stimulus approaching this size.
But there was little public understanding of why these
measures – even if approached in steps – would be likely to
turn out to be counterproductive. Many politicians, officials,
and economists throughout the world still saw demand
management, employment and prices in traditional postwar
Keynesian terms. They saw various 'hideous obstacles'
ranging from the OPEC surpluses of some years to markets
mistakenly obsessed with public sector borrowing
requirements and monetary figures. These factors were

treated as chance misfortunes; and if only they could be circumvented government could, it was supposed, go back to demand management in real terms aimed at chosen levels of output and employment. The intellectual basis of the counter-revolution was still far from widely understood.

The 'monetarist' counter-attack

The crisis in orthodox Keynesian economic policy provided, however, a hearing for all sorts of groups outside the previously reigning establishment who had never believed in the policy in the first place. The most prominent, and the ones whose teachings seemed most relevant, were the 'monetarists' associated with Professor Milton Friedman. Their counter-revolution[2] was based on three main propositions:

1 Governments cannot spend their way to target levels of output and employment. The long-run effect of boosting monetary demand (i.e. total spending) is therefore on the price level. Both the beneficial effects of demand stimulation on output and employment and the adverse effects of demand restriction on these variables are transitional.
2 The key long-running influence on monetary demand, and thus the main determinant of the nominal national product or national income, is the quantity of money. ('Nominal' means measured in cash terms and not adjusted by a prices index.)
3 More specifically, there is a clear-cut division between money and other financial assets; the supply of money can be readily controlled by central banks, and the relationship between the quantity of money and the national income is predictable and stable. Advocates of this final set of propositions can be called 'technical monetarists', in a descriptive and non-pejorative sense.

If variations in the quantity of money are the main long-run influences on demand, and if demand movements ultimately affect prices rather than output or employment, there is a clear link between changes in the amount of money and changes in the price level. Such a link is the main assertion of the *Quantity Theory of Money*, arrived at by combining proposions (1) and (2) above.

The evidence linking major historical inflations with monetary disturbances is inescapable. It requires perverse ingenuity to deny the connection between the inflation of Imperial Rome and the debasement of the denarius, or between the sixteenth-century inflation and the inflow of precious metals from the New World, or between the post-World-War-One German inflation and the billionfold increase in the quantity of Reichsmarks. Whatever the ultimate initiating force, such as the burden of defending Imperial Rome or of German reparation payments, a necessary condition on all such occasions was an increase in the quantity of currency. If the quantity of anything is increased then, other things being equal, its value will drop; and this applies to money as to other commodities even though money may be especially difficult to define.

The 'technical' monetarists who embrace proposition (3) go, however, a good deal further. They assert not merely that inflation is a monetary phenomenon but that the effective quantity of money in a modern paper currency regime can be readily defined and measured – or, alternatively, that its exact definition does not matter so long as a single aggregate is chosen and monitored. Moreover, they believe that the control of the quantity of money is a relatively straightforward technical question. They also set more store than other classical economists or quantity theorists by the claimed short-term stability of the relation between the quantity of money and the nominal national income. (Thus 'fine tuning' is neither feasible nor necessary, a matter discussed later.)

It was unfortunate for the course of the debate that Friedman formulated these more technical propositions about money before the wider proposition about the futility of governments trying to spend themselves into full employment. To make matters worse, there was an excessive emphasis both by the Keynesian and the monetarist camps on the performance of rival short-term forecasts, whereas the real debate related to the longer term. Thus public debate became hopelessly confused between (a) issues on which every citizen has a right to be informed, (b) questions of general economic theory, and (c) highly technical questions best left to specialists.

Some of the technical monetarists were scarcely helpful to the clarity of the debate. They often spoke as if hope of salvation depended on their own particular definition of money being adopted; and since different monetarists looked at different measures which moved in conflicting ways, they helped to turn off patience and support. Some of the most vociferous monetarists insisted that nothing would come right until central banks controlled the money supply by operating directly on the reserves of the banking system (a method known as 'monetary base control') instead of indirectly via interest rates. When the US Federal Reserve Board made a change in this direction in November 1979, the attack shifted to even more technical matters such as lagged accounting by member banks of the Fed. The Duke of Wellington's remark about his troops – 'I don't know what effect they have on the enemy, but by God they frighten me' – could have been applied to monetarist economists by a critical sympathiser.

No long-term trade-off

The point of a theory is in what it denies. The essence of the changed thinking, which explains the political heat of the debate, is contained in the first proposition about the inability of demand management to achieve target levels of employment. This key proposition says nothing specifically about money and can be accepted independently of belief in the other more technical contentions.

The doctrine of the long-run impotence of demand management may be labelled 'counter-revolutionary', for that is the relationship in which it stands towards the earlier postwar revolution which brought in 'Keynesian' demand management. The doctrine can be regarded as a revival of the classical tradition, which emphasised the role of real forces, rather than monetary or fiscal policy, in determining real variables such as output and employment.

The proposition that governments cannot 'spend their way' into chosen levels of employment for more than a transitory period was first enunciated – or rather revived – in 1967 by Professor Friedman (and another US economist, Professor Edmund Phelps, who was working independently).

Nevertheless, it is in no way tied to Friedman's detailed views about the role of the money supply as an instrument for controlling aggregate expenditure. Nor has it anything to do with a belief in *laissez-faire* or most of the other policies of US Republican or British Conservative governments.

A stable trade-off between unemployment and inflation, of the kind shown in the traditional Phillips curve, can exist only if wage earners continue to believe 'a pound is a pound' irrespective of inflation. The short-term trade-off is mainly between unemployment and *unanticipated* inflation. Once, however, 'money illusion' vanishes – that is, inflation is taken into account – wage earners who formerly settled for, say, 3 per cent annual pay increases will insist on 3 per cent plus an inflation premium; and, if governments pursue sufficiently accommodating financial policies, they will be able to obtain it. But, with the same policy assumptions, the higher wage increases will be passed on in still higher price rises, which will stimulate still more rapid wage increases, and so on *ad infinitum*, as explained more fully in Chapter 5.

The newly-revived classical doctrine does not say that stable prices are more important than full employment. The proposition is one about cause and effect. It gives notice that there is no stable trade-off between unemployment and inflation. An attempt to keep unemployment low and labour markets tight by financial policy risks not merely inflation but accelerating inflation. Since no country can live with accelerating inflation, the experiment will eventually have to be brought to a halt with a painful stabilisation crisis accompanied for a time by more unemployment than if governments had not been so ambitious.

The rate of unemployment at which inflation neither rises nor falls was originally labelled the 'natural rate'. There is in fact nothing natural about it; it reflects all kinds of highly imperfect labour markets and other institutions. It is now more usually called by the colourless but accurate name NAIRU – 'non-accelerating inflation rate of unemployment'. It is the lowest rate of unemployment which can be achieved by financial policy, however high or low the rate of inflation. To avoid excessive use of an ungainly acronym, I shall sometimes paraphrase it as the 'minimum sustainable level of unemployment' or just the 'underlying' rate. A further way of putting it might be the 'inflation takeoff threshold'. For if attempts are made by demand-boosting to reduce unemployment beyond that point, inflation will soar higher and higher so long as the attempts are continued.

Further reflection on the consequences of rapid inflation suggests that any long-run relation between inflation and unemployment may be in the opposite direction to that suggested by the Phillips curve. Double digit inflation is in practice never steady or predictable in its speed. The resulting instability distorts the signalling functions of the price system, making it more difficult for markets to work effectively; employment is therefore likely to suffer.

The postwar dollar standard

One question is often asked: 'If fashionable strictures on demand management directly aimed at full employment are true, why did such policies work so well for two or three post-war decades?' Those who ask it rarely wait for an answer.

The truth is that, for most of this period, neither the UK nor most other countries pursued demand management policies directed to full employment. The language of such policies was often used, but so long as the Bretton Woods system of exchange rates fixed against the dollar prevailed, the overriding aim was to maintain the currency parity.

Full employment demand management policies did not come to the United States until well into the 1960s. For most of the postwar period American administrations followed non-inflationary policies; and other countries, if they were to avoid devaluing against the dollar, had to imitate them. Thus, until the breakdown of the postwar system in the late 1960s and early 1970s, most countries followed sound money policies, although some of them did not know it; and sound money policies proved compatible with full employment. The balance of payments crises I referred to earlier, seen at the time as irritating obstacles to further growth, were in fact the way in which inflationary policies became visible under fixed exchange rate regimes. In the words of Mr Nigel Lawson, the Chancellor of the Exchequer: 'During this period foreign exchange crises served as a proxy for monetary disciplines.'[3] In the late 1960s and early 1970s, demand was boosted more vigorously both in the United States and elsewhere and inflation accelerated; but 'unsound' policies failed nonetheless to prevent unemployment from rising sharply.

The policy of counter-inflation by proxy had one unfortunate legacy in the realm of ideas. It induced many people in Britain and other European countries to suppose that the main obstacle to more expansionary demand policies was something called the 'balance-of-payments-constraint' which, if it could be surmounted, would enable demand to be expanded to stimulate more real growth. That it would stimulate inflation instead was revealed to British governments only when the correct decision to float sterling taken by Mr Heath's Government in 1972 was accompanied by overindulgence in deficit spending and monetary expansion, with results that any Friedmanite – or, indeed, anyone schooled in the older classical tradition – would have foreseen.

The moral seems to be that when underlying forces in the economy are making for low unemployment and satisfactory economic growth there is no need to embark on traditional Keynesian demand management. Indeed during the 1950s and 1960s, because of the overriding financial constraint of the exchange rate, policy was devoted to keeping British inflation rates in line with those of other countries; but because underlying unemployment was low, it was difficult to distinguish it in practice from Keynesian orthodoxy. When underlying forces are making for a low level of growth and high unemployment, Keynesian policies will be very clearly distinguishable from sound money, but they will then tend to break down.

Nominal versus real

The reason why demand management has been discredited is that policy-makers in the postwar period focussed not on *nominal* but on *real* demand – or, in terms of the published figures, not on 'Money GDP' but on 'GDP at constant prices'. The reader has only to consult a typical economic forecast to see that most magnitudes are valued at constant prices.

The emphasis on 'real demand' was a fatal error. For it begged the question of how far a boost to spending raised output and how far it was dissipated in an inflationary increase of prices and wages.* A little reflection (always easier after the event) should have shown that all that governments and central banks can hope to regulate directly by demand management consists of flows of money. The error of most postwar demand management was to assume that real things, such as output and employment, could invariably, and as a matter of course, be affected permanently by financial manipulation.

Governments were slow to realise this limitation of their powers. When accustomed injections of monetary demand no longer yielded the expected result in output and employment, but were largely dissipated in inflation, the dose was stepped up once the Bretton Woods restraints were out of the way. This is a common experience among drug addicts who need stronger and stronger doses to regain the old 'kicks'. But in contrast to drug addicts, governments did not always realise what they were doing. They thought they were stimulating or at least bolstering output and employment, when they were in practice boosting Money GDP, with the main effects on the price component.

The dissipation in rising prices of past demand increases in the UK is shown clearly in Chart 1. During the first quinquennium 1959-64, nominal demand, as measured by Money GDP, grew by nearly 38 per cent; slightly over half of the growth was reflected in increased output and slightly less than half in higher prices. The expansion of nominal demand was stepped up in successive periods, but more and more of the growth was reflected in inflation and less and less in higher output. By the time of the last expansionary period, 1974-79†, the rise in nominal demand of nearly 130 per cent was reflected almost entirely in higher prices, while output growth was less than half its rate during the first quinquennium.

The figures in the chart are neither a tautology nor a statement of the obvious, as hasty critics have suggested. As a

---

* It would be pleasant to exculpate Keynes himself from this misjudgement; but I am afraid that he encouraged bad habits by writing much of the *General Theory* in terms of a particular kind of funny money known as 'wage units'. Not all Keynesians have followed this bad habit. In the USA in particular the Council of Economic Advisers often examined past and prospective changes in *nominal* national product before estimating the breakdown between changes in price and changes in quantity.

† Considered as a quinquennium it was still expansionary – nominal demand grew much faster than before. But the change to a less accommodating stance took place in the course of the period (as explained in Chapter 11), too late to affect the broad trend.

Chart 1: The growth of money GDP in the UK

(Gross domestic product at current market prices, expenditure based)

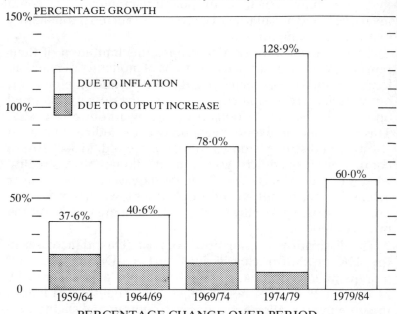

PERCENTAGE CHANGE OVER PERIOD

PERIOD	TOTAL INCREASE at current prices	OUTPUT INCREASE at 1975 prices	INCREASE IN PRICES
1959/64	+37·6	+19·4	+15·2
1964/69	+40·6	+13·2	+24·2
1969/74	+78·0	+14·1	+56·0
1974/79	+128·9	+9·3	+109·4
1979/84 Partly forecast	+60·0	0	+60·0

matter of arithmetic, successively larger demand boosts *could* have been reflected in a faster rise in output. They *were* reflected in more rapid inflation and slower real growth than ever before. The events occurred partly because of the puncturing of 'money illusion' (further discussed below) and partly because underlying *non-monetary* forces were pulling down growth rates and pushing up unemployment. These forces were misinterpreted as demand deficiency, and nominal expenditure was encouraged to gallop ahead in a vain attempt to regain previous growth and employment rates.

The chart also shows that sharp reductions in the growth of nominal demand of the kind seen in the 1979-84 quinquennium still exact a toll in lost output. Demand management was, of course, not the only influence at work; but the ideal configuration of the rectangles would be a stable series at a low height. The policy-makers in the later 1970s could be forgiven for echoing the Irishman who when asked how to reach Skibbereen said: 'If I wanted to reach Skibbereen I wouldn't start from here.'

'Monetarist' victory turns sour

The counter-revolutionary or classical school thus scored a bull's eye in predicting, well before the event, that demand-boosting policies such as President Johnson's 'guns-and-butter-policy' at the time of Vietnam and the Heath and Carter 'dashes for growth' would come to grief, ending with an inflationary explosion and no ultimate benefit to employment.

But just as the orthodox Keynesians were discomfited by the escalation of inflation, the counter-revolutionary or classical school has been embarrassed by the escalation of unemployment. Counter-revolutionary economists knew that a sharp rise in the NAIRU or minimum sustainable rate of unemployment was liable to occur, but although classical economists were familiar with a whole list of supply-side factors which *could* have raised unemployment, the massive increase *was not in fact predicted*.

They neither expected the oil price shocks of 1973-4 and 1978-80, nor were they prepared for the size of the recession which they would trigger off when they did occur. Indeed, the more obviously 'monetarist' economists did not cover themselves in glory over any aspect of the oil issue. They underestimated the effects of OPEC price increases on the general price level and on inflationary expectations, either by asserting that OPEC was a cartel which would collapse ten years before it even weakened, or by overestimating the short term downward flexibility of non-oil prices.

But whatever the *post facto* explanations, the unemployment explosion has deprived the classical school of the fruits of its victory over the Keynesians. An explanation of the transitional unemployment effects of expansionary and contractionary economic policies in terms of variations around an underlying (NAIRU) level becomes much less convincing in the face of an upward leap in that level which no one had foreseen.

No macroeconomic school has explained satisfactorily the steep trend rise in unemployment of the 1970s and 80s. The counter-revolutionaries can claim something more modest, but still important – an explanation given *long before the event* of why postwar attempts by governments to spend their way into target levels of employment would eventually fail, and why therefore such policies would be useless for dealing with problems such as those of the 1980s.

A provisional strategy

A genuine counter-revolution is not the same as mere reaction. It should be able to absorb the best elements of the revolution it is replacing; or, to change the metaphor, should keep the baby while emptying out the bathwater. In this case it should be based on the contributions of both the Keynesian and Friedmanite schools.

A financial strategy which attempts to stabilise total monetary demand has a Keynesian flavour and is far removed from *laissez-faire* or faith in automatic relationships. But the qualification 'monetary' in front of 'demand' is crucial. In contrast to orthodox Keynesianism, there can be no question of injecting unlimited amounts of spending power in the hope of achieving some previously set objective for output and employment; there is thus a built-in safeguard against runaway inflation.

For the strategy involves an undertaking that governments

will refuse to finance a permanently higher rate of inflation resulting from external or internal shocks. Indeed, any financial plan worth its salt must embody the slogan, 'No accommodation of wage or price push.' Having established this constraint, policy-makers still have a duty to try to maintain a stable growth of demand in money terms. No financial strategy can prevent a rise in unemployment stemming from an increased exercise of union monopoly power. But a preannounced policy can, if credible, minimise increases in unemployment arising from mistaken beliefs about inflation or from a sudden collapse in nominal demand.

Does lower inflation bring more jobs?

This is a suitable point at which to examine the assertion, made by governments embarked on counter-inflationary programmes, that price stability (or low inflation) promotes jobs. Is this true? The reader who would like a straight 'yes' or 'no' will have to accept that this is one of those irritating assertions which can have several meanings which need to be examined separately.

1 At its most basic, the assertion can mean that the economy will perform better at low than at high (and therefore variable) inflation rates; and that the underlying rate of unemployment (NAIRU) will be less. This proposition is probably true (it is illustrated in chart 3 in the next chapter); but there is no reason to suppose that the job gain from lower inflation will be anything like sufficient to put an end to present unemployment worries (which will remain so long as the NAIRU is high). Moreover the proposition is a long-run one and says nothing about the unemployment effects of the transition from a higher to a lower inflation rate.

2 This transition is indeed nearly always accompanied by a 'temporary' rise in unemployment (there still is a short-term Phillips curve, at least on the downward side); but given that a counter-inflationary programme is in operation, the quicker pay and prices fall the smaller will be the transitional rise in unemployment.* It is this distinction which understandably causes the most confusion.

---

* In terms of the identity MV = PT (explained on pages 128-30), if the counter-inflationary programme is represented by MV, the lower the level of P, the higher T – which is output – will be. Of course if the government is unwise enough to respond to lower than expected P by allowing or encouraging MV to fall faster than originally intended the effect will be negated.

The object of a counter-inflationary strategy is to return to a state of affairs where something approaching price stability is taken for granted. Unfortunately, many people have an excessively literal understanding of what that means.

Historically, periods of price stability were not ones of zero price change. Year-to-year variations ran to several per cent; and there were decades at a time of what would nowadays be called 'creeping' inflation or deflation. The difference from today is that the direction of movement was unknowable. Prices were as likely to fall as to rise. Stability was therefore the best predictive bet; deviations from it were not so big as to destroy a person's savings, and were in any case likely to be reversed in a single lifetime.

The result was a combination of basic stability with modest short-term flexibility. If a country's terms of trade deteriorated, or if there was a harvest failure, or if real national income fell for any other reason, the burden would be spread automatically through a temporary rise in the price level without any painful renegotiations of contracts. On the other hand, pensions could be arranged on the basis that a pound was a pound and a dollar a dollar; and wage negotiators would not be forced to add an uncertain inflation premium to their offers and demands.

The situation was in marked contrast to the post-war period when inflation has been high and variable and people have had to work with a shrinking monetary yardstick. This makes many business calculations a gamble and causes anyone who relies on a fixed money pension to pray he will not live too long.

Alternatively, indexation is introduced throughout the economy, thereby easing some of the inflationary distortions. But unless the indexation is carried out very carefully, the safety-valve of rising prices, which reduce real incomes in adverse economic circumstances, is removed; and there is a danger of appearing to guarantee to the population more than the entire value of the national income. An example of the wrong sort of indexation is an escalation clause like the Italian *scala mobile*, which automatically compensated wage earners for inflation. A sensible form of wage indexation would allow for the possibility of real wages going down as well as up in accordance with the market pressures of the time.

Both indexation and non-indexation are thus likely to be unsatisfactory alternatives in practice. Although in my view carefully introduced indexation is an essential second best in inflationary times, and can even be an adjunct to anti-inflationary policies, there will be no satisfactory solution until inflation itself has been brought down to a low or zero rate.

One reason why widespread indexation cannot solve the problems of inflation is that inflation has had a social function wherever there have been any vestiges of 'money illusion'. Governments in the 1970s could acquiesce, for instance, in a 'generous' public sector pay settlement – say to the miners – in the knowledge that much of the apparent relativity gain would soon be absorbed in general inflation. Both relativity changes and the lack of them could be drowned by a rise in the general price level and thus governments could postpone the insoluble problem of adjudicating between incompatible claims by rival interest groups. The expression of wage settlements in real indexed terms would have brought the inflation into the open straightaway.

Now, however, that money illusion is mostly gone, inflation no longer serves its social purpose of buying time by a benign form of self-deception. Little is to be lost by sensible indexation, but the systemic arguments for tolerating more than a very low rate of inflation have disappeared too.

Is the economy self-stabilising?

One advantage of an objective for total spending – or Money GDP – is that it entitles one to by-pass the fruitless controversy over whether a market economy is automatically self-stabilising.

The questions about stability *sound* interesting enough. In the absence of interventionist government policies, will the economy adjust automatically to events? Are there self-stabilising forces serving to bring it back to a normal growth and employment path after a shock? Or is the economy likely to develop an ever-growing gap between actual and potential performance – and perhaps even move into a downward spiral – in the absence of government action to sustain demand?

It is sometimes suggested that these fundamental questions lie behind the debate between the counter-revolutionary and the orthodox Keynesian. But I must confess to finding both sides extremely unconvincing and the debate between them unhelpful. The orthodox Keynesian question, echoed by many business leaders and other 'practical men' in every recession, is: 'Where is the upturn going to come from? I can't see where the demand is.' The implication is that there are no natural forces to bring about recovery in the absence of government stimulation; and that, unless it is possible to identify which specific sectors or industries will revive, the prospect is of indefinite stagnation. Indeed the prognostications of many so-called long-term forecasters make one wonder how humanity managed any growth at all in the 99.9 per cent of its existence when the theory of demand stimulation was unknown and there was no one to predict doom in the absence of intervention.

But the self-stabilising school is equally difficult to comprehend. There have been such things as depressions. That they are followed by recoveries does not of itself tell us that the system is functioning well. Without some empirical standard of the depth of depression to be expected and the time-scale for recovery, assertions about self-stabilisation are meaningless. Nor is it enough to point to government action or social institutions (such as unions) which prevent the automatic stabilisers from working. A sufficient search will always reveal some grit in the machine to an engineer who is convinced *a priori* that the machine itself is in good order. Above all, there is no way of showing non-tautologically that the actual long-term growth path is the best that could be achieved.*

A medium-term strategy for monetary demand would bypass these unanswerable conundrums. It is best stated in terms of total spending, which is represented statistically by the aggregate known as Money GDP or money times velocity. A presentation in such terms avoids prejudging complex

---

* In what sense can a counter-revolutionary believe that the economy may not be self-stabilising? He may have two worries. First, monetary demand cannot be relied upon to grow smoothly and adequately 'on its own'. Secondly, deviations from the underlying or NAIRU rate of unemployment do occur and are not always quickly corrected, especially on the side of excess unemployment. If so, large deviations in monetary demand in an inflationary or deflationary direction do matter. Technical 'monetarists' must surely share both worries. Otherwise why should they bother to advocate a stable growth of the money supply – which they think will provide the smoothest attainable non-inflationary growth of monetary demand (i.e. MV, money times velocity)? The less technical counter-revolutionary will wonder if the monetary rule is sufficient for the job.

technical financial issues and is capable of explanation to a wide public. If successfully pursued, it should ensure that depression does not occur through a mass contraction of spending of the 1930s type, although it cannot prevent unemployment rising if producer groups succeed in diverting the rise in spending into higher wages and prices at the expense of jobs.

Policy goals

There are four main themes to this part of the book.[4]

First, the object of macroeconomic policy is to contribute to price stability and, to a lesser extent, to the stability of output and employment by keeping total spending (the money value of the national income measured by Money GDP) on a steady path with the minimum of fluctuations.

Second, attempts to do this solely by focussing on particular measures of the stock of money are liable to come unstuck. The mere act of adopting monetary targets itself destabilises the relationship between the money supply and national income; and the demand to hold major currencies comes from external as well as domestic holders, which adds a new element of instability.

Third, there is a minimum underlying or sustainable rate of unemployment consistent not merely with price stability, but with any stable rate of inflation. Attempts to reduce unemployment below this level by increasing total nominal spending (that is spending in money terms) will generate ever-increasing inflation, with which no economic system can live, and thus prove self-defeating.

Fourth and most important, if this underlying rate of unemployment is too high, the only permanent way to reduce it is by supply-side measures properly understood. By this is meant not Reagan-style tax cuts, but measures to improve the working of the labour market, to reduce 'pricing out of work' and to tackle other rigidities and disturbances which discourage full use of the resources of the economy.

Lest the first point be misunderstood, let me hasten to add that I do not regard price stability as more important than output and employment. On the contrary, real variables such as output and employment are more important than nominal ones such as price levels (or exchange rates). The reason for the words 'lesser extent' has already been mentioned. Demand management is impotent, except very indirectly, to do more than reduce deviations from an underlying unemployment level, which can itself be reduced only by policies of a different kind.

The achievement of predictable, stable and low rates of inflation not only reduces economic, social and political conflict. It also on balance (and over long periods) tends to reduce the underlying unemployment rate. Vastly exaggerated claims in this regard have been made by would-be 'sound money' governments, but the direction of the relationship is as stated.

Moreover the contribution of demand management to reducing deviations from the underlying rate of unemployment is not to be underrated. Such deviations, if large and persistent enough on the upward side, are indeed known as depressions. If they continue long enough they will drag up the underlying level itself. In a depression the training of labour will fall off, the attitudes, habits and skills of the unemployed will deteriorate, making them less employable when an upturn comes, and the growth of capacity will be impaired. The process by which a high actual rate of unemployment increases the rate sustainable in the longer term is known as 'hysteresis' – an unhappy name for an unhappy phenomenon.[5]

Chapter 5 which follows will attempt to explain analytically why demand management cannot fulfil the hopes which were originally placed upon it. It is not, however, the easiest chapter and some may prefer to go on to Chapter 6 which explains what demand management can nevertheless still accomplish from a policy-maker's point of view. Chapter 7 will look at some of the instruments of policy and also why it is so difficult either to say exactly what one means by the money supply or to control it in a stable way. Those who are understandably impatient to move from the steering wheel to the engine room to discover what is faulty might prefer to move straight to Part III, which begins with an unavoidably controversial discussion of the non-monetary forces making for high unemployment.

5   Jobs, Output and Prices

The underlying unemployment rate; The shifting Phillips curve‡; Inflation and unemployment‡; Key conclusions; Fine-tuning; Queries on NAIRU‡; International transmission; Expectations, rational and otherwise‡; Gradualism and expectations; Constraints on output.

The purpose of this chapter is to explain in more detail why it is impossible to 'spend ourselves' into target levels of employment by stimulating demand and what exactly is meant by this proposition which is often mis-stated or guyed. This will show that attempts to reduce inflation do indeed have a transitional unemployment cost, and take the jobless number even higher than the underlying (or NAIRU) rate. The passages likely to be most forbidding for some readers (and insufficiently mathematical for others!) are marked ‡. The marked sections are summarised in the sections immediately preceding or following.

The underlying unemployment rate

The most famous declaration of the limits of 'demand management' was made not by Professor Milton Friedman, nor by President Ronald Reagan nor by Prime Minister Margaret Thatcher, but by a Labour Prime Minister of Britain, Mr James Callaghan. In a speech to the Labour Party Conference in September 1976, he said:

> We used to think that you could just spend your way out of recession, and increase employment, by cutting taxes and boosting government spending. I tell you in all candour that that option no longer exists, and that in so far as it ever did exist, it worked by injecting inflation into the economy. And each time that happened, the average level of unemployment has risen. Higher inflation, followed by higher unemployment. That is the history of the last twenty years.

Mr Callaghan himself quickly dropped this line of argument and by the end of the 1970s was passionately advancing the opposite view. Nevertheless, the original assertion, whether or not drafted by his son-in-law, Peter Jay, was closer to the truth, although it would have been better without the words 'out of recession' in the first sentence.

The basic doctrine is that there is an underlying level of unemployment (and associated level of output growth) which is the minimum consistent, not just with price stability, but with any non-accelerating rate of inflation. This underlying or 'non-accelerating inflation rate of unemployment' (the NAIRU)* is achieved when the economy has adjusted itself to the prevailing rate of inflation.

This underlying level of unemployment is all too likely to be both unsatisfactory and capable of improvement; but it can be changed only by structural reforms of markets which are working badly. Any attempt by governments to achieve lower levels of unemployment than this minimum sustainable level by injecting more spending power will not lead merely to inflation but to accelerating inflation, and eventually to a very nasty stabilisation crisis in which unemployment will shoot up to rates far higher than if the expansionary attempt had never been made. Of course unemployment rates can be above the NAIRU for 'short periods' measured in years. In these circumstances the doctrine of the impotence of demand-boosting would no longer apply – except for the all-important ignorance of governments and their economic advisers of where the NAIRU is and the political tendency to wishful thinking in such circumstances.

A rough idea of the size of the NAIRU can be obtained by taking the trend of unemployment over a complete business cycle and adjusting it as best one can for disturbing influences such as oil price or exchange rate shocks. In the UK in the early 1980s it was probably around 10 per cent, or 2 or 3 million, seasonally adjusted, excluding school-leavers. But any estimate is highly fallible and fortunately not essential for

---

* This underlying level of unemployment was labelled the 'natural rate' by Milton Friedman in his famous 1967 Presidential Address to the American Economic Association (reprinted in *The Optimum Quantity of Money*, University of Chicago Press, 1969). The name has eminently respectable roots; it is a deliberate analogy with Wicksell's 'natural rate of interest' determined by the forces of productivity and thrift, which would prevail if there were no expectation of rising or falling prices.

the control of *monetary* demand which is a more indirect but more reliable approach to such stabilisation as governments are capable of achieving.

The shifting Phillips curve‡

There are several different ways of deriving the concept of an underlying rate of unemployment, which cannot be reduced by boosting demand. Readers who have followed some of the academic discussion may find it helpful if I point out at the outset that the line of causation I am suggesting here runs from the state of the labour market (indicated by unemployment) to *money* wages, and from money wages to prices. This is in contrast to the more classical models, in which the link runs the other way – from misconceptions about real wages to unemployment.

My preferred explanation, in terms of the erosion of demand stimulus by wage and price increases, makes clear that the doctrine of the NAIRU in no way depends on atomistic labour markets and is compatible with wages set by collective bargaining, with union monopoly power, and with labour markets which are not cleared (i.e. surpluses or shortages remaining for considerable periods). Indeed the exposition is deliberately conducted in terms of wage bargaining.

Nor does the NAIRU doctrine depend on the view that all individuals are rational maximisers (a concept explained on page 35) or that unemployment is voluntary, or that the degree of monopoly power exercised by individual unions is constant or stable or that union militancy can be ignored or that sociological explanations are *infra dig*. These assumptions are sometimes made by over-enthusiastic counter-revolutionaries and gleefully attributed to all 'monetarists' by their opponents.

To explain the NAIRU, two main assumptions are required:

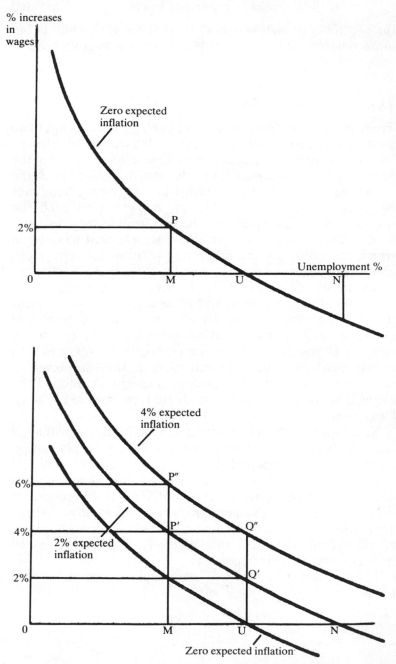

Chart 2: Phillips curves under varying expected rates of inflation

a that there is some sensitivity of price to demand in the labour market as well as in other markets;

b that no major group can be systematically tricked by inflation into accepting a lower share of the national product.*

There is no need to assume that labour demand is the only or even the principal influence on wages, but merely that it is *an* influence. It was for a long time customary to depict this influence by the single curve in the upper figure of Chart 2. Such a curve was fitted by the late Professor A. W. Phillips to British data for 1861-1913 and also for the post-war period to 1957.[1] The suggested relationship became known as the 'Phillips curve'. It led policy-makers to assume that they had a menu of choices between different combinations of unemployment and inflation – an assumption which still bedevils much political discussion.

No sooner had the Phillips curve become part of the applied economist's stock-in-trade than it began to be alarmingly misleading. It had always been difficult to fit the curve to countries other than the USA and the UK. Even in these two countries, from the late 1960s onwards unemployment rates which were very high by post-war standards came to be associated with double-digit inflation rates. Conversely, toleration of rapid inflation did not bring the low unemployment that a simple reading of the curve would suggest.

It is not difficult to see why the Phillips curve should shift. It was fitted for a period when there were expectations either of stable prices or of a stable and predictable upward creep.

Chart 2 illustrates the processes at work. It is best to begin by concentrating on the simple upper figure, which postulates a relationship between wage increases and unemployment. Other labour market indicators such as unfilled vacancies could have been used instead. Unemployment is taken because it is the most familiar and the one used in most

---

* These common-sense assertions should not be confused with technical arguments about the neutrality of money. Even an inflation which is perfectly anticipated, and to which everyone has adjusted, will affect holdings of real money balances, bonds and physical capital and, therefore, the distribution of income. Inflation will be strictly neutral only if the excess money is issued in the form of payment of interest on cash balances. (J. Niehans, *The Theory of Money*, Johns Hopkins University Press, Baltimore, 1978, p.28.) All that is asserted here is that people will not behave indefinitely as if they did not realise that inflation was occurring or changing in speed.

writings on the subject. A zero increase in productivity is assumed purely to simplify the arithmetic (the removal of the assumption does not change the argument).

I also assume a constant percentage mark-up on wages for all products, and constant terms of trade – again for simplicity. Then the rate of increase of wages is the same as the rate of increase of prices and represents the inflation rate, and there are no real wage changes except for very brief transitional periods. (The influence of real wage changes is held over for the discussion of the longer term in Chapter 8.) Because there may well be some involuntary unemployment, some economists would not regard the present level, OU, as a true equilibrium, however long it has been maintained.

Let us suppose that inflation has in fact averaged zero and is expected to remain zero in the future. What happens if the government eventually decides that the unemployment rate, OU, is too high and starts to boost demand – say by increasing its own spending or cutting taxes and expanding the money supply appropriately. So long as 'money illusion' is complete – that is workers and employers take no notice of the induced inflation in their bargaining behaviour – the story need go no further. Lower unemployment will have been purchased at the expense of some inflation. The economy is at point P on the upper figure of Chart 2. Unemployment has fallen to OM, but inflation has risen from, say, zero to 2 per cent. We can talk unambiguously of an increase in 'real demand' as well as monetary demand, the former represented by the reduction in unemployment shown by MU on the upper chart.

Unfortunately this is only the first stage. Sooner or later 'money illusion' disappears and workers begin to think in real terms. They start insisting on still higher wages to make up for the rise in the cost of living. The economy is then at point Ṕ on the lower curve of the lower figure of Chart 2. (This is known as an expectations-augmented Phillips curve, because it incorporates the expectation that prices will rise by 2 per cent.) Workers are now asking for and obtaining a 4 per cent wage increase to make up for the fact that prices are rising by 2 per cent and have eroded their initial gains. But once they obtain these increases, prices too will rise by 4 per cent. Before long the expected rate of inflation rises to 4 per cent, in line with actual inflation, and the economy shifts on to the still higher inflation-augmented Phillips curve passing through point P''.

Once that has happened workers will demand 6 per cent wage increases and, so long as demand is kept up, employers will concede them. The pay rise in turn will give the prices spiral a further twist, leading to larger and larger wage and price increases following each other indefinitely. So long as unemployment is held down at OM by government demand boosts, inflation will continue to accelerate. Thus the long-run trade-off is not between unemployment and inflation, with which we might try to live, but between unemployment and accelerating inflation, with which we cannot.

In this example, ministers and central bankers are faced with a painful dilemma. If they try to keep unemployment at the lower level OM by ever larger financial injections, they face the eventual collapse of the national monetary unit as a basis for business calculations – and with it the end of any benefit to employment from their policies – not to speak of the political and social repercussions of currency collapse. If, before this stage is reached, they try to return to the inflation rate at which they began their experiment (zero in our example), unemployment may have to shoot temporarily well *above* OU, the long-term minimum. This is because of the difficulty of reducing inflationary expectations once they have become embedded in the economic system.

Should the government be prepared to settle for whatever rate of inflation has emerged when it abandons its demand-boosting experiment, it will have to allow unemployment to return to at least OU; and some time will elapse before the system settles down at the newly-chosen position. Thus the long-term Phillips curve is (at a first approximation) a vertical line going through U, Q' and Q'' in the lower figure, and there is no long-term choice between unemployment and inflation.

The point of stability is that corresponding to the sustainable level of unemployment, OU. At that level wage increases will neither climb above nor fall below price increases. At any point on UQ'Q'' the average rate of inflation will be stable, but it can be stable with price stability or at very different (but unchanging) rates of inflation. Thus, ultimately, the rate of growth of monetary demand affects only inflation; the effects on unemployment are transitory.

The strict logic of this analysis would suggest that deflationary policies designed to drive unemployment *above* OU would eventually produce continuously *falling* wages and prices. But it is doubtful if inflationary and deflationary processes are symmetrical in today's circumstances since wages are more resistant to downward than to upward pressures. At the very least, the speed of adjustment may be slower in the face of abnormally low demand for labour than in the face of abnormally high demand.

Demand deficiency can be interpreted as a situation in which the economy is on one of the Phillips curves at a point to the right of U (which represents the NAIRU). The function of demand management (if it can be achieved) is then to return the economy to OU faster than natural processes will achieve. *The assertion of the counter-revolutionaries is that OU cannot be improved upon by demand management alone.*

Inflation can hover indefinitely around Q' or Q" provided that the country's rulers are prepared to settle for the sustainable unemployment rate OU. But politically it is probable that the impulses (such as the desire to reduce unemployment to OM) which led to the initial inflation will produce policies that culminate in successively higher inflation rates. Eventually, disillusionment may set in; or the reaction may speed up so much that even the temporary employment gain is eliminated.

Chart 2 also demonstrates the fallacy behind the question: 'What is to stop inflation restarting once the squeeze has come to an end?' The mistake is to confuse the unemployment cost of *reducing* inflation with the cost of a *permanently lower* rate of inflation. The squeeze is represented by the excess unemployment UN. Once inflation has fallen to the desired rate unemployment can safely fall back to OU (the sustainable rate) without any inflationary effect.

Inflation and unemployment‡

Some readers will have noticed that I was careful to say that the long-term Phillips curve was vertical *at a first approximation*. This was to take into account the likelihood that at very rapid rates of inflation the price mechanism and other coordinating mechanisms will work less efficiently, and that this will raise unemployment as well as impose other

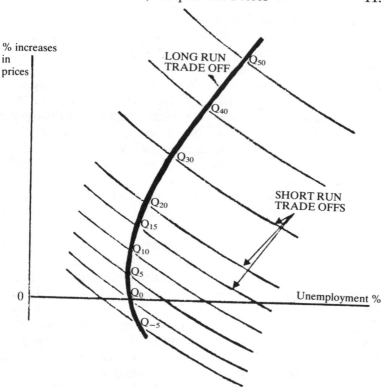

Chart 3: Phillips curves (hypothetical unemployment/inflation trade-off).

The points labelled Q are the points on the short-term Phillips curve where the expected rate of inflation is equal to the actual rate. At Q_0 these rates are both 0, at Q_5 they are both 5%, at Q_{10} they are both 10% etc., at Q_{-5} they are both minus 5%; i.e. there is both expected and actual deflation. The thin curves indicate the short-run trade-offs; the thick curve the long-run trade-off.

social losses. One reason for the distortions is that 'strato' inflation rates of 20, 30 or 50 per cent are never stable at these levels (as Latin American experience shows). The points on the charts corresponding to them are best regarded as representing averages around which the rate of inflation oscillates. A large part of the long-run unemployment costs arises from the instability and unpredictability of actual rates of inflation when the average rate is high.

On the other hand it is possible that the optimum rate of inflation is some low percentage, but higher than zero. For a positive rate of inflation avoids the necessity for reductions in absolute pay, which would otherwise sometimes be necessary to reflect the changing balance of supply and demand for different kinds of labour, especially when underlying productivity growth is low. There is no need to be dogmatic on either source of disturbance. They are mentioned to show why the long-run Phillips curve, although certainly steeper than the short-run one, need not be literally vertical all the way but may contain some slightly backward sloping sections and other moderately forward-looking ones where the trade-off would be perverse.

Chart 3 is a highly schematic attempt to show short-run and long-run relations between inflation and unemployment. Inflation rates are plotted against the vertical axis, unemployment rates on the horizontal one. Its message is that there *is* a *short-run* trade-off between inflation and unemployment. A reduction in inflation will normally require a period of abnormally high unemployment. An increase in inflation can on the other hand be accompanied by a temporary fall in unemployment – but this is much less certain (hence the abbreviated cut-off nature of the left-hand portion of the short-term Phillips curves). In the long run, however, there is little relation at all, or – at very high rates of inflation – an opposite relation. That is, very high rates of inflation are associated with high rates of unemployment. (In other words, the Phillips curve is positively sloped.) The NAIRU – or non-accelerating inflation rate of unemployment – now becomes a range with OQ_o near the lower limit.

The long run is defined as the period over which the economy has adjusted to the prevailing rate of inflation. Five to seven years may be typical for the bulk of the adjustment although for larger disturbances it may run into decades. The speed of adjustment is probably faster for increases than for decreases in the rate of inflation.

Key conclusions

The key conclusions of the above analysis can be summarised in a few simple propositions:

1   If unemployment is at its underlying or NAIRU level inflation may be high or low, but there will be no labour market influences causing it to accelerate or decelerate.

2　If demand is nevertheless boosted there may be an initial benefit to output and employment, but at the cost of accelerating inflation, which cannot last. The whole of the stimulus will thus ultimately be dissipated in more rapidly rising wages and prices.

3　If demand is curbed, there will be a 'transitional' recession with rising unemployment and falling inflation. The process is likely to be costly and painful; but once inflation has settled down at the desired lower level, unemployment should fall back to 'normal' (subject to the qualifications about hysteresis explained on page 104.)

Inflation need not return to its old level after a squeeze because the rate of price rises which workers fear and the rate which employers are able to pay are now much lower. So both the wage increases which workers desire – in a given state of the labour market and with given union power – and the increases which employers can afford to offer are lower than before. If inflation does embark on a continuing acceleration, it is a sign that the government has been over-optimistic about the NAIRU and is trying to run the economy at a higher pressure than is sustainable without more fundamental reforms in the economic structure.

4　If unemployment happens to be above its sustainable or NAIRU level it is in principle possible to secure more output and jobs by a demand stimulus. If the stimulus is sufficiently large to reduce unemployment to its NAIRU level, but no lower, inflation should not accelerate. But it cannot be over-emphasised that there is no need for the government to estimate the NAIRU directly, and that it is even dangerous for it to try. If its financial policy concentrates on maintaining a stable growth of monetary demand, the economy will eventually settle at (or fluctuate around) the underlying unemployment level. Indeed, this is the most effective way to discover how high the NAIRU is.

Obviously the above rules are a schematic simplification. In particular they ignore the effects of *changes* in unemployment. The rate of change of unemployment is important, as well as its level. Nevertheless so long as unemployment, when falling, goes no lower than the NAIRU, any rise in inflation will be a temporary one. Thus the main impact of the rate of change of unemployment (and of business activity) – as distinct from its level – is to cause oscillations around the rate of inflation at which the system will ultimately settle.*

Changes in the overall level of demand of a Phillips-curve type are by no means the only proximate influences behind changes in the inflation rate. There are many forces on the supply side which can boost prices quite quickly and also raise unemployment, thus giving a perverse trade-off even in the short term. Obvious examples include the oil price explosions of 1973 and 1979-80. Many events and policies will also raise unemployment without even a temporarily favourable effect on inflation. An increase in union monopoly power, or a worsening of the 'poverty trap', will shift the long-term Phillips curve to the right and worsen unemployment with no reduction in inflation.

The main lessons of Chart 3 are negative. Any fall in unemployment resulting from inflationary policies is at best temporary; but 'eliminating inflation' cannot in most normal circumstances be relied upon to make a large permanent dent in unemployment, unless it is inflation of the unstable and double digit variety.

Fine-tuning

Despite the assertions of the former Prime Minister, Mr James Callaghan, governments could in principle spend their way out of a *recession* – if a recession is defined as unemployment *above* the NAIRU rate (higher than OU in Chart 2) and self-correcting forces act too slowly. In principle, if governments knew enough, they could reduce fluctuations in unemployment and activity around the minimum sustainable rate of unemployment.

Critics of fine-tuning are sceptical of government's ability to perform even this limited function. Their original attack on fine-tuning   and   discretionary   demand   management

* However important the rate of change of unemployment (or any other labour market indicator) it cannot be so to the exclusion of the level. If the rate of change of unemployment were alone relevant to inflation, we would have to ask at what rate of change of unemployment inflation would be stable. If this rate were positive, unemployment would have to rise continuously, which is absurd. If it were negative, unemployment would have to fall continuously, which is also absurd. But suppose the equilibrium rate of change is zero. Then, when unemployment is stable, inflation is also stable. This implies that the rate of inflation could be anything at all, irrespective of the state of the labour market, which is again hard to believe.

None of this is to deny that we are in for a rough ride if, in the actual range in which the economy is working, the effects of the rate of change of unemployment are important relative to the level of unemployment.

emphasised the lags between the occurrence of a fluctuation, its diagnosis, the subsequent policy decisions, their implementation and their ultimate impact. The effect of these lags could be so great that would-be stabilisation measures might actually aggravate the fluctuations they were intended to reduce.[2]

The argument about fine-tuning is in a totally different dimension to that between the orthodox Keynesians and counter-revolutionary school. The latter debate is about the extent to which even perfectly timed demand management can promote employment in the longer run, whereas the former is about whether predetermined rules will provide better or worse results than discretionary government action.

There is a link, however, between the two debates, which is more psychological than logical. This is that economists who are keen on fine-tuning are either likely to disbelieve in the whole idea of a NAIRU or minimum sustainable level of unemployment, or have an overoptimistic idea of what that level is. Thus attempts at fine-tuning may not merely accentuate fluctuations in unemployment and inflation but lead over time to accelerating inflation, followed by a crisis and a violent stop.

The NAIRU is too unstable (and, therefore, too difficult to estimate) to be used directly for fine-tuning purposes or for economic management in general. Indeed, it would be a mistake to expect very much stability in forces such as union use of monopoly power, structural shifts in world demand, and perceived political and financial uncertainties, all of which influence the minimum sustainable unemployment level.

Queries on NAIRU‡

After the two oil price explosions of 1973-74 and 1979-80, it was impossible to be sure how much of the increase in unemployment represented a higher NAIRU and how far an increase in unemployment above the NAIRU was required to bring inflation back from the two-digit rates it then attained.

The most optimistic answer has been provided by the late Arthur Okun.[3] According to Okun, in a world where the performance of individual workers is variable and unpredictable but responsive to on-the-job training, it is rational for employers to maintain a given wage structure and to respond to changes in demand by adjusting hiring rates rather than moving wages sharply up or down to market-clearing levels. Moreover, when adjustments are required, it is sensible to make use of various rules of thumb, such as 'consensus' perceptions of the inflation rate and 'relativity' comparisons with other groups of workers. These administrative devices depend in his view neither on irrationality nor on union monopoly.

The net result is that the short-term trade-off between inflation and unemployment is very unfavourable (i.e. the temporary Phillips curves in Charts 2 and 3 are very flat at least to the right of the NAIRU shown by the point U). If something like an oil price shock (or a rise in indirect taxes such as the 7 per cent increase in VAT in Sir Geoffrey Howe's 1979 UK Budget) shifts the perceived inflation rate upwards, transitional unemployment will have to be long and severe before inflation returns to its original rate.

Despite much gloomy history, the Okun theory is ultimately an optimistic theory, perhaps too much so. For by implication it attributes the rise in unemployment to the transitional costs of reducing inflation after two painful but chance events, rather than to a rise in the underlying or NAIRU unemployment level. It follows from the Okun model that a favourable shock – such as the collapse of the world oil price – would set the whole process going in reverse, though not at the same speed.

If we are so ignorant of the NAIRU that it seems like a black cat in a dark room, why bother with it? Indeed it is difficult to find a single politician, however 'monetarist', who has used the concept (Mrs Thatcher specifically repudiated it in Prime Minister's Questions in 1981). But to dispense with it altogether is intellectual cheating. Once one starts to explain why attempts to 'boost demand' may lead to accelerating inflation, and thus prove futile, then one is led to the question: at what level of unemployment will inflation cease to accelerate? Nor is it meaningless to ask 'At what level of unemployment is the economy likely to settle when the counter-inflationary phase is over and absorbed', i.e. inflation is neither rising nor falling except for temporary wobbles, and there are no external 'shocks, favourable or unfavourable'? Politicians who talk about fiscal and monetary discipline and who reject demand stimulation are basing themselves on something like the NAIRU doctrine whether they know it or not; but if they insist on being ignorant physicians they are liable to inflict unnecessary pain on the body politic.

International transmission

There are many influences at work tending to speed up the transmission between expansionary or contractionary policies and the inflation rate. The immediate effect of domestic monetary expansion under a floating exchange rate is depreciation of the currency. This causes domestic prices to rise much more quickly than would occur if there were a purely domestic transmission from a tighter labour market to higher wage increases and only then to prices. The impact of depreciation is not confined to the cost of imported products. The ceiling on the prices of many goods sold in the domestic market set by imports (actual or potential) also rises. In a closed economy the short-turn effects of official attempts to contract or expand demand are mainly on output and jobs, with the price-level effects coming through later; in an open economy, under floating rates, there are important price-level effects right at the beginning, thus eroding the benefit to output and employment. Indeed in an open economy the key influence on the domestic inflation rate is the average 'world' rate of inflation, amplified or diminished in a particular country by the movement of its own exchange rate.

The international influences do not mean that we can ignore the closed economy model. After all, what determines the world rate of inflation? Excessive fiscal and monetary expansion by all the main industrial countries together will first raise output and employment, and the boost will eventually be completely eroded by inflation, as in the closed economy case. There is also a short circuit at the world level. For excessive demand growth in the industrial world leads to an acceleration of commodity prices even before wages begin to rise, thus again eroding some of the stimulus to output from the outset. There are also domestic short circuits acting through the prices of assets such as houses and land, which respond quickly to demand influences well before wages, and

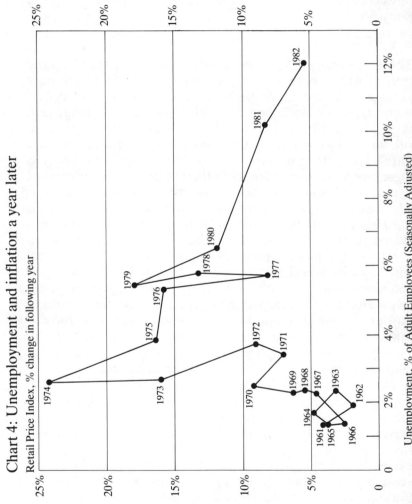

Chart 4: Unemployment and inflation a year later

before the prices of newly produced goods and services.

The net result of these and many other short circuits is that the effect on prices of expansionary demand policy can come through much more quickly via routes other than the labour market; and the more quickly higher demand spills over into prices the less there is left over to boost output and employment, even temporarily.

Yet it is very easy to go too far in describing the short circuits. The saw-tooth world recession of the early 1980s showed that restrictive financial policies have a faster impact on inflation than formerly supposed. But it also showed that a large part of the initial effect still comes through in lost output and employment.

Recent experience suggests a certain asymmetry in the transmission process. In other words, expansionary monetary and fiscal policies, based on an over-optimistic view of the underlying rate of unemployment, feed very quickly into higher inflation. Restrictive policies, on the other hand, still work partly in the old-fashioned way: first they induce a recession as well as reducing inflation, with output recovering some time later. To make matters worse, the policy cycle was superimposed in the 1970s and early 1980s on a NAIRU that was itself rapidly drifting upwards. Chart 4 shows that there is still evidence of a Phillips curve in the UK, even though it has been drifting rapidly to the right.

Expectations, 'rational' and otherwise‡

The most general influence on the speed of transmission is expectations. Once people expect a higher budget deficit or rapid monetary expansion to lead to more inflation, the effect can come through very quickly indeed as the exchange rate and government security prices are marked down, earnings are pushed up, and so on.

Crucial to expectations is the policy regime believed to be in operation. If price and wage setters believe that monetary and fiscal guidelines are here to stay, they will adjust much more quickly to demand restraint – both because they become more optimistic about inflation and because they have grown more fearful of pricing their products and members out of their markets. This, in a nutshell, is the case for medium-term objectives, together with action to underpin their credibility.

By contrast, if the targets are fixed for only a short period at a time and there is a general belief that they will be missed, or adjusted upwards at the first sign of recession, people will quite rationally refrain from changing their wage and price behaviour. Then the effects of monetary restraint will for quite a time be felt very strongly on output and employment.

These remarks embody many of the policy insights of the 'rational expectations' school of thought. Signed-up members will, of course, go a good deal further and assert that people adapt very quickly to new conditions in setting wages and prices, and that only *unexpected* changes in policy or unexpected news can affect output and employment.

They assert that people act 'as if' they have correct knowledge of economic relationships; or, somewhat more plausibly, that they do not make systematic mistakes in predicting inflation (or valuing shares) which policy-makers or forecasters can exploit. This does not mean that people adjust instantaneously to new monetary and fiscal guidelines. They may for good reasons be uncertain what the policy means or whether it will be observed. Furthermore, the existence of previous contracts inhibits instantaneous adjustment. The most controversial assertion made by some members of this school is that the economy adjusts quickly to disturbances and that unemployment soon reaches its underlying level, which (in contrast to other interpretations) is also identified with 'equilibrium'.

It is far too early to give a verdict on the rational expectations school. Rational expectations are best considered as a research technique, which may yield useful results not obtainable from a more 'realistic' theory. Its leading exponents, Robert Lucas and Thomas Sargent, have always insisted that their work is primarily a critique of conventional macroeconomic forecasting models; and they make a virtue of not having headline-policy proposals, other than the well-known Friedman programme. Professor Sargent has candidly admitted that he does not think his school has a theory which really explains depressions.[4]

'Rational expectations' are at the moment best seen as an academic research programme; and while expectations are of the first importance in policy formulation, there is nothing in the concept, either of the NAIRU or of regulating nominal rather than real demand, which depends on the 'rational expectations' doctrine. Indeed the main reason for this digression is that the reader is sure to meet some attacks on 'monetarism' based on some caricatured version of 'rational expectations'.

Gradualism and expectations

It takes no very specialist doctrine to appreciate that the cost in foregone output and unemployment of a counter-inflationary policy – or even a policy of refusing to finance a reacceleration of inflation – is less if the policy is credible than if employers, trade unionists and other agents suspect that the government will be easily blown off course.[5]

The unemployment cost of a counter-inflationary policy arises, in part at least, because it takes time for people to believe that monetary demand, and thus eventually the rate of inflation, will be held on a tight reign; and further time for them to adjust their behaviour to this realisation. The tragic 20 per cent rise in British wage levels in the 1979-80 pay round, at a time when the currency was appreciating by about the same amount and when settlements in other countries were in single figures, arose in large measure because negotiators on both sides of industry assumed that the government would and could produce enough monetary demand and depreciate the currency enough to 'validate' the 'going rate' of pay increases. By the time credibility was achieved the damage had already been done and it would have required several years of negative pay settlements (i.e. money wage cuts) to restore Britain's competitive position without devaluation.

The opponents of the UK Medium Term Financial Strategy set up a staged dialectical confrontation between two absurd alternatives. Either, it was supposed, mechanistic relations derived from the past prevailed. In that case a 10 per cent reduction in inflation would cause ten times as much unemployment as a 1 per cent reduction and the number of years a policy was in operation would have no effect on its credibility; or alternatively expectations immediately adjusted to the mere publication of a document indicating slower monetary growth in the future, and money wages immediately plunged downwards to eliminate any unemployment cost. The existing econometric models do not shed much light on what probably does happen, which is that people learn from all sources but do so in irregular fits and starts; that a credible plan can reduce the unemployment costs of disinflation but not eliminate them; that credibility has to be gained by actions as well as words; and that by the time the first battles are won it is often too late to prevent the bulk of the unemployment increase.

Constraints on output

In most of the argument between the postwar Keynesian establishment and the counter-revolution, the constraint on output was seen in the labour market. The Keynesians thought that output was limited by what could be produced at full employment and the other camp by the point at which pressures in the labour marked reached the take-off threshold for inflation.

Since the early 1970s, however, the constraint has tended often to reveal itself in other markets. During the boom of 1972-4, for instance, primary product prices started to accelerate on a world scale earlier and more rapidly than wages. In the developing countries of the Third World non-labour constraints have always operated. In many of them there is not enough capital or enterprise to employ available workers at wages even as high as subsistence. In such countries excessive demand expansion will manifest itself in the goods rather than the labour market, with higher prices, shortages and increased imports as evidence.

The above analysis of accelerating inflation in the labour market is thus a stepping stone to the more general idea of a sustainable rate of growth of output, irrespective of the nature of the constraint. Persistent attempts to boost output above its sustainable growth rate will lead to accelerating inflation, and the bottlenecks can be in any market. There will still however be an underlying or minimum sustainable rate of unemployment, wherever the bottleneck which prevents full employment being reached happens to arise; and attempts to go below it by demand-boosting will, if governments persist with them, lead to escalating inflation with no other benefit to show in return.

6   The Case for Money GDP

Why not a price target?; A stable framework; The meaning of 'monetary demand'‡; Expenditure and income‡; Instruments and objectives; Fiscal policy; A balanced budget?; The Meade strategy; Setting GDP objectives; Treatment of shocks; Union wage push.

Why not a price target?

If the position of the underlying or NAIRU rate of unemployment were known and the shape of the shifting short-term trade-off between unemployment and inflation were also known, then it would not matter how the objectives of macroeconomic policy were stated. If (short-term) objectives for output and unemployment were stated, it would be possible to read off the corresponding changes in the rate of inflation. If instead the objectives were stated in terms of inflation, one would know the corresponding movements of output and unemployment around their underlying level. An objective for prices could be translated into one for output, and vice versa; and as a matter of arithmetic the two could be combined to show what was implied for Money GDP.

If these information requirements were fulfilled it would be very attractive to set a price target, as prices are the only variable that demand management can be confident of influencing in the longer term. A target of price stability, or of some given low rate of inflation, would be simpler and more attractive than any national income or monetary aggregates. Just as the Romans said 'If you want peace, prepare for war,' it might be tempting today to say 'If you want high employment prepare for price stability.' Recessions would be minimised and slumps avoided by adopting a sufficiently gradual path in reducing inflation and by being careful to avoid actual deflation. An event like an oil price shock should be met by tolerating a temporary rise in the inflation rate before resuming the planned downward path.

The basic objection is that we do not have the required knowledge. Over short periods that run into years, the price level is affected, not merely by major shocks such as an oil price or wage explosions; there is even in normal years a good deal of 'noise'. Price levels are influenced by chance events such as harvests, indirect tax changes, the timing of state industry pay and price increases, import price changes (which may originate abroad rather than from exchange movements), and so on almost indefinitely. These may be, at least in their timing, outside the framework of macroeconomic policy or the general pressure of demand in the goods and labour markets. Any attempt to gauge whether policy is or is not too tight (or not tight enough) by examining only whether the inflation rate is accelerating or decelerating can, therefore, lead to highly perverse signals. This is especially so if the short term Phillips curve happens to be fairly flat in the face of reductions in demand pressure (i.e. if output and employment fall a great deal, but inflation drops only slightly).

An exchange rate target is a way of achieving a price target by proxy (as explained in Chapter 4). It will have all the problems of a price level target, plus the added difficulty of knowing exactly what exchange rate path corresponds to a given price objective.

The lack of knowledge required for steering an economy by means of a price target is not merely an unfortunate deficiency of information which may one day be remedied. Neither the sustainable long term rate of unemployment nor the short term trade-off between inflation and unemployment is given deterministically by such forces as the degree of unionisation, social security benefits, or quantifiable measures of mobility of labour and structural change. There is a great mass of indeterminacy where attitudes, values and beliefs about policy can all make a difference. The division of any increase in Money GDP between output and price changes depends on the responses of employers, trade unionists and other economic agents; and it is desirable to stress this aspect.

A stable framework

One way of emphasising the point is to announce that the government will keep the growth of total national expenditure (and therefore income) on as stable a path as possible. The division of this growth between extra output and rising prices is not one that governments can influence directly. They can, however, provide a stable framework within which people can adjust their own wage and price decisions in the knowledge that they will not be bailed out of their mistakes by inflationary injections of demand.

A reduction in the rate of inflation is normally highly desirable. But with a nominal GDP target it is clear to policy-makers that such a reduction has created room for more real output growth. So unions, for example, can be assured that wage restraint will lead to more jobs rather than less, and that greater productivity will not just lead to more unemployment. One trouble with a price level target is that 'undershooting' does not emerge as a problem – it is just the bonus of lower than expected inflation. No further action seems to be needed, so there is no pressure to restore monetary demand even if output might thereby return more quickly to its trend path.

A target for Money GDP would also be much easier for people to understand, once they got used to it, than the bewildering variety of money and credit measures now placed before those who penetrate into the business columns of the newspapers or who read financial circulars. A 'national cash objective' (on the lines of public sector cash limits) might be a suitable catchphrase. An objective of this kind involves retaining demand management so long as this means *monetary* demand or money times velocity (MV). It cannot mean guaranteeing *real* demand irrespective of the level of wages and prices that producer groups succeed in obtaining.

A target stated in terms of money GDP rather than real GDP may be a step back from the over-reaching ambitions of recent years. It is, however, a return not to the 1920s but to the spirit of the 1944 White Paper on *Employment Policy*, hailed in its time as a revolutionary document. The White Paper's key paragraph 40 located the source of depression in the lack of a 'sufficiently large expenditure on goods and services. . . . The first step in a policy of maintaining employment must be to prevent total expenditure falling away.' The quotation is referring to expenditure in actual money, not 'real demand', 'volume terms', 'wage units', or any other kind of funny money. This is surely clear from paragraph 43 which warns that 'action to maintain expenditure will be fruitless unless wages and prices are kept reasonably stable.' A nominal GDP target would involve a commitment by government to try to avoid a collapse of nominal income and expenditure such as occurred in the Great Depression. If monetary demand were inadequate, measured against some medium term objective, government would act to increase it.

No kind of financial strategy can reduce the unemployment rate for long below the minimum NAIRU rate. All that can be expected from a financial strategy, once it has been in operation for some years, is an avoidance of unnecessary fluctuations in output and unemployment and a reasonably low and stable rate of inflation. Success on these two fronts will provide a background against which underlying structural problems can be tackled with a higher chance of success.

The argument against Money GDP that has given me most pause is that while most people instinctively sense that in the case of the money supply 'more means worse', in the case of Money GDP there may be a tendency to say 'more means better.'[1] I would accept this danger and say that people will have to learn that there can be too much as well as too little Money GDP, as of most other things. Many of the problems in the area of economic management arise from the search for easy slogans; and a public relations problem needs to be faced rather than dodged.

The meaning of 'monetary demand'‡

Since so much has been said about 'monetary demand', 'nominal national income', 'Money GDP' and allied concepts, it is necessary to give a little more detail about what they mean and how they relate to each other.

Let us start with 'demand', or 'aggregate expenditure' as it is often termed. In an analysis of the movement of national

‡ As in the previous chapter, this mark signifies a passage which some readers may find more difficult than the surrounding text. Skimming rather than skipping is recommended.

Table 1: GDP at current market prices:
Incomplete list of near synonyms

UK usage	*US usage*
Money GDP	Nominal GDP
Total Demand \} at current prices	
Aggregate Demand	
Monetary Demand	Nominal Demand
MV (Money times velocity)	
Total Spending	Nominal Spending
Aggregate Expenditure at current prices	Nominal Expenditure
Money National Product	Nominal National Product
Money Value of National Output	Nominal Output
Money National Income	Nominal National Income
Money Incomes	Total Nominal Income
Total Incomes	Nominal Incomes

income statistics monetary demand or 'aggregate expenditure' has to be identified with the total flow of spending actually observed. Total spending is in practice measured by the 'Gross Domestic Product at Current Prices' which is usually called for short 'Money GDP'. In America or American-influenced parlance 'Nominal GDP' is often used instead.

Money GDP can be conceived in two ways. It is the product of the quantity of money multiplied by its velocity of circulation in current transactions; or, in symbols, MV: money times velocity (of circulation). It can also be broken down into 'Real GDP', i.e. the GDP expressed at the prices prevailing in some particular year, multiplied by a price index. Thus T is 'Real GDP' and PT or MV is 'Money' or 'Nominal' GDP.*

There are many other synonyms (listed in Table 1) in use for 'total spending' or 'Money GDP' or MV. One reason for this proliferation is that, in national income accounting, the circular flow of spending can be measured as expenditure,

* Most official series and analyses using money GDP are calculated at current market prices. This is the case for instance for calculations of the 'velocity of circulation' which is defined as Y/M, where Y is Money GDP and M is some measure of the money supply. I have followed official practice. But there is a strong case for using GDP at factor cost, as the measure would be immune from the effects of indirect tax changes. Increases in value added tax designed to depress monetary demand may be wise or unwise; but there are advantages in a measure which makes them distinguishable from expansionary measures designed to boost demand.

output or income. The three methods ought in principle to yield closely related figures, although in practice there are bound to be discrepancies in measurement. 'Total spending' or a 'national cash limit' is probably the best term for popular presentation and 'Money GDP' for reporting economic statistics. 'Total Incomes' or 'Money Incomes' is often used in discussion, but risks giving the false impression that the speaker is talking about what the public knows as 'incomes policy' when he is really referring to demand management.

Expenditure and income‡

Strictly speaking, the exact measure which governments can influence through domestic financial policy is not Money

Table 2: Relation between main national income measures
(Expenditure based) 1982

		£bn
	Consumer Expenditure	165·1
	Government Consumption	59·7
	Gross Domestic Fixed Capital Formulation	41·7
	Increase in Physical Stocks	−2·0
	TOTAL DOMESTIC EXPENDITURE	264·5
ADD	Exports	+73·0
	TOTAL FINAL EXPENDITURE	337·5
DEDUCT	Imports	− 67·1
	GROSS DOMESTIC PRODUCT (GDP) AT CURRENT MARKET PRICES (EQUALS MONEY GDP)	270·4
ADD	Overseas Investment Income	+ 0·2
	GROSS NATIONAL PRODUCT (GNP) AT CURRENT MARKET PRICES	270·6
DEDUCT	Expenditure taxes (net of subsidies)*	− 42·4
	GNP AT CURRENT FACTOR COST	228·2
DEDUCT	'Capital Consumption'	−33·0†
	NATIONAL INCOME or NET NATIONAL PRODUCT	195·2†

* known as 'factor cost adjustment'
† estimate

GDP but a wider aggregate known by the name 'total final expenditure'. The relation between the two is shown in Table 2. An expansionary monetary and fiscal policy can boost total final expenditure; but the impact on Money GDP will be diminished if a disproportionate amount leaks into imports.*
Arguments between British Chancellors and their critics about whether monetary demand is rising fast enough have sometimes turned on the distinction between total final expenditure and Money GDP.

Let us suppose that the government's objective is a 10 per cent annual increase in monetary demand and that total final expenditure indeed rises by this rate, but because of leakages into imports, Money GDP has only risen by only 5 per cent. Has the growth of monetary demand been inadequate or not?

The 10 per cent figure which the government is likely to quote represents demand from the point of view of purchasers irrespective of whether they buy UK goods or not. The 5 per cent rise in Money GDP, which the critics are likely to quote, represents demand as it is experienced by UK producers for goods they can afford to supply at current costs, selling prices and exchange rates. The latter concept of 'demand' is the key one from the point of view of stabilisation policy. Thus it is the critics who are nearer the mark.

While nobody can know for sure whether the economy is above or below the NAIRU, a growth in Money GDP of 5 per cent compared with a target of 10 per cent is (in this example) a clear sign that policy is tighter than intended and can be relaxed (just as a growth in Money GDP of 15 per cent would be a sign it should be tightened). Moreover, the particular example given above will point to some measure of exchange depreciation as an appropriate mechanism for raising Money GDP.

Instruments and objectives

The stock response to the suggestions for a Money GDP target when – with no claim for originality and in the wake of many other economists[2] – I put forward the idea in a Hobart Paper[3] was to ask 'how do you control Money GDP?', as if I

---

* The remedy of import controls for this leakage is counter-productive because, apart from many disadvantages, they will tend to boost the exchange rate and thus defeat their own object.

were asking for a completely new set of instruments which did not yet exist. This was to misconstrue the nature of the proposal.

Governments and central banks have always engaged in operations to influence interest rates or to influence the credit or money creating potential of banks. They have always used fiscal policy (i.e. changes in the balance of the budget) and sometimes exchange rate policy (the latter itself requiring further instruments to implement). These are the instruments required for influencing (not 'controlling') monetary demand. Monetary demand and Money GDP are not gimmicks nor panaceas, but rough guidelines for the use of existing instruments.

It is convenient to use public sector borrowing (or the general government deficit) as a summary of fiscal (i.e. budgetary) policy and money supply (the total notes and coin and bank deposits) as a measure of monetary (i.e. central banking) policy. Both these magnitudes can be defined in many different ways and there is nothing sacrosanct about a particular definition.

Money supply and public sector borrowing are termed intermediate targets since – if my argument is correct – they are useful mainly as a means of influencing Money GDP, which is the final objective. But, just as it is wrong to be carried away by over-ambition and to conduct the whole discussion in terms of 'real' objectives which governments cannot determine, it is equally mistaken to become too technocratic and to think only of the intermediate objectives. In the last resort, the Money GDP objective should be the overriding one; and there should be no cries of 'blown off course' or 'U-turn' if changes in the specification of intermediate objectives prove necessary, i.e. *really* necessary and not merely convenient. In the words of the US Council of Economic Advisers in its 1983 Report: 'The principle of targeting money growth rates is not an end in itself but only a means of achieving control of nominal GDP.'[4] It went on to suggest that the observed behaviour of Money GDP should in future be used 'to guide a gradual recalibration of the monetary growth targets, recognising that there are uncertain lags between monetary and GDP change'.

As the toleration of monetary overshoots by the British

THE HIERARCHY OF OBJECTIVES

Instruments

Government Spending

Taxation

Money Market Operations
and Debt Management

Intermediate Targets

Government Borrowing

Monetary Aggregates
or Interest Rates

Final Objective

Money GDP

authorities in 1980 and 1981 and by the Fed in 1982 suggests, when monetary growth is offset by a fall in velocity, monetary targets are indeed overriden. Once national authorities start looking at money in conjunction with velocity they are using Money GDP as a guide whether they know it or not. A conscious avowal of that fact might enable action to be taken more promptly and with less sense of guilt. It would also provide a better guide to how far to go in relaxation (or in other circumstances in tightening up) than the more usual meaningless formula of 'taking all indicators into consideration'.

I can understand the objections of traditional Keynesians, who would like direct objectives for real variables such as output and employment, but I have less sympathy for the objections of monetarists. For a Money GDP objective would have exactly the same effect as the successful achievement of money supply objectives, if the right monetary aggregates could be discovered and if velocity were as stable as had been hoped. All monetarists are being asked to do is to shift their headline utterances, and their top-line advice to politicians, from intermediate objectives to those final aims which government has a hope of influencing. Such a shift would also have the, not entirely negligible, dialectical advantage of showing clearly how wage moderation would promote output and employment.

A major advantage of talking in terms of total spending or Money GDP is that the precise definition of 'money' becomes a secondary issue. We can say that in 1982 the average outstanding stock of money measured by Sterling M3 was £88 billion and velocity was 3·1. We can alternatively take the narrower M1 definition of money, which excludes deposit (in US parlance 'savings') accounts, and say that this amounted to nearly £36 billion and that velocity was about 7·6. Either way we arrive back at a Money GDP of just over £270 billion.

Some people have misunderstood this suggestion by responding: 'It is difficult enough to control money; do you want to regulate velocity as well?' The last thing we need are

---

*   M1 consists of notes and coin in public circulation plus sterling sight bank deposits ('current accounts') of the UK private sector. Sterling M3 consists of M1 plus UK residents' sterling time deposits ('deposit accounts'). M2 consists of M3 minus large time deposits held for investment purposes. It is an attempt to measure transaction balances and has only been available since late 1981.

separate targets for M and for V. The government and the central bank are all the time influencing total spending (MV) when they determine the size of public sector deficits and the way they are financed, when they act to influence interest rates or the ability of banks to lend, and sometimes too when they intervene in the foreign exchange market. The suggestion is that these operations should have as their ultimate target Money GDP, i.e. MV considered jointly as a flow.

As institutional financial change will continue, views will always be shifting on the appropriate monetary aggregates to use (and their relative weighting if more than one is used) and on the relationship of these aggregates to Money GDP. The choice is between giving central banks a free hand to make these technical adjustments and insisting on some *guiding principles* and on a time horizon longer than a year.

Fiscal policy

Fiscal and monetary policy must in the long run be in harmony. A future where larger and larger budget deficits are offset by tighter and tighter money with no inflationary effect is not easy to credit: and a good deal of empirical work suggests it is unlikely.[5] When prospective US budget deficits approximated to the entire national savings total, it was hardly surprising that long-term yields on government bonds suggested a disbelief that the inflationary effects could be completely offset.

Nevertheless, over short periods, central banks have shown themselves to be successful in offsetting the potential inflationary impact of quite high budget deficits, although a heavy interest rate price has been paid for lopsidedness in the use of instruments.

A tighter fiscal policy can help monetary control in two ways. It can lower the interest rate cost of observing money supply limits. This is an effect that the most technical monetarists will recognise, even though they sometimes suggest it is small. Secondly, lower budget deficits might themselves curb monetary demand, independently of any effect on the money supply – which would show itself in a lower velocity. This second effect would be rejected by most technical monetarists.

On either way of looking at it, there is a trade-off between fiscal and monetary policy, both when it comes to stimulating demand and when it comes to reining it back. The best short-term composition of the mix for demand management varies with time and place as examples in Chapter 9 will illustrate.

A balanced budget?

The idea will certainly have occurred to some readers that governments should simply balance their budgets and forget the complications. But it has no clear meaning in today's circumstances. Mr Gladstone's budget was small and simple enough, and sufficiently undistorted by inflation or nationalised industries, to be treated as a single current account to be financed from revenue. Today there is no one right way of measuring the balance.

Do today's budget balancers want to eliminate the whole Public Sector Borrowing Requirement (PSBR) or do they want to exclude the nationalised industries? Some people want to exclude all public expenditure classified as capital. (The objection to this argument is that most government capital spending produces no ascertainable revenue and a social return which can only be guessed; it is thus not really comparable with the kind of spending that commercial enterprises will reasonably finance by borrowing.) Such questions could be posed indefinitely. If the public sector accounts are presented on an inflation-adjusted basis, the UK PSBR disappears completely in many years when the published figures show it to be high. It also disappears if a sufficient correction for business cycle distortions is made.

These questions are not hair-splitting conundrums. They can make all the difference – to take the year 1982-3 in the UK – between a Public Sector Borrowing Requirement as published, of £9 bn, equivalent to just over 3 per cent of GDP, and an adjusted repayment or overall surplus of almost £26 bn or about 9 per cent of GDP. People instinctively keen on 'sound money' would be well advised not to push the balanced budget argument too far, as it will only play into the hands of their critics who will gleefully produce one calculation after another purporting to show that the budget is already in excessive surplus.

Table 3: Alternative estimates
of UK budget balance, 1982-83

	£bn	% of GDP
Public Sector Borrowing Requirement	−9·2	−3·3
General Government	−10·1	−3·7
General Government, cyclically adjusted	+2·1	+0·8
General Government, cyclically and inflation adjusted	+9·6	+3·5
As above deducting capital expenditure	+25·6	+9·3

Source: Simon and Coates

The Meade strategy

This is a convenient point to relate the advocacy of a Money GDP target in this book to Professor James Meade's pioneering work on the subject.[6] Professor Meade, of course, has the distinction of being a very early advocate of the idea; and he was among the economists whose analysis encouraged me to come out explicitly in favour of this objective. Moreover he has, together with David Vines, carried out a very detailed study to determine both the desirable path of Money GDP and the means of achieving it.

The main technical difference between the Meade proposals and other proposals for a Money GDP objective is that Meade would use fiscal policy as his main instrument of control, leaving interest rate policy to maintain a 'competitive exchange rate'.

The more fundamental difference lies in Meade's stress on wage-fixing. Unless wage-fixing institutions are reformed in an employment-creating manner, so that a given Money GDP gain is channeled into output and employment instead of being dissipated in wage and price increases, Meade is unwilling to lay down or endorse any financial strategy at all.

However, the more one thinks about it, the clearer it becomes that even if one accepts the Meade incomes policy without reservation, there will be no Day One on which it can be announced that wage-fixing institutions have been reformed sufficiently for the financial side of the Meade strategy to go ahead. The erosion of wage-fixing practices detrimental to full employment will be a long and gradual process of attrition, whatever the route chosen.

In the meanwhile, the proposed 'national cash target' should itself contribute to the greater awareness of the link between pay and jobs which Meade would like to see and thus help gradually to reduce underlying (or NAIRU) unemployment. Admittedly the main attack on very high unemployment levels will have to come from labour market and not demand management policies; but I would be willing to go ahead with the stabilisation of monetary demand as a good deal better than nothing.

Setting GDP objectives

The most difficult problem about Money GDP objectives is the level at which they should be set. Yet hardly any of the critical discussion has focussed on this point. This is, of course, less of a problem if we start from a position of price stability or low and stable inflation, which has lasted so long that it is expected to remain, and there have been no upward or downward productivity leaps. Money GDP objectives could then be set on the basis of past trends.

Even then the technical job of monitoring and correcting deviations would be far from easy. UK estimates of Money GDP appear about 2½ months after the end of the quarter to which they refer, and are subject to considerable revision. Moreover, the quarter-to-quarter path is highly erratic even when fully known.

Normally attention will focus on Money GDP trends over two or three years. Indeed attempts to achieve a precise quarter-to-quarter path would be positively undesirable even if it were possible. If deviation were apparent over an intermediate period, say a year, the authorities should 'stop, look and think' – which is the purpose of guidelines and plans, government or private.

If Money GDP is well below the guideline at a time of severe recession, partly because output is low, the balance of risks may suggest stimulative action. It may be too dangerous to wait two or three years to ascertain more certainly if Money

GDP really is off trend. Again if a major overshoot of Money GDP is due to the price component rising, and if indicators such as interest and exchange rates suggest the development of inflationary psychology, a risk should probably be taken on the side of prompt action.

It is not difficult to pose trick questions, e.g. 'suppose the Money GDP objective were 10 per cent, what would you do if Money GDP were rising say at 12 per cent, but this was all due to a rapid rise in output of 9 per cent with prices rising by approximately 3 per cent?' Remembering what was said in the last chapter about inflation responding to the rate of change of business activity as well as its level, a sudden spurt in output growth could indeed be a sign of overheating and later inflation; early restrictive measures might avoid a violent slamming down of the brakes later. But by looking at prices and output together, the authorities avoid having to hold an absolute judgment on how much of a rise (or shortfall) in output is too much.

The government is not being asked to 'throw away' information about output and price components of Money GDP; on the contrary, it would use information on both to decide the direction in which risks are to be taken in corrective action. Why not just stimulate output in a recession and forget about Money GDP? Because if the government does this, it will either stimulate too little out of overcaution or stimulate too much and have to bring the brakes screeching down after an acceleration of inflation. If you like, Money GDP is a guide to how far the government can safely go in stimulating output when it is concerned about recession; and how far it can wisely apply the brakes when faced with inflation.

Thus, official influence over Money GDP can never be a simple progress towards straightforward targets. It involves rather the use of numbers to illustrate a general direction, which is bound to be achieved jerkily. It does not help to ascribe to numerical objectives an automaticity they cannot hope to possess, however great one's philosophical preference for rules over discretion.

One major problem is the transition from one kind of regime to another. Even if output and employment would eventually be higher under a non-inflationary than under an accommodating regime, they are likely to be lower during the transition. While the credibility of a new monetary and fiscal regime is in question the economy may get the worst of all worlds, with more unemployment than under either accommodating or fixed rules. Events which shake belief in a pre-announced strategy or monetary regime without utterly destroying it are extremely expensive in terms of output and employment. The result is likely to be greater pessimism about inflation, and encouragement to pressure-groups to 'have a go' with both wage claims and demands for fiscal assistance. Thus the curbs which remain depress output and employment far more than if credibility had been maintained. The advocates of retreat under fire are among the main begetters of the unemployment of which they complain.

Treatment of shocks

A sudden deterioration in the composition of Money GDP is liable to occur, raising the price component and reducing the output one, as a result of events entitled supply 'shocks'. A supply shock affects the PT side of the identity $MV = PT$. It can occur as a result of price shocks – say the success of an oil cartel or a wage breakthrough by a number of major unions. It can also occur as a result of an output shock. The traditional example is a bad harvest; today it could be the result of a war in the Middle East holding up oil deliveries. In the postwar period shocks on the prices side have been more frequent.

The general price level does not suddenly leap upwards of its own accord. A price shock is possible because individual prices or wages are slower to adjust themselves to downward than to upward pressure. This is often called 'downward wage and price rigidity', but sluggishness or resistance is a more accurate description. It therefore follows that sudden and unexpected rises in major costs or prices will provide a shock to the system. The failure of other prices to fall straightaway in compensation will lead to an initial rise in the overall price level (P) and thus to a decline in activity and employment (T) if the government stands firm in its control of MV. Should the government stand firm on monetary demand, or should it accommodate inflationary impulses originating elsewhere whose initial effect is to boost the price level?

Union wage push

Union wage push is best understood as one example of a supply shock. An existing degree of union monopoly power or strike-threat power affects the distribution of *relative* wages between occupations and industries. Wages will be higher and employment lower in the more effectively unionised sectors than they would be in a competitive market, while wages will be lower and employment higher in the less effectively unionised or non-unionised sectors. But there is nothing here to start off a new inflationary trend or aggravate an existing one.

Suppose, however, that a major group of unions increases its degree of monopoly power or makes more use of its existing power. This can be the result of a thousand and one factors. For instance, there may be increased organisation or membership, or more militant tactics. Such changes may be a reaction to a period of government wage control. They can stem from pressure on real take-home pay due to a worsening of the nation's terms of trade. They can be due to legislation, such as that in Britain in 1974-76, deliberately designed to increase union power. Nor is there any reason to rule out changing political currents or key personalities.

Whatever the initiating force, the result is the same as with other shocks. As wages and prices outside the union sector are most unlikely to fall immediately to anything like an offsetting extent, prices will rise even if MV remains stable, and activity and employment will fall; i.e. P will rise at the expense of T.

For domestic shocks of a wage-push kind, the general rule should be 'no accommodation' (a formula which was recommended by the middle of the road McCracken Report for the OECD).[7] But, if it is to benefit rather than harm employment, it is essential for the rule to be known in advance and to carry credibility. The hallmark of the counter-revolutionary's approach to demand management is not a denial of the possibility of cost-push but his view of the appropriate response by policy-makers. If domestic shocks are not accommodated, they will not, he claims, give rise to a sustained inflation (or acceleration in the inflation rate). They will certainly be costly and should be avoided as far as is within our power; but, with relatively fixed demand management rules, such explosions will generate only short-term and temporary inflationary boosts. Above all, if unions know beforehand that there is scant possibility of wage push being accommodated, they will be less inclined to engage in it and there will be fewer episodes of either rising inflation or transitional unemployment above the 'underlying' level.

Where the shock is external, as with the oil price rise, there is a case for some minimal accommodation so that price and wage cuts (or drastic reductions in their rate of increase) are not forced onto other sectors.* But it should be made clear that there can be no financial accommodation for pay rises which attempt to recoup real income losses brought about by changed world conditions. Even for external shocks, minimal accommodation should be reserved for very rare major and unpredicted upheavals. If every transient influence on the price level is treated as a 'shock' and demand expanded accordingly, irregular but frequent increases in monetary demand will come to be the norm and inflationary expectations will worsen, with all the problems that accompany such expectations.

---

*   Strictly speaking no accommodation is required if a Money GDP objective is being followed. For GDP is the sum of all domestic value added and does not include imports. But it is difficult to avoid some inflation of domestic costs in such circumstances, for instance through the practice of applying percentage mark-up at the wholesale stage, which does not distinguish between domestic and imported components. Inspection of GDP deflators in the relevant periods does not suggest that they rise much less than ordinary consumer price indices, if at all.

7 Money in Longer Perspective

The Friedman rule; Historical stability misleading; Goodhart's Law; International portfolio shifts; Challenge and response; The gold standard; Competitive money.

The Friedman rule

There are, we have seen, difficulties in measuring the money supply and in finding a stable relationship between money and national income that will be useful for policy. Are these difficulties temporary problems in a period of rapid change, or do they have deeper roots?

A policy of frequent adjustments in the definition or definitions of money used for target purposes and in the targets themselves may or may not turn out to be the least imperfect way of regulating Money GDP (which is what the technical monetarists wish to do). It is, however, very different in spirit from the automatic-sounding Friedman rule of a fixed annual growth of the quantity of money based on the indisputable historical association between monetary changes and price movements. With the Friedman rule the money supply is dictating the course of the economy (in the long run nominal magnitudes alone; in the short run a mixture of real and nominal ones). With the pragmatic adjustments often in use, it is the course of the economy which is determining the monetary rule.

It is still possible that the surprising fall in velocity in the early 1980s was just a reaction to a drop in inflation. As Friedman and Schwartz themselves emphasise[1], such a drop would itself increase the amount of money people would want to hold relative to income, as the penalty for holding the non-interest bearing component of money, relative to interest bearing assets, would decline. During the transition to the new higher level of desired money holdings, Money GDP must for a time undershoot, as people are making a once-for-all adjustment. In that case the Friedman policy rule might be

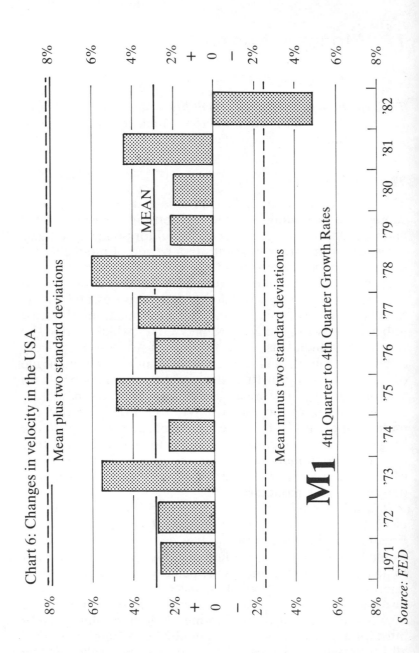

Chart 6: Changes in velocity in the USA

Mean plus two standard deviations

MEAN

Mean minus two standard deviations

M1 4th Quarter to 4th Quarter Growth Rates

Source: FED

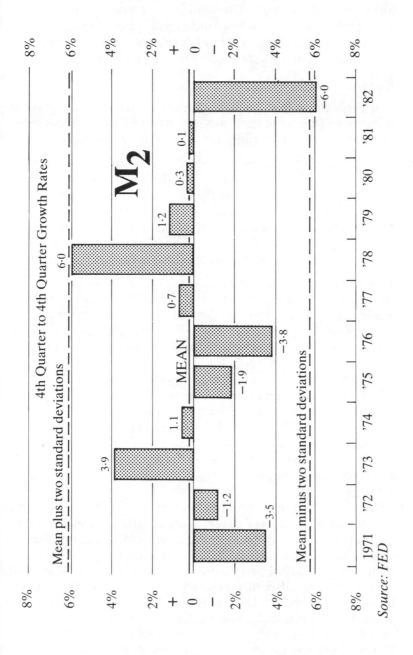

4th Quarter to 4th Quarter Growth Rates

M₂

Source: FED

too severe for periods of transition, but would come into its own again once a new low and stable rate of inflation was established. But we certainly cannot *rely* on the re-establishment of a stable money to income ratio.

Historical stability misleading

The problem is that we have almost no experience of price stability arising from man-made control of a purely paper or fiat currency inconvertible into a particular commodity.

> [The] fundamental objection to the adequacy of the pure quantity theory of money is that, even with a single currency in circulation within a territory, there is, strictly speaking, no such thing as *the* quantity of money, and that any attempt to delimit certain groups of the media of exchange expressed in terms of a single unit as if they were homogeneous or perfect substitutes is misleading. . . .

This is a quotation from Professor F.A. Hayek[2] but it could equally have come from the UK Radcliffe Report of 1959, notorious for its downgrading of monetary policy. The mistake made by Radcliffe, but not by Hayek, was to suppose that, because money was difficult to measure, the limitation of its supply was unimportant.

Historically, periods of price stability have been those in which the monetary unit consisted of precious metals (stamped into convenient units of standard weight known as coins) or of IOUs, notes or bank deposits convertible into specie. Superficial rationalists have rebelled against the idea of the amount of money being determined by anything as arbitrary as the supply of certain metals. But it never was as arbitrary as that.

When the money stock threatened to be inadequate, the real value of gold and silver rose, creating an incentive to develop banking and credit facilities and to economise on bullion supplies. Columbus set out in search of gold and silver at a time of deflationary pressure, when the commercial revival of the fifteenth century was being hampered by insufficient supplies of those metals.

During the two and a half centuries of broad price stability that England enjoyed from the reign of Charles II to World War I, there was no conscious attempt to regulate the money supply; it was automatically checked by the link with gold. In none of the periods covered by Friedman and Anna Schwartz in their monetary history was there a conscious money supply policy. The Federal Reserve, established in 1913, acted to maintain the gold value of the dollar or – especially in later decades – to influence interest rates.

During the Bretton Woods period, after World War II, the US authorities always denied that gold convertibility had any effect on their internal monetary policies, which, if true, explains why the system did not last. What is certain is that the Fed did not pursue a conscious money supply policy, but rather an interest rate one, which by fortunate coincidence led for a while to fairly stable monetary behaviour. When the Vietnam War and the budget deficits of the late 1960s rendered conventional interest rates incompatible with stable US monetary growth, the whole post-war monetary order came to an end.

There is one other historical finding to be mentioned. The record suggests that, despite all the banking crashes, financial bubbles and other crises resulting from the exuberance of unrestrained profit-seeking, the great and persistent historical inflations originated in the financing of government.

Those technical monetarists who want to play down the US budget deficits of the early 1980s could claim that heavy government borrowing *need not* lead to rapid inflation if it was financed outside the banking system. The difficulties with this view, if the deficits are long sustained, have been discussed.

The negative proposition is stronger. It is difficult to find long-lasting inflationary episodes which persisted in the absence of heavy government borrowing. The main exception is the sixteenth-century discovery of precious metals in the New World, which was the result of the profit-seeking quest for gold and silver. Even then the inflation rate averaged less than 2 per cent a year – very slow and creeping by the standards both of the currency debasements engineered by contemporary monarchs and of twentieth-century experience.

Can we not profit from the experience of the days of rough-and-ready stability of gold and silver standards to design rules for a superior conscious control of a managed monetary standard?

Unfortunately, the basic truth of the quantity theory of money does not mean that it is easy either to measure the effective quantity of money under any standard or to control its growth in a non-inflationary way. For the purpose of examining a period when there was no conscious policy of controlling the quantity of money, the exact definition of money does not matter. The amount of money was determined by the gold or silver base and by the credit pyramid erected by competitive banking institutions. Official policy was concerned at most with the convertibility of bank deposits and not with their size. Individuals decided whether to hold cash, 'checking' or 'savings' accounts. These might be subject to different long-term velocity trends; but it makes little difference whether the historian claims that a rate of growth of 2 per cent in narrow money or 3 per cent in broad money was consistent with price stability. Slightly different monetary rules can be formulated retrospectively; but overwhelmingly the most important principle seems to be that monetary growth should be kept at a modest rate. A wrong definition would seem to lead merely to slowly creeping inflation, easily correctable by a modest downward adjustment of the monetary target.

Similarly, the problem of whether to monitor money, financial assets or even total wealth did not arise. There was no large dead-weight government debt (i.e. debt not backed by productive assets), and financial assets might be expected to grow roughly in line with the nation's real wealth multiplied by the price level. Any tendency to flood the market with bond issues would have been corrected by a debasement of their value relative to that of money and real things, and a consequent increase in their yield and therefore cost of issue. Currency, financial and real assets would grow in rough proportion to the nation's wealth in periods of stability; and prolonged inflationary or deflationary episodes would reveal themselves whatever asset was used for measuring purposes.

Goodhart's Law

Historical experience is not necessarily a good guide to the behaviour of a purely token system when one particular range of financial asset classified as 'money' is being controlled through central bank targets. 'Goodhart's Law' (named after some *obiter dicta* by a Bank of England economist Dr Charles Goodhart) states that any monetary indicator becomes distorted as a guide to monetary conditions once it is selected for target purposes.

The defects of monetarism, in the narrow sense of the fixed rule for domestic money supply, are that it concedes too much power to official intervention, underrates the influence of competition in providing monetary substitutes, and takes official statistics far too much at their face value. 'Friedmanites' are often very good at analysing how controls and regulations in the economy generally will be avoided or will produce unintended effects quite different from those their sponsors desire; but too often they evince a touching faith in governments in their own special sphere.

The invention of new monetary instruments to replace old ones – and competition between currencies – is becoming more important as communications improve further and capital markets become even more closely linked. The abolition of exchange control in Britain in 1979 was bound to create complications for the measurement and control of the quantity of money, as the evolution of the Eurodollar market had already done for the USA.*

International portfolio shifts

Monetarist theory is also formulated in excessively parochial terms. Even so-called international monetarists who make the exchange rate the main transmission mechanism between a country's monetary policy and its inflation rate operate in terms of what Professor Ronald McKinnon has called the 'insular economy',[3] in which it is assumed that the demand to hold a country's currency comes mainly from its own citizens and is fairly stable. The development of a unified world capital market has made nonsense of this assumption – especially after the two oil price explosions led to the accumulation by OPEC countries of hundreds of billions of dollars worth of foreign exchange reserves, often footloose

---

* Eurodollars are deposits in non-US banks denominated in dollars. They arise, for instance, when an American transfers his dollar deposit to a foreign bank, but keeps it in dollars. 'Euro' versions now exist of most prominent currencies.

and ready to go wherever the prospects seem best.

It is still true that, other things being equal, low inflation countries (with inflation related to prices of goods which appear in international trade) are likely to have rising exchange rates relative to high inflation ones. But a great many other things tend not to be equal. Political hopes and fears, stemming for instance from the effects of Polish events on Germany, or the vulnerability or safety of energy supplies, are also important; and the evaluation even of economic policies can change overnight.

Nevertheless it is upside-down logic to suggest it was therefore wrong to abolish exchange control or reduce barriers between capital markets. The reluctance of people to hold a freely-tradable world-wide currency which depreciates rapidly and erratically is a bigger long-run constraint on inflationary policies than monetary targets achieved by controls and manipulations which distort the meaning of the aggregates controlled.

Challenge and response

There have been two main types of response to these challenges from those central banks which have been seriously interested in preventing the overissue of their currencies. At one extreme there has been the attempt to tighten up control methods to stop leakages – exemplified by the US Fed. Not only does the Fed monitor several definitions of money; it has also often adjusted the definition of the measure of M1, which has often been its principal monetary target.

The Fed has tried to plug other leaks by extending its jurisdiction to non-member banks. Under the Depository Institutions Deregulation and Monetary Control Act of 1981, non-member banks must submit periodic reports to the Fed and also begin to hold deposits with it. The Fed has also tried to persuade overseas central banks to impose reserve requirements on the dollar operations of non-American banks, so far without success.

At the other extreme, the Swiss National Bank has adjusted its operating techniques to the practices of financial markets. It imposes no official reserve requirements on the commercial banks. They choose freely the ratio of their deposits with the National Bank to their total deposits. The National Bank engages in open-market operations – in practice, foreign currency purchases from and sales to the banks – on the basis of its own estimates of the ratio of total deposits to reserves which the banks will want to hold.

The two approaches are not mutually exclusive. It is possible to have fairly tight control *à la* Fed but also to make the legal requirements correspond as closely as possible with what the banks want to do on the basis of commercial prudence. The most effective riposte for central bankers and governments would be to make mandatory and prudential reserve requirements correspond more closely.* Then there will be less incentive to invent new financial instruments (such as money market mutual funds in the USA) outside the existing definitions of money or outside the scope of central bank regulations. It may also help if the incentive to avoid mandatory reserve requirements is reduced by paying market-related interest rates on deposits with central banks.

Such attempts to work with, rather than against, the market will help to plug unnecessary leakages in monetary control. But they are not in the last resort intellectually satisfying. If people wish to issue more IOUs to each other and use them for making payments, they will eventually find a way. Central bank efforts to stop this are likely to result mainly in the transfer of activities from New York, Frankfurt, Zurich or London to the more exotic financial centres outside their effective jurisdiction.

When banks are prevented from expanding at home by reserve asset requirements in excess of their own prudential limits, they will expand overseas where such restrictions do not apply. This is the most fundamental explanation of the evolution of Eurodollars and other Eurocurrencies.

The growth of Eurocurrencies has probably not yet become a major threat to control by central banks over the world's money supply. But it could become so; and is in any case illustrative of the leakages in methods of monetary control which operate against the self-interest of existing or potential financial institutions. (In 1980 the stock of Eurocurrencies representing deposits by, or lending to, the non-bank public,

---

* The UK since 1981 has had no mandatory reserves for monetary control purposes, but the Bank of England maintains a close check on the banks' prudential provisions.

and not included on the national estimates of the monetary aggregates amounted to about 6 per cent of the 'broad' money supply of the main banking countries.)[4]

The gold standard

Why then do I not, in the face of these problems, join the supporters of a new gold standard? The first cause of suspicion is its link with so-called 'supply side economics' in the USA. Panacea-mongers look at the headline economic problems – high real interest rates, the unpleasant choice between higher taxes and public spending cuts in countries with excessive government deficits, and above all recession and unemployment – and offer the gold standard as a nostrum in the way that others offer planning, import controls or deficit finance. This is another way of saying that its advocates make claims which put it into the category of a free lunch: the golden morsel.

A successful gold standard would be no more than a method of controlling the quantity of a particular kind of money. Judicious advocates of stable currencies, of either the commodity or paper currency kind, claim no more than that they would contribute to broad price stability – certainly not year to year constancy of the price level.

A 'return to gold' would ease the transitional pains of reducing inflation if and only if it transformed inflationary expectations. Would people henceforth expect stable prices, now that the money supply was supposed to be on an automatic pilot and no longer under the discretionary control of irresponsible governments and unreliable central bankers? They might. But closer investigation of both a 'weak' and a 'strong' version of the gold standard idea reveal the difficulties in achieving such a transformation of expectations.

Many who talk of going back to the gold standard mean no more than a return to the Bretton Woods system of 'gold parities' for currencies, which would be used to determine exchange rates but would not make national money convertible into gold for private holders. Gold movements would take place only to settle payments imbalances between national authorities.

Even to maintain such a 'weak' gold exchange standard a

new official price would have to be fixed for gold – which, in view of recent market movements, would have to be between 10 and 30 times the 35 dollars per fine ounce level of 1971. People could hardly fail to notice that all currencies had been devalued against gold to this extent, and it would therefore be nonsense to talk of an immutable standard such as prevailed in the UK for two-and-a-half centuries before 1914.

Everybody would know that a major devaluation of all currencies against gold had happened very recently and could happen again. Since such a vestigial gold standard would operate like a Bretton Woods exchange-rate 'peg', it would at most be only a moderate inhibition on a government inflating above the world rate. Devaluation would be available as a not-so-last resort.

In the more radical form of the gold standard proposal, domestic currencies would also be convertible into gold on demand for private holders. This would impose a stronger constraint on inflation. But it would still come up against the lack of incentive for governments to maintain convertibility at a pre-ordained rate when the going became rough. The original gold standard depended on the belief that money was not merely convertible into gold or silver but in fact *consisted* of those precious metals, for which on occasion IOUs might be created. It depended on the myth that catastrophe would occur if a country 'went off gold'; and a myth by its nature cannot be artificially re-created.

These uncertainties about the system would be compounded by the well-known difficulties of deciding the right price of gold even for the moment. If it were too high, gold would pour into central banks and we would have more rather than less inflation. If it were too low, holders of paper money would redeem currency, deplete official gold reserves and engender a deflation. Knowledge of these possibilities would hardly contribute to confidence either in the stability of prices expressed in national currencies or of the new gold price.

The one chance that I see of overcoming the re-entry problem would be to announce an intention to restore a specified form of gold convertibility in say ten years' time based on the then market price of metal. It will take at least that long to iron out the effect on the gold market of years of attempted demonetisation and uncertainty about its future.

But even the most subtle transitional mechanism would not dispose of the most fundamental difficulty of all. This arises from the desire to economise on stocks of precious metals. As in the nineteenth century, it would lead to multiple reserve banking, i.e. the creation of large deposits on a small reserve base known as 'pyramiding'. In the heyday of the gold standard in 1914, £145 million in specie were outweighed by £45 million in bank notes and £1,076 million in bank deposits – the latter, of course, being convertible by the Bank of England into gold.[5] This pyramiding was not excessive, judging by the fact that the convertibility of sterling into gold at the established rate was then not threatened and the national price level was broadly stable. But there must be some amount of pyramiding that would unsettle confidence; and the performance of a new gold standard would depend on whether there were built-in incentives to prudence on the part of financial institutions with considerable money-creating power.

Competitive money

The disadvantages and possible lack of credibility of a new gold standard lead us to consider Professor Hayek's proposal (already alluded to in Chapter 3) for free competition between currencies, so that Gresham's Law can be reversed and good money drive out bad. Hayek has made two proposals. The first is for the free circulation of existing national currencies across the exchanges. This, of course, is already possible in countries without exchange control, which include the USA, the UK and Germany. Why then do not people already switch to good currencies when their own are seen to be subject to risks of depreciation? Taxation may be part of the reason. The UK owner of an investment in an alternative currency which had maintained its real value and appreciated by, say, 10 per cent against sterling would be taxed as if he had made a capital gain. The whole tangle of tax and accounting complications, relating to the valuation of corporate overseas assets when exchange rates change, would invade national business transactions as well.

Many of the advantages of alternative currencies for unit-of-account purposes could be obtained through contracts linked to a general price index or expressed in a stable foreign currency, even if the medium of exchange remained the domestic currency. Yet such contracts seem to become widespread only when strato-inflation has persisted for a long period, as in Latin America. People will pay a high price to stay with a familiar unit of account.

The second, and more far-reaching, form of Hayek's proposal would allow the introduction of private enterprise currencies, not necessarily related to an official unit. The proposal takes us into uncharted territory. There is no widely accepted theory of the results of free competition between privately-issued currencies. During periods in the past when different currencies circulated side by side they were nearly always gold and silver coins of varying weight and purity.

Modern experience in frontier areas has been of competition between official currencies. There is hardly any experience of competition between true private enterprise token currencies; it is highly likely that any successful private enterprise currencies of the future will turn out to be commodity-based.*

Price stability in the very long run probably depends on the simultaneous fulfilment of two conditions:

a the availability of commodity-based currencies; and
b free choice between alternative means of payment and standards of value to allow the reverse of Gresham's Law to hold and provide a deterrent to undue pyramiding on the commodity base.

It would be a characteristic 'rationalist fallacy' to try to lay down a blueprint for fulfilling these conditions. All we can do at present is to minimise the obstacles put in their way by unwise policies.

---

* Gold is not the best candidate for a commodity-based currency. In the USA, a commodity basket containing 33 cents worth of ammonium nitrate, 12 cents worth of copper, 36 cents worth of aluminium and 19 cents worth of plywood (all at 1967 prices) has moved in close relation to the US cost-of-living index since World War II, performing in this respect much better than gold. (Robert E. Hall, *Explorations in the Gold Standard and Related Policies*, National Bureau of Economic Research, Washington DC, 1981.)

PART III

The World Economy After the Golden Age

8 Unemployment and Pay

The 'lump of labour fallacy'; The satiation bogey; The price of work; Capital shortage?; Objections to 'pricing out'; Disequilibrium theory‡; Why pay is out of line; Social aspects; The role of unions; The social security floor; Housing and mobility; Incomes policies; Central European consensus.

The 'lump of labour fallacy'

Most popular discussion of unemployment is governed by the belief that there is a limited amount of work to be done and that society is threatened by a chronic and increasing shortage of jobs as technology advances. This is known as the 'lump of labour fallacy'. It is typified by remarks such as: 'Once we bring all this overmanning to an end, there just won't be the jobs to go round;' or 'I cannot see where the people who have been displaced from contracting industries like steel or railways are going to work.' It is a maddening fallacy because, if believed and acted upon, it could halt all improvement and impoverish us all quite needlessly.

The 'fixed amount of production fallacy' might be a more accurate name for it, for it presupposes there is a fixed amount of goods and services to be produced and that, if anything happens to enable that work to be done with fewer hands or to increase the supply of labour, the result must be more unemployment or compulsory work-sharing. The fallacy rears its head when trade unions call for a shorter working week to combat unemployment, or when so-called experts look with alarm at the likely growth of the European labour force, wondering 'where the jobs to employ it will come from'. If it were true, the man who 'could make two ears of corn or two blades of grass' grow where one grew before, far from being worth 'more than the whole race of politicians put together', would be the enemy of mankind.

The same kind of attitude underlies the recent concern about the micro-chip computer, the desire to reduce retiring ages or push young people into more years of full-time education, and much other nonsense. Alarm has been expressed whenever an apparently labour-saving invention has appeared. Few people now remember the scare when the earliest types of automation appeared in the motor industry in the 1950s; but other examples go back much further – well beyond the Luddites who roamed the country after the Napoleonic Wars destroying machinery. In the sixteenth century sheep were believed to be 'eating up' jobs on the land. No doubt the same charge was levelled at the inventors of the plough and the wheel.

Unfortunately no amount of technical or professional training is proof against this type of thinking in the absence of a feeling for the outrageous absurdity of certain propositions. Indeed, some of the worst offenders are people whose expertise in statistical projection, and flair for flesh-creeping headlines, exceed their economic common-sense.

Many doom-watch unemployment forecasts are based on little more than a projection of the rise in population of working age plus a rapidly rising trend productivity attributed to the micro-chip or some other fashionable invention. Suppose the addition of the two suggests in some country that output will need to grow in the future at an annual rate of 4 per cent compared with a growth trend in earlier decades of 2 per cent. Projecting the two rates generates an ever-increasing 'employment gap' of 2 per cent a year compound until ultimately everybody is out of a job.

Calculations of an ineradicable 'employment gap' are an example of the 'economics without price' which clouds so much thinking. Such calculations take no account either of the possibility of growth (counting *voluntary* leisure as a form of growth) speeding up to take advantage of a bigger supply of labour; or of the effects of a surplus of workers in reducing the rewards of labour relative to those of capital, and thus promoting the use of more labour-intensive methods. None of this means that adjustment will work well or will happen without policy adjustments. My criticism is that silly arithmetic is substituted for the analysis of labour markets.

It is possible to argue that new policies (other than work sharing) are required to bring idle hands to serve unsatisfied wants; or alternatively that the market will look after the process, or something in between the two. The attitude outrageous to reason is that neither approach, nor any compromise between them, has any chance of success; and that people, who could be contributing to the wants of others, must be forced to retire early, stay longer at school or have their hours of work cut against their will, because no way is seen of using their contributions.

There is nothing in the historical record to suggest that either technological progress or growth in the working population must lead to more unemployment. In the century from 1860 to 1960 UK output per head nearly trebled and the labour force doubled. The result was not mass unemployment but a near six-fold increase in total output. Between 1932 and 1937, during the recovery from the Great Depression, employment increased by 2¼ million, equivalent to about 3 million on today's population figures. After World War II, Germany absorbed millions of refugees; and in most of Western Europe a large rundown in the farm population was not only easily absorbed, but millions of guestworkers were drawn in from Southern Europe, Turkey and North Africa. No such miracles were predicted in the gloom of devastated postwar Europe where economic pessimism was at least as great as it is today.

The satiation bogey

The 'lack of work' view is sometimes justified in terms of the satiation of human wants. This means that as productivity rises there will be nothing more, apart from leisure, that people are willing to buy with extra income. Such a state of affairs is not *a priori* impossible. If it occurred, working hours would indeed fall; but the reduction would be voluntary, for, not having any use for the extra take-home pay, people would by assumption prefer to take out the fruits of higher productivity in the form of extra leisure. If people wanted to carry out activities which are now called work – whether driving trains or advising the foreign minister – for their own satisfaction, these activities would count as hobbies rather than jobs. I once tried to sketch the economics of a society of this kind,[1] but there is not the slightest reason to suppose that this is our present state of affairs. The reader who is in doubt should ask how many people he knows who are indifferent to their pay, or who seek increases exclusively to pile up savings which they neither intend to spend later nor bequeath or donate to others who will spend.

If satiation did arrive, we would be in a state not of depression but of economic bliss. Technical progress would then be enjoyed by workers in the form of reduced working hours without loss of take-home pay; and this would happen quite voluntarily through normal bargaining. Thus it would not be unemployment in the sense of enforced idleness.

If satiation were really here, few would be interested in winning the football pools; and people might well continue to work in their chosen occupations regardless of reward. We are a very long way from such a state of affairs. Satiation of wants – even in western industrialised countries, let alone in the poor Third World – does not pass muster as an explanation of present-day unemployment.

If a few computers or robots could satisfy all our material wants, there would be no need to worry about increases in the money supply or budget deficits. For there would be nothing on which people would want to spend extra purchasing power and its inflationary impact would be non-existent. So City monetarists who 'wonder where the jobs are coming from' need to rethink their mixture of ill-digested and incompatible ideas.

The price of work

Having in earlier chapters emphasised that there is an underlying rate of unemployment or NAIRU consistent with a stable rate of inflation, and having now rejected the notion that technology is making labour redundant, the question remains: what does determine the underlying rate of unemployment?

The clue to an answer is that the quantity of labour of different kinds demanded and supplied depends, like any other service, on the costs and prices in the relevant markets. Some people react with fury to any mention of the point. On one occasion I mentioned in a *Financial Times* article that if the price of bananas were kept above the market-clearing level – the price which balances the demand and supply for bananas – there would be a banana surplus. Similarly if the price of labour were kept above the market-clearing rate of pay, there would be a labour surplus – i.e. unemployment.

This analogy so inflamed a number of English economists that they asked their students to write essays to refute it. Some of the people who reacted in this way were, I suspect, so up in arms over the proposition that they did not bother to read on, or notice that I had explained the differences as well as the similarities between the market for bananas and the market for human labour.

If the cost of labour of given productivity is increased, less of it will be bought. This, incidentally, has nothing to do with 'capitalism'. It applies to state socialism and to the market in direct services where people engage craftsmen, plumbers, gardeners and others to do jobs without the intervention of an employer or other intermediary.

The real wage on which the demand for labour depends is not quite the same as the real wage from the point of view of the worker. The real wage, seen as an employer's cost, is best expressed as a proportion of value added per worker or, as it is sometimes called, the 'product wage' (and it includes employers' social security contributions). Higher taxes on consumer goods, or import price rises, which reduce real wages for the worker do not change the cost of employing him, unless he demands and obtains higher pay in compensation.

The demand for labour depends of course not merely on the average level of real wages but also on the pattern of *relative* wages for different skills, occupations, industries and areas. Even if the average pay level is appropriate, people can still be priced out of work if relative wages are not at market-clearing levels. In this case unemployment in some areas is likely to coincide with labour shortages in others. The two types of distortion aggravate each other, since the shortages hold down total output and thus reduce the demand for workers in the areas of labour surplus.

There is a good deal of evidence about the way in which particular groups and categories of workers have been priced out of jobs. One of the worse examples is the insistence that young people be paid the full adult wage irrespective of productive performance. The low level of youth unemployment in Germany compared with other European countries has been attributed by the OECD not only to the apprenticeship system but to the fact that wage levels of new entrants are adjusted to their productive capacity. Denmark has had a German-type apprenticeship system, but the rate of youth unemployment there soars suddenly at the age of eighteen when a minimum wage corresponding to two-thirds of average manual earnings becomes obligatory.[2] Numerous American studies have shown how minimum wage legislation has increased unemployment particularly among blacks, teenagers, and other minority groups.

Another way in which the labour market is more complicated than the banana market is that labour works together with capital; and capital structures take time to plan, organise and erect. Much long-lived equipment cannot easily shift to new production methods. The term 'putty-clay' is sometimes used to indicate that, at the drawing board stage, production can be carried out in many different ways; but once the investment has been made, production methods are fairly rigid until the next generation of equipment comes into use.

The moral is that some of the main influences of real wages on employment are long-term. Just as it took time for workers to price themselves out of jobs, it will take time to price them back into work. Employers will have to be convinced that the new trend of real wages will not be reversed if they are to translate their beliefs into new plant and facilities of a more labour-using kind.

Not all employment is so dependent on specialised equipment. We should not underrate what can be done meanwhile in personal social services, the cleaning and decorating of our cities and a host of other services which we could afford in greater amounts if labour were cheaper. There are many areas from gardening to retailing where the labour-to-capital ratio changes quickly in response to relative change in labour and capitals costs, and where pricing into work can be quite speedy.

In other areas – services as well as manufacturing – technological change is a matter of years and it takes a long time for labour to price itself into or out of work. It is wrong to look for the main effects of real wages on employment in year-to-year changes. The movement is rather from one business cycle to the next. The worrying aspect of unemployment has not been its rise in recession but its long-term upward drift in

Europe since the early 1970s – and in some countries the late 1960s.

Capital shortage?

In the developing countries the availability of capital and enterprise (including entrepreneurship and skilled personnel as well as physical structures) limits employment. Although there may be a market-clearing wage which would price all who wanted to work into jobs, it would not be relevant if it turned out to be below subsistence or even negative, as it could be. Nor would it be very satisfactory (whether or not technically an equilibrium) if large numbers of people found their best openings selling a few shoe laces at street corners.

Developed countries can regress into states of capital deficiency if for any reason capital investment has dropped behind the requirements of population and technology, or – more likely – if high real wages have given investment an excessively labour-saving bias (excessive because premature). It would be beneficial for robots to do more and more of our menial and routine work, but not before reasonable full employment has been achieved. Then we could enjoy the benefits of the robots in the shape of more take-home pay, more voluntary leisure or more congenial working conditions. But to mechanise while there is still a labour surplus is likely to be as wasteful and inefficient as it would have been to build the Great Wall of China with computer-controlled excavating equipment instead of men with picks and shovels.

Capital shortage can of course exist, even when industrial surveys show considerable unused capacity, if that capacity has become obsolescent in relation to technology, market demand or changes in input costs (e.g. energy intensive machinery can become obsolescent when oil prices rise). Unemployment due to capital shortage can be remedied by a combination of investment and a sufficiently restrained level of real wages to impart a labour-using bias to the capital installed.

Objections to 'pricing out'

Why does the 'pricing out' hypothesis engender so much hostility? The answer goes back to the Wenceslas thesis of the first chapter. Instead of suggesting that an entity called 'government' should spend on job creation in a supposedly costless manner, the 'pricing out' hypothesis puts the onus on those already in jobs to make a sacrifice. It is saying that many of the 35 million out of work in the OECD countries are in that position because some of those in jobs are being paid too much. That is not what those who make the greatest hue and cry want to be told – nor those waiting in the wings to advise present and future governments on economic management.

Nevertheless, it is worth going through the standard objections. The oldest and most familiar is voiced as well as anywhere by the British Trades Union Congress in its 1983 Annual Review.[3] A wage cut, it argues, will also curb purchasing power. So although goods and services might be cheaper, consumers will have less money in their pockets to buy them. No extra demand will have been created, so firms will have no incentive to produce more by taking on workers.

The trap to avoid is getting into an argument about whether the economy is self-stabilising or not. The technical monetarists assume that aggregate cash expenditure is related to monetary assets and not just income, so that expenditure will not fall in proportion to the cut in wages. But there is no need to depend on this problematic relationship for an answer to the TUC objections. If the government has a commitment to maintain monetary demand on a stable non-inflationary path, it will boost spending in some other way should the TUC view turn out to be near the truth. If a Money GDP objective is in existence, lower pay and prices will mean more jobs; and by refusing to commit themselves to try to maintain monetary demand (the baby in the Keynesian bathwater), governments throughout the west are handing over a debating victory to their opponents on a plate.

This issue, however, relates to demand management; and our concern in this chapter is with the underlying rate of unemployment which remains when demand management has done its best. The more important difficulty about wage cutting is that after it has occurred prices may fall in proportion, thus failing to reduce real wages as an employer's cost. To price workers back into jobs over the average of one or more business cycles, wages have to fall more, or rise less, than prices (abstracting from the productivity trend). Why this does not happen is the major unsolved problem of macroeconomics, which will be discussed below in terms of particular instances, but not, I am afraid, definitively 'solved'.

Disequilibrium theory‡

The most sophisticated objection to the 'pricing out of work' thesis arises from the interaction between different markets. This body of thinking is often known as 'disequilibrium theory'.

In brief, it is based on the fact that if any prices become stuck away from their market clearing levels, unemployment is liable to arise. The prices which are out of line can be in the goods market (or capital or foreign exchange markets) as well as in the labour market. If the price of steel is 'too high' there will be unused steel capacity, a reduced national income and a correspondingly reduced demand for both labour and other products – unless the price of those other products can fall low enough to capture the market lost by the steel producers.

In principle a non-market-clearing price in any part of the economic system can affect any other part; but if we are to learn anything we have to take the matter further. Let us assume that an international cartel has raised the price of steel (unfortunately more than an assumption). Steel prices will be higher, but less steel made and sold, and fewer workers employed in the industry. What prevents other product prices from falling in the more competitive sectors to allow the resources displaced from steel to be employed elsewhere?* It is surely the downward rigidity of costs – above all labour costs; for material prices are determined in world markets and do respond (even over-respond) to supply and demand changes. Pay levels on the other hand are slow to respond to demand changes in a downward direction, and this limits the responses of final product prices.

If the price of steel – or oil – is increased and other product prices do not fall enough to compensate, the general price level will be too high in relation to the money supply (or, as I should prefer to put it, to monetary demand, money times

---

‡ Once again, marked passages involve more 'academic' argument than the rest of the text.
* Why do steel trade unionists, as well as employers, favour higher steel prices at the cost of less output? Perhaps because they expect to share the monopoly gain with the industry in the shape of higher pay for those who remain employed. Another reason is that union leaders in individual European countries or North America associate low prices with Japanese and Third World steel which they correctly see as a threat to their own earning opportunities.

velocity). For an individual country, prices may be too high in relation to the exchange rate. Indeed the main examples that disequilibrium Keynesians tend to give of product rather than labour overpricing relate to events such as the overvaluation of sterling after 1925 and in 1980 and of the dollar in 1981-82, and of disequilibrium in the world price level after the oil price explosion of 1973 and 1979-80. Respectful as they are of institutional rigidities, they would recommend devaluation in the one case and world monetary expansion in the other to validate prevailing price levels.[4]

In a general depression all factors of production, capital as well as labour, are likely to be underemployed and the national product reduced. It is therefore not all that surprising that statistical studies, especially in the United States, often show that real wages fall rather than rise in recession. So too does the return to capital. When output is well below the sustainable long-run rate, a great many groups are likely to be worse off.

The distinguishing feature of a depression is that *nominal* prices and wages are too high in relation to monetary or exchange rate conditions; and I have already discussed in Chapter 7 the extent to which it might be sensible to adjust monetary policies rather than force prices down. (The big problem arises when we are dealing not with absolute price levels which are too high, but with rates of increase which have become embedded in behaviour and expectations.) The most important influence of real as distinct from nominal wages on unemployment relates to the trend (or NAIRU) level of unemployment rather than to short-term movements within the business cycle.

When a recession is superimposed on a secular rise in unemployment, it is possible to say that 'monetary demand' is too low, but real wages are also too high. ('Keynesian unemployment is superimposed on classical unemployment' is the way that some theorists would put it.) When monetary expansion (or moderation in nominal wage and price increases or some combination) brings recession to an end, unemployment will still be too high by standards of earlier decades or by the common sense criterion of jobs being available for those who want them; and further progress depends on an adjustment of real wages to the market value of marginal contributions to the productive process.

Why pay is out of line

To say that real wages over a run of economic cycles have diverged from market-clearing wages is a statement of the problem, not an answer. The important issue is *why* they have diverged.

Being priced out of work is not necessarily the consequence of aggressive union pressure for higher real pay. It may result from passive resistance to *downward* shifts in the market-clearing real wage, either in the whole economy or in particular sectors. Here the much-despised banana analogy can be helpful. A price of bananas above the market clearing level can be due to an initiative by a growers' cartel; but it can also be due to a reduction in demand or a very good crop making the previous equilibrium price obsolete. The responsibility of the growers' cartel is then the passive one of sticking to its old price in the face of changing circumstances.

There is no shortage of plausible explanations for why pay has moved out of line with market-clearing levels; on the contrary, a wealth of suggestions has been offered. The difficulty is to discriminate between them and give each of them its appropriate weight.

The root of the problem lies probably in the structural changes which have reduced the medium-term growth of real wages compatible with high employment and the growing out-datedness of received ideas on relativities. There have clearly been important changes since the 1960s which have affected the demand for various categories of workers. The oil price explosion itself made a good deal of existing equipment obsolete, thereby reducing the ratio of usable capital to labour.

The fall in the real price of oil which began in 1982-3 may make older equipment viable once more. It is also possible however that this equipment has already been scrapped or become decrepit; then the main effect may be to make some of the new energy-saving plant (and investments in oil substitutes) uneconomic. It is anyone's guess which effect will predominate.

In the special case of Britain, the development of North Sea oil production to the point of self-sufficiency (achieved in

Chart 7: OECD and UK unemployment (percentage rates, seasonally adjusted)

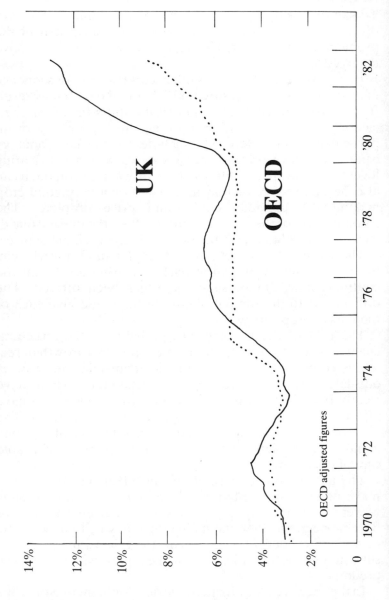

OECD adjusted figures

1980) was bound to change the structure of demand for labour in Britain. This conclusion follows from the fact that the current account on overseas payments must balance, except to the extent that there are net exports or imports of capital. The country became wealthier as a result of the oil. Fewer non-oil exports were needed to pay for the imports required to support a given volume of activity. It is because manufactures constituted a higher proportion of exportable goods than of final sales in general that they bore the brunt of the readjustments.

According to one estimate a new equilibrium at a constant level of real activity would have required a level of manufacturing output 9 per cent less than it would otherwise have been, offset by an 8 per cent rise in the level of other activities – private services, construction, housing and public administration in whatever mixture voters and consumers desired.[5] Because of a mixture of recession and structural rigidities, these adjustments were not made. Manufacturing production fell by 20 per cent between 1973 and 1982 but there was too little offsetting rise elsewhere.

The impact of North Sea oil is, however, only an intensified case of a broader structural shift away from manufacturing affecting most of the advanced countries and not just the UK. A major element lies in the take-off which occurred in the 1970s in the growth of the so-called Newly Industrialising Countries (NICs). The developed countries are still large producers of manufactures, but have costs of production (measured at equilibrium exchange rates) far higher than the NICs for at least some of the main standard products. Of course, to speak of manufacturing *versus* service activities is itself an oversimplification. There will be trends within manufacturing away from old-fashioned 'heavy' industries, such as steel and cars, to electronic software and other activities which are much more skill-intensive and are likely to remain profitable in the older developed countries, as are speciality products of many kinds.

In view of all these adjustments, even with a well-functioning labour market there would probably have been several years of relatively high unemployment while the required shifts of resources were taking place. To preserve full employment in the face of these shifts, wage costs in many sectors would have had to fall as a proportion of value added.

It is by no means easy to say what actually did happen in view of the many pitfalls in the interpretation of movements in relative income shares. The European Economic Commission uses the concept of the 'real wage gap' which is the difference between the actual growth of real wages and the growth rate which would maintain constant shares for labour and capital.[6] During the 1960s there was relative stability in these shares for the EEC as a whole, but between 1971 and 1975, the gap widened by 4 per cent. It narrowed in the late 1970s, but jumped back again in the second oil-induced recession of 1980-81. The main discordant note is struck by Germany which suffered a severe increase in unemployment without any rise in the real wage gap – leading some market-oriented German economists to conclude that the wage share consistent with full employment had fallen owing to structural change.*

There have been some econometric estimates of the effect of real wages on employment. One exercise suggests an elasticity in the range of 0·7 to 1·4, applying to a group of European countries, North America or Japan. (In other words a 1 per cent increase in the product wage will reduce employment by around 1 per cent.) Estimates for the UK range from 0·5 for the whole economy to a tentative 2 for manufacturing.[7] But in view of the extreme difficulty of arriving at these estimates and their sensitivity to the exact methods of derivation – not to speak of the ability of all schools of thought to come up with econometric calculations in their own favour – I would rather rest my case more loosely on the observed movement of employment, pay and profit shares in the context of structural changes tending to depress the market-clearing wage.

* The data on relative shares of the national income are extremely difficult to interpret. In its Economic Review for 1983, the British Trades Union Congress (TUC) argued that the proportion of domestic income deriving from employment had not increased over the two preceding decades. The Confederation of British Industries (CBI) cited alternative data to show that the employment income had risen from 75 per cent in the late 1960s to 81 per cent in 1981.

The difference was that the figures cited by the TUC were a proportion of Gross Domestic Product plus stock appreciation, and the ones cited by the CBI were a proportion of Net Domestic Product. The biggest difference between the gross and the net is that the latter deduct an allowance for 'capital consumption'. In principle the net measure is surely right, but an argument on the side of the gross measure is the extreme difficulty of measuring capital consumption. If North Sea oil profits were excluded the share of income from employment rose further to 87 per cent in 1981.

Indeed even a stable level of factor shares is no refutation of the 'pricing out of work' thesis. It is all too easy for the capital-to-labour share in the national product to become stabilised at a level consistent with a large or even growing rate of unemployment.

In political discussion and in representation of the employers' case, the relationship is usually stated positively as one between profits and employment, rather than negatively between real wages and unemployment. Why not follow the common practice of the political arena which is much less politically provocative and would often gain the support of Socialist politicians, instead of being received with embarrassment by nearly all public figures? The answer I am afraid is that posing the issue in terms of profits is not always 'just as accurate'. Changes in the relative share of profits and wages in value added help to show what is going on during a period of change; but once capacity has been adjusted to a particular pattern of real wages, one might see a stable long-run relation between profits and wages, but a pool of unemployed people remaining who could not find work at prevailing wage levels. Moreover, outside the corporate sector where there are no profit figures, more people could be employed if pay per head were less.

Social aspects

Of course there are many social problems in adjusting wages to market clearing levels. The trend rise in real interest rates throughout the world since the middle of 1970, together with slack labour markets, suggests that capital is now the scarce factor (despite the deceptive evidence from industrial surveys of under-utilisation) and labour the plentiful one. To secure a return to full employment, the share of wages in the national income may have to fall and the share of profits and the return to capital rise more than past statistical relationships suggest would be necessary. As a result the distribution of income and wealth could become more concentrated and adverse to the poor. The art of policy will be to attempt to correct this switch without aggravating unemployment.

It will help to bear in mind that the relationship between pay and poverty is much weaker than generally supposed. In the UK only one in five of the poorest 10 per cent of families are in the bottom 10 per cent of the earnings range. The discrepancy is accounted for by matters such as family size or number of earners per household.[8]

So keeping wages above market-clearing levels not only destroys employment but is a very inefficient method of protecting the poor. It would be best to leave wages to the market and use fiscal and social security measures (e.g. raising child benefits and the tax starting point) to redistribute income. More radical measures should tackle the ownership of property and not the pattern of market rewards. If the return to capital is to rise, it becomes more important to find ways of spreading capital ownership to more ordinary citizens other than just through pension funds. The reprehensible feature of 'unearned' (i.e. investment) income is that too few of us have it; and opportunities of correcting this should be taken by distributing capital more widely, a theme to which I return in the final chapter.

The role of unions

So far little explicit mention has been made of labour unions. In discussing their role it is necessary to say at the outset that whatever other evils are attributed to them, they are largely guiltless of the most common charge of causing continuing inflation. Of course, if the government imposes a squeeze on the growth of total spending, or MV, the more unions retard the downward adjustment of wage settlements, the higher will be prices and the lower output and employment. So for a short period of a year or two it well might seem that union power adversely affects both inflation and unemployment. But we are here talking about transitional effects. In the long run the main influence is on unemployment, not inflation. Indeed, if union power was the dominant force behind continuous inflation, it would suggest that union leaders were interested in money wages – i.e. numbers on pieces of paper – rather than real wages. They are not so irrational.

The belief that monopoly of any kind, whether enterprise or union, causes continuing inflation is based on a confusion between *higher prices* and *rising prices* and between the *general price level* and the *relative prices* of particular commodities. If there is a monopoly in, say, soap powder, this product will be more expensive and other products cheaper (because consumers have less to spend on them) than under competition. Even if the soap power firm has only just acquired its monopoly and raised its price yesterday, and if the prices of other goods are slow to fall in compensation ('downward price rigidities'), there is at most a knock-on effect on the price index. Inflation, by contrast, is a *continuing* rise in the general price level, year after year.

Nevertheless, although union monopoly power does not lead directly to inflation, it can cause a good deal of damage. If wages and prices are higher in the strongly unionised sectors than in the weaker and non-unionised ones, workers can be crowded into these sectors and confronted with the choice between inferior or fringe employment and living on social security.

All monopolies work by reducing volume to obtain higher prices (not rising prices) and unions are no exception. Union monopoly raises wages per hour at the cost of reducing the number of man-hours worked in the unionised sector. There is a conflict of interest between people who have jobs and expect to retain them – who gain from successful union monopoly action – and the unemployed or new entrants, who would do better with less payment and more jobs.

The danger to employment has nothing to do with extremism or subversion. It is in the nature of labour monopoly and can be exercised just as much by rational self-interested moderates. The socially beneficial role of unions is to represent individual employees and protect them from harsh treatment or discrimination. The monopolistic collective bargaining function is at best a promoter of a dual labour market – a better paid unionised sector and a secondary submerged sector into which the less fortunate are crowded. If the displaced workers are unwilling or unable to find places on the secondary labour market, unionised pay settlements serve to increase unemployment.

Unemployment will worsen if either union power increases or unions make more use of their existing power. The former influence can be established easily enough from the growth in union membership. According to official figures, the number of union members in the UK grew from 10·5 million in 1969 to 13·5 million in 1979, representing an increase from 45·4 to 56 per cent of total employees. Much of the growth was in the public sector. This supports the general impression that union monopoly power is largely, but not exclusively, a public sector problem where it is a reaction to the existence of a monopoly or semi-monopoly employer who cannot go bankrupt.

It would be too mechanistic to measure the union effect only by the percentage of workers unionised. The extent to which union monopoly power is applied depends on prevailing norms of behaviour as well as on market calculations. The electricity supply workers, for instance, clearly do not use their full power to extract higher wages and raise electricity prices through the strike threat. Nor is this pure grace-and-favour on their part. Union monopoly power is not a fixed, known quantity but something uncertain which can be increased by investing resources in organisation and strike funds.

In a highly unionised society some tacit conventions about acceptable relative wages have to be followed if Hobbesian anarchy is to be avoided. The rules of the game have never been spelt out; but what are felt to be legitimate relativities probably embody a mixture of market and historically determined differentials and traditional ideas of status (such as the relativities between the Archbishop of Canterbury and York). The quasi-moral element attaching to the result is an essential part of the enforcement mechanism. This situation is very different from the usual idea of a market equilibrium. I would prefer to call it a 'balance of forces', not exclusively economic. (There is no reason for an advocate of market forces to sign up for that union of economists which regards all mention of sociological factors as an act of intellectual blacklegging.)

If we are prepared to accept that unions use their monopoly power to varying degrees in different times and places, we can make better sense of the awkward fact that the stagflation problem, or the underlying NAIRU rate of unemployment, has worsened alarmingly in countries with widely varying degrees of unionisation, widely varying legal and effective shop-floor power of unions, and widely varying degrees of 'responsibility' in the use of that power.

It is not only unions which price people out of work. Regional and industrial policy in many countries has often aggravated the shift towards excessively labour-saving and capital-using techniques by subsidising capital-intensive investment in regional policy grants and by taxing labour. Even if all the taxes and subsidies are shifted onto the final price, there is still an artificial stimulus to capital-intensive, as distinct from labour-intensive processes and products.

In many countries there are legally enforced minimum wages and in the UK there have been Wages Councils which set minimum wages in the 'sweated trades'. More widely, there is a 'pricing out of work' culture in Europe and perhaps parts of North America. Some employers boast for instance that they would rather take on fewer people and pay them 'reasonable' wages. The approach acts as a rough quality control on the manpower taken on, but it reduces employment.

Again, however, to blame these attitudes and institutions for the threefold jump in OECD unemployment, one would have to show that they intensified in less than a decade in countries with the most diverse history and institutions. The implausibility of such an assumption makes it worth entertaining an alternative hypothesis of Richard Layard and his associates at the London Centre for Labour Economics. This traces the rise in the NAIRU to economic circumstances making for an increased use of union monopoly power.[9] The idea is that unions have a real wage target which they try to achieve for members; but that this target can be revised downwards under the influence of depressed labour markets and high unemployment. He argues that the combination of a productivity slowdown in Europe, and the effects of two oil price shocks on the terms of trade, reduced by 2½ per cent the annual growth of earnings consistent with a given degree of employment. Thus joblessness has had to increase for several years to reduce unattainable real wage aspirations.

The social security floor

The price of labour can be raised not only by pay rigidities in the place of work, union imposed or otherwise. It can also be raised by forces on the supply side, which raise the minimum reservation wage which an unemployed person will need to accept a job. The supply of labour depends *inter alia* on the cost of not having a registered job. The latter is determined by such factors as benefit levels, work expenses and tax thresholds, as well as by the value of and opportunities for 'unofficial' work, whether perfectly legal 'do it yourself' activities or unregistered jobs in the black economy.

The social security and tax systems have two potential

effects on work incentives. They establish a floor wage below which it is not worth taking a registered job. (A 'registered job' means that it is registered for income tax and social security purposes.) But, even for people with a wage above that floor, the net gain from taking a job is reduced by that combination of lower benefit and liability to tax which constitutes the 'unemployment trap'. The two effects together can lead not only to more 'search time' – that is, to people picking and choosing over a longer period to find the right new job. They can also result in more long-term unemployment if people find they have little to gain from taking the sort of job they are likely to be offered, however long the search.

To make the matter concrete, it is worth quoting estimates from Britain in 1982. An average household with two children was said to be no better off with the breadwinner in rather than out of work for earnings up to £120 per week.[10] At £140, which was the average pay level, the family was only some £17 better off. For a family with four children the break-even point came at between £140 and £150. On these estimates 15 per cent of householders were in the no-better-off category and another 23 per cent no more than 10 per cent better off in a job.

The subject is both highly emotive and full of technical pitfalls. The figures cited are for representative cases and assume full take-up of all benefits. In fact individual circumstances vary widely. Survey evidence suggests that many of the unemployed are much worse off than might be supposed from hypothetical calculation of benefit entitlement. On the other side, the shadow economy and the benefits of do-it-yourself activity raise the 'reservation wage' for some people some of the time (i.e. the wage below which it would not pay them to take a registered job) but there is no doubt that some of those workers most prone to unemployment have little opportunity for unofficial work in the black economy and suffer great hardship without a job. A rational analysis of the labour market is not a denial of social hardship and has little to do with campaigns against scroungers.

Indeed social security benefits are far from being the only influences on the unemployment trap. There are other influences on which people ranging from Professor Patrick Minford (a consultant to the Thatcher Government) to the British Low Pay Research Unit could and did make common campaigning cause.

One of the biggest contributors to the unemployment trap in the UK was the fall in the real tax starting point. In 1955 a head of household with two children paid income tax if he was on average earnings or above. In 1965 he started paying tax at 72 per cent of average earnings, and in 1975 at 44 per cent. By 1981 the threshold was down to 38 per cent and even after the widely advertised concessions of the 1983 Budget it had still only gone back to 44 per cent. The problem occurred in most countries where tax thresholds and bands were not indexed to inflation. Partial indexation came to the UK in the late 1970s, but too late.

The problem with raising real tax thresholds is that it is very cost-ineffective. The benefit extends right up the scale and is obviously largest for the highest-rate tax-payers. A much more cost-effective approach is to increase child benefits, which improves the incentive to work, quite apart from its other social effects. For the higher child benefit is the less the head of a family has to lose in income support on transferring from the dole to a job. The measure is particularly cost-effective because households most affected by the unemployment trap are heavily concentrated among large families.

The main analytical importance of the social security floor is that it answers the question that every good market economist will wish to pose about trade union influence: 'Why don't those who are priced out of work find a job in the non-unionised sector?' The workers who are crowded out of the unionised sector could depress wages for any occupation in the rest of the economy towards the social security minimum. This is quite plausible in a highly unionised country such as the UK, where many of the non-unionised manual jobs are in peripheral sectors (laundries, kitchens, cleaning, etc.).

Average pay levels for male manual workers in Britain in November 1982 were estimated at £140 per week. If average union pay in the UK was £160 in 1982 as Minford suggests, it is not implausible that typical non-union manual pay was £100 or less – which for many families after tax and work expenses would not have been much if at all above the social security floor.

The moral I draw from this is decidedly *not* that the 'dole' should be cut, but that the union effect needs to be weakened. It is not a criticism of dole payments that they discourage people from 'work' such as selling shoe laces at street corners.

In the meanwhile the case for unemployment palliatives such as marginal labour subsidies or public employment schemes cannot be cast aside.[11] The logic of a job subsidy is that, instead of unemployed people being expected to price themselves into jobs by working for lower pay, the employer is given a subsidy to achieve the same effect. But it is not a costless option; and it will work only if taxpayers are prepared to accept lower net real incomes to pay for the subsidies.

The various work-sharing gimmicks such as reduced hours or early retirement might, if earnings per hour were not raised, increase the demand for labour. But if the demand for labour is already as high as is consistent with a non-accelerating rate of inflation, any further increase will be temporary and self-defeating. If, on the other hand, it is safe to increase the demand for labour, why not do so directly by expansionary monetary and fiscal policies rather than by wasteful work-sharing methods?

Above all – and this is where we come to the nub of the matter – work-sharing would not resolve the problems of labour market frictions, monopolistic wage-setting and union wage-push which make it impossible to have full employment. Indeed, if the working week were reduced to twenty hours for everyone next year, there might well be no reduction in unemployment – and possibly even an increase.

Housing and mobility

Not all the distortions in the labour market come from pay itself. If housing costs are maintained at below market levels by controls and subsidies, and the benefit is not transferable to another location, then labour mobility will suffer.*

An unemployed steel-worker with a wife and four children occupying a council house in Durham in the north of England

---

* This might be a good example of a non-wage disequilibrium price. But for some, not very surprising reason, it is rarely mentioned by 'Keynesian disequilibrium theorists'.

will, quite rationally, think several times before moving to and retraining for a job in the south. Less often discussed are distortions supported by the political right as well as the left. Examples are tax relief for mortgage interest payments and the absence of tax on the rented value of an owner occupied house. Not only do these 'bourgeois' aids make it politically difficult to phase out the subsidisation of the rents for council dwelling and rent controls and make it hard to treat housing as a private good; they also encourage overinvestment in residential accommodation relative to other assests, which can hardly be good for mobility.

Housing obstacles to labour mobility vary from country to country. In the UK there is evidence of a deterioration. The privately rented sector has traditionally housed the youngest and most mobile part of the population. The decline of this sector under the impact of rent controls gathered pace in the 1970s when one third of privately rented units were lost. This must have been discouraging to geographical mobility, already low enough. According to the MSC estimates, only 1 per cent of the working population moves home each year for job or training purposes.

Incomes policies

The reader will not imagine that these brief remarks have solved the problem of why labour markets do not clear to avoid involuntary unemployment. But I have tried to show that the simple rule, that employment offered is a function of pay per unit of effort, is a better guide than the complexities and exceptions which have captured the attention of some theorists, especially when we are thinking not of temporary slumps and booms but the underlying performance to be expected in periods of normal growth. The reasons for non-market pricing will vary a great deal and may be more easily brought out by the case studies which conclude this book.

Not surprisingly, however, many economists are impatient with the slow and uphill task of reforming the labour and other markets which are working sluggishly and would like to take a short cut by means of incomes policies. The logic of the incomes policy case (rarely stated baldly for reasons of political prudence) is: (a) union power has added to the sustainable rate of unemployment by distorting the market pattern of real wages; and (b) incomes policy can reproduce something more nearly approaching market wages.

It is at least a step forward that it is now recognised that the logical role of long-term pay policies (and pay restraint in general) is to reduce unemployment, not inflation. Incomes policy enthusiasts have not, however, helped understanding by pandering to popular delusion in describing proposals designed to lower underlying unemployment as an 'inflation tax'.

As I have written extensively on incomes policies elsewhere, I shall be brief here.[12] Governments may or may not be strong enough to tackle union and other influences which prevent wages and other prices from approaching market-clearing levels. But if they are unable to do so directly, it is extremely unlikely that they will be able to do so by the back door of controls or deals with federations of unions or employers.

Unions have contributed to the trend rise in unemployment in most countries, not only through their direct industrial activities but, along with other producer lobbies, through their political influence. For instance, as a result of their insistence on UK Wages Councils which fix minimum wages, less-skilled people have been priced out of work in low-pay industries. The union influence on the Manpower Services Commission (which has a tripartite board) ensures that it treads very gingerly with measures which will price young people *into* work. Policy concessions to union leaders have in practice been a feature of every post-war incomes policy. Nor can an incomes policy without such concessions be realistically conceived. Trade union leaders will not abandon their real or supposed control over wages, which is the basis of their prestige, except in return from some other gain.

Policy measures to reinforce union power in Britain have included state encouragement of the closed or union shop and the exclusion of union immunity from the normal processes of contract law. Concessions in return for promised wage restraint have also included controls on prices, profit margins and dividends, which merely discourage risk investment. Other examples are higher council house and mortgage subsidies and the tightening of rent control. Further, some phases of incomes policies have tried to squeeze pay differentials, both by differential pay norms and punitive taxation (i.e. purely political taxation which has no significant revenue yield).

The main effect of all these measures has been to inhibit the efficient functioning of the relevant markets (and thereby to aggravate, to take one example, the housing shortage). The reason why so many of them destroy productive jobs and create unemployment is that either they directly reduce the incentive to satisfy potential demand (price and rent controls) or they involve deliberately punitive taxation. The latter is either passed on, and therefore fails in its objective, or reduces the supply of key factors of production – whether skilled workers, top quality specialists, or managers of physical capital in risky ventures. Such people have tended to vote with their feet – by emigrating, moving into the black economy, or settling for a quiet life. Incomes policies have also sought to 'level up' the incomes of the lower-paid. While a laudable intention, the effect, like that of minimum wage laws in the United States, is to price out of work a large number of less-qualified workers.

The proliferation of projects for market-based incomes policies, in which the use of monopolistic power will be discouraged by a tax or by 'almost compulsory arbitration' does not change the basic evaluation. The drawbacks of incomes policies do not arise from the inadequacies of their formulae or incentive mechanisms but from the political and social forces making for monopolistic pay settlements which are not countered by them and may even be indirectly encouraged further.

Central European consensus

Another very different suggestion is that the employment-reducing effects of organisations like the British trade unions arise from their fragmentation and that a centralised union movement would be able to cooperate with governments and employers in employment-promoting pay policies.

The suggestion arises in relation to Mancur Olson's hypothesis[13] which states that interest groups embracing a large part of the population will do *less* damage than numerous fragmented groups. An organisation which represents half or two thirds of a country's income-producing potential will largely bear the burden of any social losses brought about by its action; it will thus have an incentive to pursue its members' interests in a way which does not harm and, if possible, benefits overall national prosperity.

The distinction between all-embracing collective interest groups and narrowly fragmented ones throws light on the widely varying fate of incomes policies and attempts at social consensus. In countries such as Austria and some of the Scandinavian group, there are highly centralised union organisations which cover a large proportion of the working population and have at least some incentive to avoid policies which price people out of jobs or reduce national income by restrictive practices or protection. At the other extreme is Britain where the trade union movement has at times been strong, but always as a confederation of disparate individual unions with little central power. The British Trades Union Congress therefore finds it difficult to enforce wage restraint for more than short periods; and in return for its occasional efforts has insisted on a shopping list of demands detrimental to efficiency and sometimes to human freedom. In between there is the German trade union movement, which is more centralised than the British but less so than the Austrian, and which has tended to follow consensus policies but without the detailed Austrian-type machinery of 'social partnership'.

A social consensus based on a strong centralised union movement is likely to be most effective when two conditions are fulfilled. First, the real wage consistent with full employment must be on a rising curve – or at least not on a falling one in the great majority of years. Several governments have found it possible to persuade union movements that wages must not rise more than prices in a particular year, but engineering a substantial fall in real wages – or even a pause of several years – has not so far proved possible.

Second, there must not be sharp relative changes in supply and demand in different parts of the labour market. A trade union federation finds it much easier to agree on a roughly uniform increase for all kinds of workers (which is also convenient for employer groups) than on major changes in differentials among different groups of workers. The turmoil of the years following the oil price upheavals, which has produced big changes in relative prices and wages and has at times required lower real wages, has put great strains on social consensus policies. Up to now, this has been more apparent in Germany than in Austria, where the central union organisation is more powerful and more involved in national policy formulation, but it is doubtful if any country will be able to escape the stresses.

Even in favourable conditions, centralised, widely-encompassing organisations, whether of union movements or other kinds of interest groups, are by no means a universal panacea. Not only is there a danger that they will fragment, but they will work better at some times than at others. If a state is dominated by a few widely embracing organisations, there is less diversity of opinion and fewer checks on misguided policy or on inadequate appreciation of information by the leaders. The larger the country, the greater is the danger.

The real harm of pay policies, both 'hard' ones based on wage and price controls and 'soft' ones formulated in national forums (i.e. dialogues among leaders of unions, industry and government), is that they encourage the belief that each person must look to the political process for his well-being. This strengthens the interest-group pressures by which the citizen has to press his case under a politicised system. Far from reducing conflict as their sponsors intend, the policies introduce political issues into every nook and cranny of personal and business life.

Thus, quite apart from the overwhelming difference in historical background, it is unconvincing to suggest an Austrian-type incomes policy as a contribution to the solution of stagflation in the United States or even Britain or France.

9 Economic Stresses in the West

The great deterioration; The banking crisis; Lending to the Third World; The transitional costs of reducing inflation; US policy shifts; International goals; The challenge of the NICs; 'Common interest groups'; Conclusion.

> 'The financial position is almost irretrievable: the country has lost its way. In the worst of the war I could always see how to do it. Today's problems are elusive and intangible, and it would be a bold man who could look forward to certain success.' – *Winston Churchill, on returning as Prime Minister in 1951*[1]

Substitute 'the western world' or even 'the whole world' for 'the country' that 'has lost its way' and Churchill's words could be equally applicable to the world economy since the end of the Golden Age of post-war growth, an end which became apparent at the time of the first oil price explosion of 1973. The strains which developed were neither foreseen nor particularly illuminated by any school of economic thought.

Even within the period since 1973 there have been changes; and the recession following the second oil price shock of 1979 proved quite different from the first. The most obvious symptoms of crisis were the concern, which first came to the fore in 1982, about the stability of the world banking system and the solvency of major Third World borrowers. Like many symptoms these were liable, if neglected or mishandled, to aggravate the disease and turn recession into depression. Even without a banking collapse, the bank debt problem was causing nervousness and financing difficulties which were depressing world output and trade.

There are three groups of explanations of the underlying problems. First there are those which focus on monetary and fiscal policy and the pains involved in expelling inflationary psychology. The second set of explanations focuses on real disturbances, such as energy price switchbacks and the challenge of Third World industrial development to the established industries of the west. The third set focuses on real factors of a different kind: rigidities, producer interest groups and other obstacles to the functioning of market forces in western countries which induce a kind of sclerosis and resistance to change. These explanations are not mutually contradictory and all shed light on the 'pricing out of jobs' discussed in the previous chapter.

The great deterioration

It was from 1973 onwards that growth rates slowed down, and unemployment and inflation both rose, and in a number of countries political instability increased as well. In some countries there seemed to be a swing to the left; in others to the right. The only common feature was a swing against the government which had the misfortune to be in power.

The crude growth indices illustrate the change in economic performance. During 1960-73, the average annual growth of real GDP in the developed market economies was roughly 5 per cent. In the cycle after the first oil price shock, 1973-79, growth in the developed world averaged only 2½ to 3 per cent. In the 1979-82 period (which does not make a complete cycle) growth was virtually zero.

Throughout the developed world the rate of inflation increased markedly after 1973; and it was the resultant combination of low growth, high unemployment and high

Table 4: Growth of real GDP (Annual average compound growth rates %)

	Golden Age 1960-1973	First oil shock 1973-1975	Recovery 1975-1979	Second oil shock 1979-1982	Wharton Forecast 1982-1987
Developed countries	5.0	0.3	4.0	0.8	3.0
United States	4.1	−0.8	4.5	−0.1	3.3
Japan	9.9	0.6	5.2	3.2	3.4
Europe	4.8	0.8	3.4	0.8	2.4
West Germany	4.5	−0.7	4.0	0.6	1.7
Oil exporting	8.2	2.3	5.4	0.1	4.2
Other developing	5.5	4.8	5.4	2.0	4.2
Centrally planned economies	7.2	5.6	4.6	2.9	3.3

Source: World Economic Outlook, Wharton Econometric Associates.

inflation that gave rise to the ugly word 'stagflation'. But a close examination of the table below shows that inflation was already increasing before the first oil price explosion. This suggests that the oil shock itself was in part at least a delayed response to inflationary forces in the developed world, rather than an entirely independent event solely due either to physical constraint or the Yom Kippur conflict of 1973.

The two oil shocks took the percentage inflation rate in the developed world into double digits. But just as the recession following the second oil price shock proved worse than that after the first oil shock, the shakeout in inflation went further.

The economic cycle following the first oil price explosion consisted of a sharp downswing from 1973 to 1975 and an upswing from 1975 to 1979. The next cycle began with another recession which was triggered off by the second oil price explosion in 1979, following the deposition of the Shah of Iran. At the beginning the second oil-induced recession looked very similar to the first. It seemed, if anything, that the world might get off more lightly. The recession seemed to be shallower. Inflation rose less and subsided more quickly and most oil importing developed countries adjusted their current balance of payments more quickly.

Unfortunately events in 1982 showed these better tidings to be wrong or at least premature. The post-1973 oil-induced recession was V-shaped: a steep plunge followed by a quick recovery – admittedly to a lower growth path than before. The post-1979 one turned out to be at best W-shaped. A hardly perceptible recovery in 1981 soon petered out and was followed by a second unexpected phase of recession in 1982.

The second phase of that recession had the following specific features.

Table 5: The inflation shakeout

Annual Increase in Consumer Prices %

Countries:	1960-67	1967-73	1973-80	1980	1981	1982	1983†
USA	1.8	4.5	7.9	13.5	10.4	6.1	4
Main 7 OECD countries*	2.5	4.9	9.2	12.2	10.0	7.1	5

*USA, Japan, Germany, France, UK, Italy, Canada.
† estimate.   Source: OECD

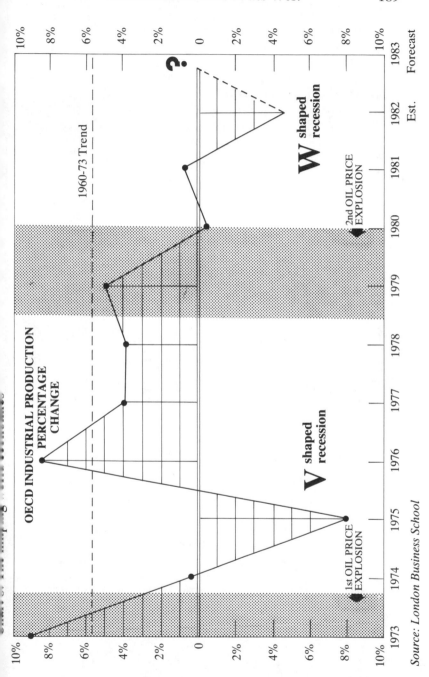

OECD INDUSTRIAL PRODUCTION PERCENTAGE CHANGE

1960-73 Trend

1st OIL PRICE EXPLOSION

V **shaped recession**

2nd OIL PRICE EXPLOSION

W **shaped recession**

Source: London Business School

Chart 9: Short-term interest rates

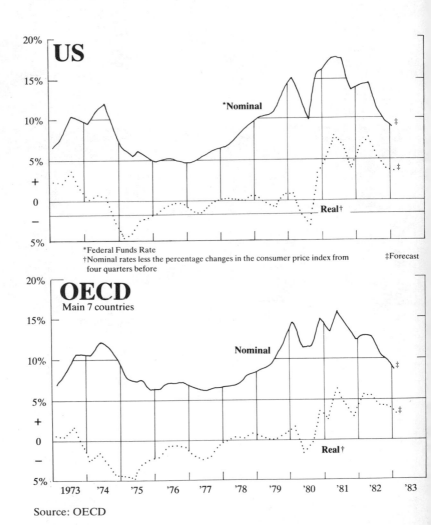

*Federal Funds Rate
†Nominal rates less the percentage changes in the consumer price index from   ‡Forecast
four quarters before

Source: OECD

First, inflation subsided much more quickly than expected.

Second, nominal interest rates were slow to adjust. As a result *real* interest rates (i.e. the excess of the interest rate over the rate of inflation) rose to record heights. This was in sharp contrast to their behaviour in the first oil-induced recession, when they were negative. Short-term real interest rates averaged about 5 per cent for much of 1982 for the USA, and about 4 to 5 per cent for the other main developed countries, according to estimates made by the Organisation for Economic Co-operation and Development (OECD).*

The extreme height of real interest rates in 1980-82 probably reflected the combined pressures of overstringent monetary policies and inflation-anxious financial markets. But even when monetary disturbances are reduced, real interest rates are likely to stay much higher than in the 1973-81 cycle, when their average level was negative, even before allowing for tax. The rise in real interest rates since 1979 may well be a sign of a growing shortage of capital, as well as of monetary forces.

Third, the world's main currencies moved far out of line with anything that could be expected on the basis of costs, prices or previous historical trends. The Morgan Guaranty index of 'real' exchange rates (i.e. exchange rates adjusted for international differences in inflation rates)[2] showed a 25 to 30 per cent real appreciation of the dollar and sterling in the four years to autumn 1982, and a scarcely credible real *depreciation* of the yen in excess of 30 per cent. The combination of prolonged recession and high real interest rates in the United States was in large part responsible for the currency distortions and the squeeze they exerted on world real economic activity.

Fourth, although it is normal for non-oil commodity prices to fall in a recession, they fell particularly severely in 1981-82. Relative to the prices of manufactures and fuel, the prices of non-oil primary products reached their lowest level since the

---

* Long-term real interest rates were also estimated at similar levels; but the calculations here are suspect. To derive them one would need to know the views among the borrowers and lenders about the path of inflation rates for many years ahead. One piece of direct evidence widely ignored was the yield of UK Government indexed bonds which fluctuated around 2 to 3 per cent. Unfortunately, these lower real long-term rates had little practical effect. For nearly all corporate and most country loans were either on a short-term or variable rate basis.

mid-1960s.[3] Oil prices did not begin to weaken seriously until the winter of 1982-83. It was an example of the prevailing pessimism that, although the violent rise in the price of oil from $2 per barrel in 1972 to $12 in 1974 and $34 in 1981 triggered off two major bouts of stagflation, the 1982-83 weakening of the oil price was also received with cries of alarm although OPEC was able, for a while at least, to stem the fall.

Fifth, needless to say, protectionist pressures continued to grow. Each government tended to think that other governments were taking unfair advantage; and, because of high and rising unemployment, sensitivity to Japanese and low-cost Third World competition became intense. Protectionism remained backdoor and selective, but it was creeping forward with proliferating trade squabbles and 'voluntary' restraint agreements. One estimate suggested that the proportion of 'managed' world trade – the proportion subject to non-tariff control, such as quotas or OPEC production ceilings – had risen from 40 per cent in 1974 to 48 per cent in 1980.

An example of the self-inflicted wounds was the agreement negotiated by the EEC Industry Commissioner, Viscount Davignon (who enjoyed a sycophantic press from journalists who equated activity with wisdom) for voluntary restriction on Japanese exports ranging from quartz watches and videos to fork lift trucks and machine tools.

A related response was the efforts of many governments to snatch at every export contract, however poor the terms, generous the credit, or dubious the political implications. Yet underlying this whole obsession with exporting was a mistake of economic analysis. If it is inflationary to expand domestic demand, as many governments fear, it is also inflationary to boost overseas demand by boosting arms sales to Latin America or cheap credit for the Soviet bloc. It may be argued that purely domestic demand expansion may have a larger, or at least earlier, inflationary impact because it is likely to reduce the exchange rate. Even that argument would be much weaker if the OECD countries expanded demand in concert. This is not to argue that they should (or should not) do so. It would be extremely easy to push inflation up again with very little lasting effect on output and employment. I am simply making the analytical point that overseas demand has no special virtue which makes it less inflationary than domestic expenditure, whether on roads, schools, consumer durables or any other desired public or private object of consumption or investment.

Fortunately, a full-scale trade war was averted in the 1980-82 recession. Some policy-makers and their advisers were at least dimly aware that the Smoot-Hawley tariffs of May 1930, which raised US duties to a record high, were followed within a few months by retaliatory tariffs elsewhere, quantitative restrictions in 26 countries by the end of 1931, and the UK switch to Imperial Preference early in 1932. Although the precise interconnections remain a matter of academic debate, this trade war, together with the banking crises, was among the events which turned the world downturn of 1929-30 into the Great Depression of 1931-34.

Sixth, there emerged during 1982 the first signs of the international banking crisis, as a product or symptom of the other problems mentioned. A few projects which bankers had queued up to finance in the 1973-81 period were inherently questionable – as such projects always will be when easy money is available and few questions are asked. But slump, high interest rates and low commodity prices, plus protectionism in western markets, caused many Third World and Soviet-bloc nations (above all, but not only, Poland) to have the greatest difficulty in servicing their debts, quite apart from any errors of over-borrowing or misuse of funds on their part.

Seventh, during 1982 the actual and perceived impact of high American interest rates, and especially their repercussions on exchange rates, increased the feeling of dependence on the US in the rest of the non-communist world. It was thought that only the US could lead the world to lower interest rates either by reducing its prospective budget deficit or by relaxation on the part of the Federal Reserve. After two decades of talk of the relative decline in US influence on the world economy, commentators in one country after another vied with each other in emphasising the dependence of world recovery on US fiscal and monetary policy. In the words of a distinguished former president of the Bundesbank, Dr Otmar Emminger, 'It was a return to the

Pax Americana, at least in the monetary field.'

Thus the rest of the non-communist world was looking to the US for a lead out of the second severe recession to have hit the world since the 1973 oil price shock – and one marked by high real interest rates, currency distortions, trade tensions and an international banking crisis. Indeed fears about the financial system almost certainly depressed business sentiment and aggravated the world recession which in turn aggravated Third World payments problems in a mutually reinforcing way.

The banking crisis

For the first time since the 1930s the world economy faced the spectre of national, banking or large-scale corporate insolvencies. These posed a new kind of threat, over and above the normal effects of boom and recession, or mistakes in demand management by national governments.

The seriousness of the banking threat first became apparent in 1982 as a number of minor US financial institutions, such as the New York firm of Drysdale Government Securities and Penn Square, failed. Some of these owed money to larger banks. A much bigger institution, the Italian Banco Ambrosiano, also went down that year, with its affairs in an impenetrable tangle and unpaid debts owed by fourteen foreign subsidiaries.

The biggest shock of the year came, however, on Friday, 13 August 1982, when Mexico announced that it was no longer able to service $80 billion of foreign debt. If Mexico had defaulted, 70 per cent of the common equity of two of the largest US banks would have vanished overnight. By the end of 1982, an IMF Letter of Intent had been agreed with Mexico. Another was agreed with Argentina and negotiations were in train to reschedule the debts of still more countries, of which the most important was Brazil with outstanding debts of $90 billion. The problems extended, however, well beyond country (or 'sovereign') lending. Many bank loans were to corporate borrowers, who themselves were having difficulty in staying in business, and the quality of the loans was therefore in doubt.

When it came to diagnosis and prescription, a distinction

needed to be drawn between (a) the threat to the world's banking system and (b) the threat to world economic activity and the flow of world trade. They interacted, but needed to be analysed separately. The direct banking danger came from the external loans made by the world's chief banks. Outstanding medium-term bank credit to the non-OPEC developing countries rose from $40 billion at the end of 1975 to an estimated $180 billion at the end of 1982. There are no comprehensive figures for short-term credit, but OECD estimates put the end-1982 total at $120 billion (mostly but not entirely, emanating from banks), giving a grand total of around $300 billion. If one includes official debt, loans from multilateral organisations, export credits, bond issue and miscellaneous loans, the OECD estimate of the total disbursed debt of non-OPEC developing countries come to about $640 billion at the end of 1982. Four countries – Mexico, Brazil, Argentina and South Korea – accounted for nearly half of this sum. Two thirds of these countries' debts consisted of floating rate debt – compared with one third for other developing country borrowers – and nearly a half was theoretically repayable within a year. At the same time as bank assets became more risky, the equity-to-assets ratio (that is, the portion of assets not corresponding to deposit or fixed-interest liabilities and therefore available to shareholders) of the US banks in the American financial centres fell.

There are particular reasons why, in sovereign or country lending, there is a divergence between the self-interest of an individual bank and that of the banking system as a whole. In much domestic lending any one individual bank is likely to be responsible for a larger proportion of an establishment's borrowing than is the case with internationally syndicated country loans, where each individual bank provides only a very small proportion of the country's total borrowing.

Each additional loan to a vulnerable country increases the degree of risk not merely to the particular lending bank, but to all banks that have already lent to that country. However, it is only the former cost that will be taken into account in decisions on whether to lend and on what terms. A good analogy is with the congestion costs imposed by each additional vehicle in an urban centre, not merely on itself but on other vehicles. In each case there is an 'adverse externality', i.e. the imposition of costs which the responsible agent does not himself bear.

There is another source of divergence between the individual and collective interest. This is the information problem. Information about a debtor's position is a *public good*. Each bank has an interest in being a 'free rider' on the investigations of others. The externality and public good aspects together provided a case for some umbrella organisation, whether the IMF or the Ditchley Group which a number of international banks formed in 1982, to provide information and concert strategy towards particular countries.

Precautionary action was left very late. The banking danger arose from the possible effect on the banking system of the default of one or more major borrowers, perhaps combined with domestic bankruptcies during a bad phase of the economic cycle. One key question was whether 'lender-of-last-resort facilities', which were supposed to exist for domestic banking, were adequate in the international field. In particular, were there plans to meet not merely a *liquidity crisis*, but a *solvency crisis*, when the amount of bad debt could exceed the equity capital of major banks?

Central banks were, for far too long, reticent about their international lender-of-last-resort obligations. One proffered justification was on grounds of moral hazard – the fear that they might encourage imprudent bank lending. But by the early 1980s, the pretext was no longer credible. The imprudent lending had *already* taken place. Moreover the same arguments could be used against domestic lender-of-last-resort facilities.

A more convincing explanation for reticence was that central banks had been slow to make adequate contingency plans for stemming or offsetting any major failure among international banks. Until well into 1982 the main publicly disclosed efforts had gone into only partially successful efforts to bring regulatory practice in different countries together.

According to the Basle Concordat of 1975, each central bank was responsible for regulating the activities, home and overseas, of banks with headquarters in its own country. By extension, it was also supposed to be morally responsible for lender-of-last-resort operations, although this was never formally admitted. But the problem of consortium banks or partially owned subsidiaries was left unresolved. So, too, was the question of what was to count as a bank.

Both these problems were exemplified on a small scale by the crash of the Italian Banco Ambrosiano whose affairs were revealed to the world when its chairman Roberto Calvi was found hanging from scaffolding under Blackfriars Bridge in London on 18 June 1982. The Bank of Italy set up a pool of seven banks to provide liquidity to meet the demands of creditors and depositors of the Banco Ambrosiano, which was declared insolvent by a Milan court on 26 August. But the Italian central bank did not accept responsibility for debts worth over $140m of Ambrosiano's 69 per cent owned subsidiary, Banco Ambrosiano Holdings of Luxemburg.

The biggest problem facing lender-of-last-resort operation was of a different kind. This was that a central bank may run out of foreign exchange reserves if there is a run on deposits of banks for which it is responsible, and which are denominated in an external currency. It could still act as a lender of last resort but only by activating a swap network with the central banks whose currencies were being demanded by depositors. Here was a further reason for clarifying lender-of-last-resort arrangements – even if it were better not to reveal the size of swap lines lest they be thought insufficient in a really big crisis, when larger sums could probably be arranged on the telephone.

A deeper thought came to mind. Was it reasonable that cash balances for household transactions or domestic business should be put at risk because of problems that had arisen in lending OPEC surpluses to Third World industrialising countries? There was an old far-out academic proposal, promulgated by Irving Fisher[4], that the provision of balances for monetary transactions should be strictly separated from borrowing and lending operations. Under this concept, known as '100 per cent money', banks would be required to have liquid reserves sufficient to repay their deposit liabilities at sight if requested; and they would be remunerated by service charges. In other words fractional reserve banking would be forbidden. The difficulty of this idea is that the interest-paying liabilities of other investment institutions would tend to circulate as money in preference to the obligations of the reformed banks. The advent of money market funds in the US and checking accounts for UK Building Societies are examples of what can happen.

Lending to the Third World

The threat to world trade and activity can occur without any banking collapse. Indeed it can be precipitated by the attempts of bankers to maintain solvency by cutting down on new lending to the Third World either because they are worried about exposure or because they want to rebuild their own equity. Similarly contractionary forces can come from Third World and other debtors either if they lose their borrowing power or if they try to satisfy the IMF and other lenders by adopting policies of domestic retrenchment.

The statements made by western finance ministers and central bankers at the IMF meeting in Toronto in September 1982 in response to such fears might have been calculated to induce neurosis in a Pavlovian dog. Commercial bankers were lectured on prudence – and they were also told for the sake of world activity not to be too prudent. Paul Volcker, Chairman of the Federal Reserve, tried towards the end of the year to resolve the dilemma on the expansionist side, by saying that where loans facilitated 'the adjustment process' the 'new credits should not be subject to supervisory criticism.' He ran into trouble, however, from Congress which was very reluctant to bail out bankers from the consequences of their own mistakes.

As part of the same process of relaxation, the US dropped its opposition to a major increase in IMF quotas ahead of time; a 47 per cent increase was agreed in principle in February 1983, which should effectively double the Fund's stock of usable currencies. In addition the General Arrangement to Borrow (GAB) under which the Group of Ten major members stood ready to lend to the Fund was raised from $7 billion to $19 billion. A third element, strongly urged by outside financial opinion, was that the Fund should be ready to borrow on the private markets.

A much more difficult task than IMF enlargement is to determine the criteria for the distress lending it undertakes. This is especially important as an agreement with the IMF is regarded as a seal of good housekeeping and helps to restore the creditworthiness of the borrowing country in the international market. The normal IMF country-by-country approach is outmoded at times when a particular country's problems could reflect world problems rather than its own imprudence.

Lending as such is neither good nor bad. The best approach would be to determine a global stance on the basis of whether the total level of world expenditure on goods and services in money terms is rising so quickly as to pose inflationary dangers or whether, on the contrary, the main danger is that it may fall (or rise inadequately), thus posing a recessionary threat. If world demand is deficient the main remedy does not have to be to encourage unwise spending by, say, Mexico or Argentina. Relaxation of monetary and fiscal policy in the major world economies would do as well or better. If the IMF 'seal of good housekeeping' is given too readily to help out panic-stricken western creditors it will become devalued and less capable of attracting private lenders into problem countries.

The emphasis in western financial policy, as it developed in response to the banking crisis, was neither on lender-of-last-resort operations nor on the global management of monetary demand, but on case-by-case patching up operations to 'reschedule' the debt of countries unable to pay. It would be a brave man who would have condemned these operations in the fragile state of the world's financial markets.

What was required, however, was not an ill-thought-out monetary stimulation throughout the world or panic-stricken increases in the IMF resources on the scale advocated by the Brandt Commission, but a long-term reconstruction of Third World debt. The main problem with this debt was not that it was excessive. The real rate of increase of Third World debt in the decade after 1973 was actually slightly less than in the 1960s. The main problem was that it had become too short-term in response to years of very high nominal (as well as real) interest rates. There was an arguable case for a conversion operation, without waiting indefinitely to see how far interest rates would fall back. One proposal was that the debt should be bought from the banks at a 10 per cent discount by some official international intermediary in return for 10 to 20 year bonds, which the borrowing countries would amortise. One problem could well be to persuade the borrowers to accept the conversion at a realistic interest rate.

The hand-to-mouth approach to each debt crisis adopted in 1982-83 put economic power in the hands of potential defaulters. It is true that a country which declared default would indeed risk cutting itself off not merely from world financial markets, as normally understood, but from export credits and a whole network of financial services such as banks and insurance on which modern commerce depends. (Even communications, shipping and telephones are often dependent on bank finance.) On the other hand, borrowing countries can go a long way in threatening default because they know that western governments and banks are terrified of the potential consequences to the world financial system of the threats being carried out. Thus there is a large element of crying 'chicken' on both sides. A more systematic approach to rescue operations, with clear-cut guide-lines, and publicised fall-back plans to support the international banking system in the event of a major default, would give the west more bargaining power in dealing with threats made by fanatical regimes of all kinds.

It was not a very good advertisement for western capitalism that the decision on whether to reschedule both banking and official debts to General Jaruzelski's Poland could not be made on broad foreign policy considerations, but was guided by fears of the consequences to the western financial system of a Polish financial collapse. To take another instance, it was far from certain that a complete financial clampdown on Argentina would have persuaded the Buenos Aires government to negotiate a peaceful withdrawal from the Falklands in 1982. But the fact that this was *never even put to the test* and a thousand people were killed in the conflict is a shaming instance of what happens when western countries cannot afford a financial showdown with petty dictators of the right or left.

The transitional costs of reducing inflation

The banking and international indebtedness problems were symptoms of underlying problems. The most obvious arose from the pains involved in the transition to a lower level of inflation and the expulsion of inflationary psychology.

In principle the task of reducing inflation is fairly straightforward. Inflation and deflation are monetary phenomena: as explained in Part II of this book, there is no reason to suppose that there is any long-run choice between inflation and unemployment. Output and employment will be no lower – they could easily be higher – at a low rather than a high inflation rate. But the process of reducing inflation is a painful one, nearly always involving a transitional recession. In addition, two severe oil price shocks followed by two tight money periods were bound to take their toll. The experience of the world economy since 1973 was thus a case study in the costs of the transition to a lower rate of inflation. While some of these costs were virtually inevitable, there were also policy mistakes exacerbating the difficulties.

It is a fundamental feature of the world economy, as of individual national economies, that different kinds of prices react with different speeds to demand restraint. Primary-product prices react most quickly and have to take much of the strain. Wages are slowest to react. Final products and services are somewhere in between. They are more sensitive than wages to recessionary pressures – and therefore profit margins are inevitably squeezed – but they are not as sensitive as primary products. Thus any transition towards lower inflation is likely to include high levels of unemployment, as real wage levels adjust only slowly, and also financial difficulties for Third World commodity producers, the price of whose exports may fall dramatically.

But policy mistakes have been superimposed on these structural problems. Instead of focussing on monetary demand (money GDP), policy-makers in many countries focussed on particular narrow aggregates. They took from the technical monetarists the mistake of assuming that it was easy to measure the effective quantity of money and that there was a reliable mechanistic relationship between their chosen monetary target and total monetary demand.

The earlier fear about the monetary approach to inflation was that it would fail due to the growth of money substitutes, the greater ability to economise on cash balances as a result of computer developments, and so on: in other words, that velocity of circulation of money would rise and monetary policy would fail to restrain spending as sharply as intended.

But in fact the problem, especially in the US and Britain, was the opposite: velocity fell and the whole stance of demand management – despite large fiscal deficits in the US – was a good deal tighter than intended. The characteristic criticism of technical monetarism thus turned out to be precisely the reverse of the strictures which were justified by events. Two major economies thus suffered a much tighter domestic monetary squeeze than was either intended or desirable.

Partly because American and British labour markets take a long time to react to exchange rate changes and partly because of excessively tight monetary policies, the dollar and sterling became overvalued. This aggravated the recession by transmitting their tight stance to other countries. The central European countries and Japan felt they had to keep a tight rein on money and credit, because they were worried about the inflationary impact of further depreciation. So they were not able to reap the full benefit of the trade stimulus which normally comes from undervaluation.

The combination of domestic policy mistakes with the new international transmission mechanism caused the pace of disinflation to be much faster than intended. As a result of human action but not human intention we did not have Friedman's well known policy of gradualism, but something more like the less well publicised policy of a sharp shock advocated by Hayek.[5] Growing recognition of this led to changes in the stance of policy in the US. It also demonstrated the case for a new kind of international monetary cooperation.

US policy shifts

From the beginning many in the US Fed understood the weaknesses, in changing conditions, of technical monetarism based on a target for one or more monetary aggregates. The main factor preventing an earlier relaxation in the Fed's monetary policy terms was fear of the US budget deficit. Indeed calls for higher US taxes or lower government spending became a feature of international meetings, and were expressed by governments, such as the French, which were committed to expansionist fiscal policies in their own countries (at least until their own currencies weakened on the foreign exchanges).

What exactly was the US fiscal problem? About a third of the 1982-83 US budget deficit was officially attributed to recession. The trouble was that the non-cyclical structural element was on a strongly rising path. The Council of Economic Advisers feared in its 1983 Report that without policy changes it could amount to 6 per cent of the GNP in the years up to 1988, compared with a net personal and business savings ratio of only 7 per cent. Built into the structure of US bond prices was an insurance element to protect investors against the risk of either real interest rates being bid up or of inflation rising once more. But just as lenders were worried that inflation might rise, borrowers were worried that it might stay low, or fall even further, and were reluctant to borrow long-term at prevailing interest rates. So a part of what would otherwise be long-term borrowing was transferred to the short end of the market; and base or prime rates also stayed high for a long time.

By about the middle of 1982 both President and Congress seemed at least agreed on the need – if not on the actual measures – to shift the US budget deficit onto a downward track as a proportion of national income. The earlier, so-called 'supply side' belief that budget deficits either did not matter if the Fed held to its monetary targets, or would be automatically reduced as a result of the stimulating effects of tax cuts, was abandoned decisively when Professor Martin Feldstein took over as chairman of the Council of Economic Advisers. Corrective action was, however, slow to come.

Nevertheless by October 1982, the Fed had relaxed, and Chairman Paul Volcker announced at Hot Springs, Virginia, the suspension of US monetary targets. In the same month the Chancellor of another supposedly monetarist government, Britain's Sir Geoffrey Howe, coined the slogan 'flexibility without laxity'. Meanwhile American monetary policy was shifting from a 'technical monetarist' focus on specific monetary aggregates to a still unspecified broader range of indicators. An earlier statement by Paul Volcker on 20 July had already broken with all the canons of the more technical kind of monetarism.

The Fed Chairman had then identified the following influences which would determine the judgment on monetary growth. 'We will look to a variety of factors in reaching that judgment including such technical factors as the behavior of different components in the money supply, the growth of credit, the behavior of banking and financial markets and more broadly, the behaviour of velocity and interest rates.' In other words instead of using predetermined monetary growth to regulate the economy, the Fed would use the behaviour of the economy to formulate its aims for the growth of the money supply. Mr Volcker wondered aloud whether the rising trend of velocity of the previous ten years (which were mostly periods of rising inflation and interest rates) was not being reversed. He very reasonably did not pretend to know; but this very agnosticism was bound to increase the discretion of the Fed both in determining monetary targets and deciding how far they should be observed. It was not at all clear what the Fed's new longer-term yardsticks were to be, whether they were to be the newer and higher monetary targets announced in 1983, interest rates, output and employment or Nominal GDP. Nor was it clear how these variables were to be weighed against each other. The Fed was feeling its way.

It is very important that the new flexibility should not either be or appear to be going back to traditional postwar demand management which attempted to underwrite any level of wages and prices which happened to emerge in the market place. The reason for this is not puritanical anti-inflationary virtue, but severely practical. For if a return to inflationary finance is foreseen, interest rates will rise and not fall in response to monetary and fiscal stimuli, which will therefore 'not work'. There were indeed many signs that the Fed – like financial authorities in many other countries – was not at all sure how to implement 'flexibility without laxity' in practice.

Unfortunately, leaving the size and scope of action completely to central banks' discretion is not likely to be adequate. Without guidelines they cannot be depended upon either to do enough to maintain monetary demand to offset a slump or to restrict it enough to prevent a reacceleration of inflation in the longer term.

International goals

One constructive response to the new uncertainty and instability in the 'demand for money' is to have a combined international money supply objective.[6] It need only involve the countries with the world's main currencies – say the US, Japan, Germany and perhaps Britain. This would be a step forward, as the demand for a central group of currencies is almost certain to be more stable than for any one currency alone.

If it were politically possible to have a joint money supply objective for a few major countries, it would be an improvement on the experience of the last few years. Nevertheless I question whether even the demand for a key group of currencies will be stable enough to provide a reliable target. There will be occasions when the central banks may have to inject liquidity into the world financial system without too obsessive and immediate a concern about the money supply numbers. But a series of piecemeal adjustments to the pressures of the moment is most unlikely to bring the stability of expectations which the world so badly needs. Although the demand for a key group of currencies such as the dollar, yen, mark and sterling is likely to be more stable and predictable than the demand for any one of them, it still may not be stable enough. Money GDP would serve better as an objective of policy, internationally as well as domestically.

An objective for Money GDP for, say, the inner group of five summit countries – the US, Japan, Germany, the UK and France – may sound a tall order; but it is doubtful if anything less will suffice. Long-run guidelines for the growth of Money GDP in the core countries of the industrial world are, of course, no substitute either for intermediate objectives for monetary aggregates, for public sector borrowing limits, or for official international lending and emergency operations to bolster countries or banks facing temporary difficulties. A Money GDP objective would, however, prove the best guide to using these instruments so as to combine firm long-term guidelines with maximum short-term flexibility for central banks and finance ministers.

The fact that such an objective makes sense mainly over a period of years is a positive advantage. For it enables short-term discretion for central banks to be combined with coherent long-term guidelines. It is not a gimmick, but merely a way of expressing policy objectives which experience suggests have some, admittedly imperfect, chance of being achieved.

The challenge of the NICs

Although new guidelines for macroeconomic policy are urgently needed, the problems of the industrial economies go deeper. An explanation of the traumas of the 1970s and 1980s entirely in terms of the transitional costs of reducing inflation is at bottom too optimistic. If inflation and tight money policies were the only problem, it would be possible to move back towards earlier levels of performance once inflationary expectations were eliminated.

Apart from being optimistic such a view leaves many questions unasked. Why was it so much more difficult and costly to puncture inflationary expectation after the oil-price explosion than, say, after the post-Korean inflation in the early 1950s, let alone in many earlier periods? Why are wages and some prices quite so sticky in the face of reduced demand?

It seems pretty clear from the experience of recovery periods that the rates of employment and growth consistent with stable non-accelerating inflation have fallen in most western countries. The 16 per cent fall in British manufacturing output in 1979-82 (and the fall of over 20 per cent compared with 1973) has been paralleled by similar if less spectacular difficulties in the established industries throughout Europe and North America. It is unconvincing to blame all this either on the inevitable costs of disinflation or on the mistakes of President Reagan, Prime Minister Thatcher or Helmut Schmidt (German Chancellor from 1974 until 1982). There are clearly 'real' non-monetary forces at work.

There are a good many indications that the large amounts of unused capacity revealed by industrial surveys are deceptive. No doubt the physical plant and equipment are there – but much of it may be economically obsolete and not likely to come back into operation even in a period of normal growth. The most important single pointer is the prevalence of high real interest rates, which cannot be accounted for entirely by monetary policy mistakes. High interest rates are normally a sign of capital shortage.

Another remarkable phenomenon has been the clamour of complaints from so many western countries that most of any increase in demand is sucked off into imports with little benefit to domestic industry. If this were so only in one or two countries, it might be a sign merely of wrongly aligned exchange rates. But such reports come from many countries; and the beneficiaries from rising imports always seem to be Japan, southeast Asia, the other newly industrialising countries, and the low-cost plants of southern Europe.

One reason for the obsolescence of so much capital has been the shifts in relative prices of different inputs into the production process.[7] The golden-age growth period before 1973 was accompanied by fairly stable price relativities. Since then the most spectacular changes have been in energy prices. Capital costs have, as already mentioned, risen. On the other hand the market clearing price of labour (the price at which demand and supply are brought into line) has clearly fallen, if not its actual price.

A major force behind all these changes and the economic obsolescence of so much capital equipment in the west has been the emergence of the developing countries as major manufacturing countries. They have been acquiring a comparative advantage in an increasing number of industries formerly the preserve of the west. This so-called transition thesis, which has been most fully developed by Professor Michael Beenstock of the City University, does tie together a number of developments.[8]

The most obvious effect is the growing uncompetitiveness of many parts of traditional industries in the west, not just textiles but a large range of metal and engineering goods and even services, such as shipping. Manufacturing has, however, been the prime victim. As manufacturing is also the most capital-intensive sector, the downward pressure here has contributed to a general fall in the share of profits in the national income of most western countries. The pressures on the rate of return in the old countries and the competitive advantages of the new centres have directed investment towards the developing countries, where fixed investment grew in the 1970s at an average annual rate of 7·8 per cent compared with 1·6 per cent in the developed world. Thus, Third World indebtedness is a natural development – but, like similar investment a century ago, it is prone both to fits of over-exuberance and to setbacks whenever a global recession puts a check to the growth of markets. It is something of a paradox that the long-term success of the developing countries should have intensified a world economic setback which has itself reduced Third World borrowing power, but it is perhaps a paradox with which we may have to live.

The strongest evidence for the Beenstock 'transition thesis' is the simple fact that, taking the decade since 1973 as a whole, Third World countries have performed better than the advanced ones. Non-oil developing countries were only slightly affected by the 1973-75 recession and did better than the developing ones in the 1975-79 recovery. The Third World countries' 5 per cent growth rate in the 1973-79 period was twice as good as the performance of the developed western economies then. Developing countries suffered a substantial check in the 1979-82 recession; but even so they fared considerably better than the western world. The Wharton projections to 1987 again show the Third World countries outstripping the First by a substantial margin.

It is true that in the early 1980s the non-oil developing countries accounted for barely 10 per cent of OECD imports of manufactures (up from 6½ per cent in 1973). The Third World competition so far seen is only the beginning of the beginning. Moreover in all markets, domestic and international, a marginal low-cost supplier does not have to be large to bring a downward pressure on profitability among existing producers.

The shift in comparative advantage to the NICs for traditional industries does not mean that western countries are doomed to be uncompetitive. It is impossible for one country to have a comparative advantage over another in every product; and there normally exist terms of trade at which a country can pay its way in the world and sustain a normal level of economic activity.

But countries which respond with alacrity and ingenuity to the new pattern of comparative advantage will do better than those which do not. Among developed market economies, responsiveness to new technological opportunities seems to increase as one moves west from Europe to the USA and from the USA to Japan (the process may also be seen as one goes west or south-west across the USA). For instance, one estimate of the number of 'programmable robots' in operation at the end of 1981 put Japan ahead with 14,000, the US next with 4,100, followed by Germany with 2,300, France with 1,000 and Britain with 500 (just below Sweden). The seven main semi-conductor companies are American or Japanese.[9]

The implication is *not* that Europe should copy Japan or that governments should bribe companies to imitate Japanese patterns. The moral is simply that a capacity for rapid economic change is helpful to economic success.

Beenstock's main explanation of why the development of LDC competition should have caused unemployment in the west is what he calls 'mismatch'. Redundant steel or garment workers cannot transform themselves into computer programmers overnight: and inflexibility of relative wages, and controls and subsidies in the European housing markets, hinder mobility. There still remains the awkward fact that redundancies in traditional industries do not seem to be matched by comparable excess demand for labour in the service sector or in the newer industries. Moreover the rise in real wages in Europe relative to productivity, and the decline in the rate of return to capital and the share of profits, seem to be too great to be accounted for merely by a relative shift away from the older capital-intensive industries.

Third World competition and even energy price changes would not have led to such prolonged stagnation and inflation without institutional rigidities, which prevented relative prices from adjusting enough to secure full employment. These rigidities are particularly great in the labour market. At this point, some distinction must be made between Europe and North America.

During the period of postwar growth, a rapid rise in European real wages was possible with little disturbance. Some of the factors which made this possible were: straightforward gains from catching up with the best US methods; a demand for more and more of the same types of goods which encouraged economies of scale; cheap energy and as yet little resistance to growth from any 'green' environmental lobby. In addition, 'money illusion' – the habit of treating tomorrow's dollar as equivalent to today's – enabled Finance Ministers and central banks to keep real interest rates and unemployment below the levels at which they could be sustained in the long run.

There have always been strong social, political and institutional forces in Europe tending to resist either reductions in average real wages or changes in relative remuneration. But these did not matter so much when the above mentioned forces, which made rapid real wage growth compatible with full employment and with minimum disturbance, were in operation. When these unusually favourable factors ceased to operate, the structural rigidities began to cause far more harm.

In the United States these forces were less powerful; and despite the record postwar unemployment rates of the recession the unemployment *increase* was much less than in Europe. The US labour market has been able to absorb over the last decade a rapid increase in new entrants, youths, and women, at the expense of lower real wages and lower productivity. Average real earnings per hour for US private sector workers were lower in 1981 than ten years earlier and had not shown any net growth since 1967. All the rise in American output in recent years has come from increases in the employment of labour with hardly any net gain in productivity or per capita real earnings.

In Europe real wages have grown much faster for those who have retained their jobs; and many people have been priced out of work. In Japan and still more in southeast Asia, real wages have been even more flexible than in the US, and they, rather than employment, have taken the strain. So European economies have reacted to external measures with falls in employment, whereas in the USA and still more Japan and southeast Asia there have been adjustments in real wages.

'Common interest groups'

Why then has institutional sclerosis crept up on the west, but at different speeds in different countries? The most plausible theory relates to the politics and economics of common interest groups and collusive associations. These cover a great variety of organisations and informal groupings: professional associations, trade unions, price rings, industrial lobbies that campaign for protection from foreign competition and for government subsidies. The list is endless and their distortionary influence on representative democracy has

Chart 10: Employment

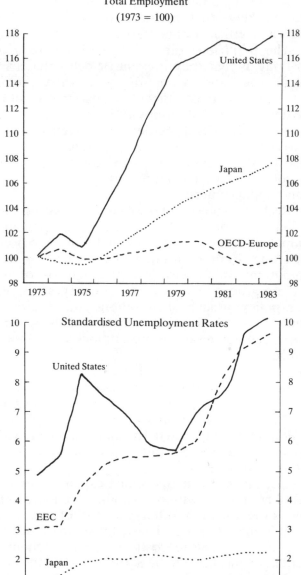

Total Employment
(1973 = 100)

Standardised Unemployment Rates

Source: OECD

already been discussed in Chapter 3.

Some of these associations may strengthen the cohesion of society by creating a network of local professional loyalties intermediate between the citizen and the state. But they reduce growth, efficiency and the capacity to adapt to outside events. The pernicious direct effect of 'common interest organisations' is that they prevent or delay the changes in *relative* incomes and prices required when productivity changes or the system is subject to an external shock. So the damage done by interest groups is likely to be greatest in the circumstances described earlier in this chapter – when inflation is being reduced and the transitional costs depend on the capacity of economic agents to adjust, and when large amounts of capital are becoming obsolete as new patterns of prices and trading emerge.

The effect of common interest groups resisting economic adaptation is greater than that arising from the pure influence of monopoly power efficiently wielded. For the power of the interest group is not even efficiently wielded. Some of the most important effects arise from the high cost of decisions within these groups. Major external changes will alter the optimum policy of such organisations and require difficult bargaining with other organisations and/or the government. Thus cartelised organisations are cautious about innovations and change.

As important as the direct effects in the market places are the political by-products of interest-group lobbying. The complexity of regulations and the scope of government are increased. Increased resources are devoted to lobbying, negotiations and political activity; and individuals with these abilities will be favoured relative to those with technical or entrepreneurial abilities.

The most plausible theory which explains why collusive organisations and interest-group politics are more important in some societies than others is that of the American economist Mancur Olson.[10] These organisations are costly to maintain and even more costly to start. Each individual member has an incentive to be a 'free rider' on the actions of others. Participation is costly whether in the form of membership dues, strike action or lobbying. For interest groups to become effective, the leaders have to provide 'selective incentives' such as professional information or social insurance benefits which make participation individually worthwhile. Alternatively, moral pressure or coercion may be applied. The relevant incentives, loyalties and pressures all take many years to evolve, but once they have become established, interest groups tend to maintain themselves almost indefinitely at much less cost. From this we derive Olson's Law:

> Stable societies with unchanged boundaries tend to accumulate collusive organizations and interest groups over time, and thus tend to lag behind in their growth rates and capacity to adapt in comparison to newer and more dynamic societies.

Thus it is not surprising that a country such as Britain which pioneered the Industrial Revolution and has had the longest record of political freedom and settled institutions should have been among the first to succumb to economic stagnation (whether it will be the first to emerge is another question), closely followed by the industrial mid-west of the United States. On the other hand, countries 'where common interest organizations have been emasculated or abolished by foreign occupation, totalitarian governments or political instability' experience rapid rates of growth 'after a free and stable legal order is established'. The countries of continental Europe in the 1950s and 1960s are the obvious examples.

But as World War II and its aftermath receded, and settled democratic institutions moved into their second generation, it was only to be expected that producer-interest groups would gain ground in western Europe as well. The countries now experiencing the most rapid growth are in the Pacific Basin where industrial development is still a novelty and untrammelled by collective or political pressures.

Olson has now extended his theory to cover unemployment and prolonged recession as well as low growth. He starts from a state where there is involuntary unemployment, i.e. there are workers who would be willing to work for less than the going wage but still cannot find jobs. Mutually advantageous job contracts could in principle be made between employers and unemployed workers at a wage below the going rate, but above the value of the unemployed person's free time. Who,

Olson asks, might have an interest in blocking such transactions? The answer, of course, is 'workers with the same or competitive skills'. Existing workers can only prevent such contracts if they are organised into a cartel or lobby or are informally able to exert collusive pressure. If we recall the earlier argument that collusive organisations find it particularly difficult to react to changed market conditions, for instance those requiring lower real wages, it is not difficult to see how the impact of shocks such as oil price increases or Third World competition or counter-inflationary policies can be felt in a prolonged and deep recession.

It seems clear that the collusive groups with the most power to price workers out of jobs, or stop them pricing themselves into jobs, are the labour unions in western Europe at least. In the USA it is probably the political lobbying of a great variety of producer groups from the American Medical Association to corporations threatened by imports. The European variety is the more harmful.

Conclusion

The deep-seated structural problems of the older industrial nations are neither parochial nor international, but common problems, which have to be tackled on the spot by whoever has the opportunity to act. They are thus not easily amenable to summit diplomacy.

International economic cooperation can help to minimise the financial and macroeconomic disturbances which make the real problems worse. It can also help to keep down the economic arms race in trade restrictions, subsidies and other costs and distortions. These are particularly pernicious, because, although they are imposed to protect employment in particular sectors, their ultimate effect is to delay adjustment and to worsen either employment or living standards or both.

Progress on the international economic front will require not only a more coherent response to default risks and to lender-of-last-resort operations; it will also require a concerted demand-management and monetary policy by at least the three or four major countries of the system. But the result of all these financial actions will be extremely disappointing if there is not a great improvement in the ability of the developed countries of the world to respond to changes in demand, technology and costs – in what is known as the 'supply side' of the economy, using this term for once in its correct sense. Exhortations, committees and training schemes may have their place in such improvement; but far more important is to allow the price mechanism – in the labour as well as in the goods market – more scope, to provide incentives to produce the products of the future rather than the past, to price workers into jobs and to move resources from areas of surplus into areas of scarcity.

PART IV

The British Instance

10 How British is the British Sickness?

Long-run problems; Recent problems; Suggested explanations; Spending and taxes; State intervention; Incomes policy and inflation; The argument so far; The class system; Union power; Democracy and interest groups.

There are at least two separate problems about the British economy, which are not sufficiently distinguished. First there is the long-standing gap between the growth rate of the United Kingdom and that of other industrial market economies. This goes back over a hundred years. Alfred Marshall remarked that by the 1860s and 1870s 'many of the sons of manufacturers' were 'content to follow mechanically the lead given by their father. They worked shorter hours; and they exerted themselves less to obtain new practical ideas.'[1]

Secondly, there is the simultaneous occurrence of high unemployment, high inflation, and incipient protectionism that has affected most western countries since the early 1970s – 'stagflation' – which has put a check to many hopes after a generation of postwar prosperity.

The recurrent inflationary disorders, the depth of recent recessions, and the troubled and unsatisfactory nature of most recoveries have been problems common to many countries. But, partly because they were superimposed on an economy which in any case had a low growth rate, they affected Britain with particular severity and gave rise to an orgy of pessimism and self-doubt among British leaders. It was this phenomenon, so surprising in a country of such long-established political culture, which impressed many foreign visitors and which made the diagnosis of the 'condition of England' such a growth industry in the United States.

The so-called British sickness is thus a mixture of different maladies – slow growth, a severe recent attack of stagflation and accompanying political strains. Although I hope to find common elements in the explanation of these phenomena, it is first necessary to distinguish them from each other.

Table 6: UK long-term growth rates, measured by real
gross domestic product per head of population

	Average of 16 Advanced Countries*	United Kingdom
Growth % per annum		
1870-1976	1.8	1.3
1870-1913	1.5	1.0
1913-1950	1.1	1.0
1950-1970	3.8	2.3
1970-1976	2.4	2.0
1976-1981	1.6	0.5
GDP per head in 1970 US dollars		
1870	$666	$956
1976	$4258	$3583
1981	$4610	$3674
Ratio of UK to average GDP per head		
1870	–	1.44
1976	–	0.84
1981	–	0.80

* Arithmetical average of United States, Canada, Australia, Japan, United Kingdom, Germany, France, Italy, Switzerland, Netherlands, Belgium, Sweden, Denmark, Norway, Austria, Finland.

Note: The only country with a slower growth rate than the United Kingdom over the century was Australia where GDP per head in 1976 was 1.19 times that of the United Kingdom. US growth over the century 1870-1976 was 1.9 per cent per annum, the Japanese 2.5 per cent, the German 2.0 per cent and the French 1.9 per cent.

Source: Angus Maddison: *Phases of Capitalist Development*, 1977 Banca Nazionale del Lavoro Q Rev 103. Financial Times Statistics Division

Long-run problems

The lag in British growth rates goes back at least a century. One estimate made by Angus Maddison[2] suggests that the average level of output per head in sixteen industrial countries rose sixfold between 1870 and 1976, but only fourfold in the United Kingdom. Estimates going back that far have, of course, a heroic dimension, but neither the study of alternative estimates, nor that of subperiods, nor attempted corrections for working hours, upsets the relative orders of magnitude. The estimates are of course of output, not of happiness or welfare.

In 1870 the United Kingdom was the second richest country in terms of output per head among the sixteen, surpassed only by Australia which had a uniquely favourable ratio of labour to land and natural resources. Later the United States overtook Britain. But during the nineteenth century and the first three-fifths of the twentieth century the United Kingdom remained ahead of nearly all the main European countries, and the low growth rate was a matter for concern only to sophists, calculators, and economists.

Since 1960, however, an absolute gap has emerged – whether measured by output, or real wages, or whether the comparisons are made at market or purchasing parity exchange rates, or by the fallible impressions of personal travel. One comparison of gross domestic product (GDP) per head at purchasing power exchange rates suggests that by 1973 most European Economic Community countries were 30 to 40 per cent ahead of Britain.[3]

International corporations are in a good position, compared to merely national concerns, to minimise productivity differentials between plants in different countries. Yet a study of such international corporations in the 1970s showed net output per head to be over 50 per cent higher in German and French plants than in corresponding plants in the United Kingdom. Only about half the Anglo-German difference could be attributed to product mix, scale, or capital equipment. The remainder was due to 'differences in efficiency'.[4] Much more lurid comparisons could be given by selective evidence from particular industries, or anecdotally.

Recent problems

Although the lag in the British growth rate is historically deep-seated, the country's special troubles with jobs and prices are, by contrast, recent. The 1949 devaluation of sterling was part of a common adjustment of the parities of most war-devastated countries relative to the United States dollar. Between then and 1967 there was little out of the ordinary in the UK macroeconomic experience. The British inflation rate was only very slightly above the average of the twenty-four nations of the OECD. Registered UK unemployment averaged scarcely 2 per cent; and even in the worst recessions, seasonally adjusted adult unemployment rarely touched 3 per cent.

British inflation rates began to rise substantially above the average of industrial countries only in the decade after the 1967 devaluation of sterling. It was in the second half of that decade, from 1972 to 1977, that British inflation really soared. This was a highly inflationary period for the world economy, but while the OECD price level rose by 60 per cent in five years, the British level rose by 120 per cent or twice as much.

The 1970s also saw a reversal of comparative unemployment experience. The British unemployment rate, put onto common definitions, climbed by late 1977 to about 7 per cent and to over 12 per cent by 1982. Thus there was for a time neither price stability nor low unemployment to set off against a low-growth performance. It was not a coincidence that political and social stability seemed threatened in the mid-1970s. I am using the past tense because on the inflation front, at least, this period could be over, and the United Kingdom may no longer diverge from the OECD average.

Suggested explanations

Why has British performance fallen so far behind other countries? A great deal of fun could be had from the many and often contradictory suggestions offered. Both the inequities of British society and excessive egalitarian zeal have been blamed; so too have inadequate competition and insufficient government intervention. Some people cite the enormous institutional obstacles to change and others the excessive ease with which policies are reversed under a two-party winner-takes-all system; and one could go on indefinitely.

Some of the suggested explanations of British economic performance may shed light on recent years, but cannot conceivably explain the long-term lag in growth rates. Some dwell on transitory phenomena already disappearing or unlikely to last. Some are factually dubious on any basis whatever.

For instance, a once popular diagnosis was that British growth was held back by cyclical fluctuations in output, caused by stop-go financial policies. Numerous studies have, however, shown that deviations in UK output, measured in relation to trend, were less than in most other countries.[5]

A related explanation was low investment, especially in manufacturing, since World War II. Close examination reveals, however, that gross investment in manufacturing, as a percentage of value added, was no higher in Germany than in the United Kingdom. Where the United Kingdom did come clearly at the bottom of the league was in the effectiveness of investment in terms of output generally. It is therefore not surprising that profitability and the return on investment were low by international standards. (The ordering in the second column of Table 7 is still roughly appropriate.)

A contemporary vogue diagnosis is 'deindustrialisation',

Table 7: Investment in manufacturing 1958-1972[a]

	Investment Ratio[b] %	Increase in net output[c] per unit of investment. Index nos. UK = 100
UK	13.0	100
USA	12.2	145
Germany	13.0	190
Sweden	14.4	145
France	16.3	163
Japan	24.6	157

Notes: [a] Or nearest comparable period to eliminate cyclical distortions
       [b] Manufacturing gross investment as % of value added
       [c] Incremental output to capital ratio

Source: Confederation of British Industry, *Britain Means Business 1977*, 38 (1977).

The British Instance

Table 8: Changes in employment in the UK
(in thousands of employees)

	1959	1959 to 1971	1971 to 1976	1976 to 1981
Private Industrial Sector	9137	−296	−755	−1251
Other Private Sector	6912	+175	+396	+533
Public Sector (non-manufacturing)	5108	+721	+817	−79
Total Employees	21417	+705	+421	−834
Unemployment	512	+184	+569	+1130

Source: Central Statistical Office

which has been used to describe a pathological fall in the ratio of industrial to total employment. But comparative international figures make it clear that if this is a disease at all, it is a very new one. The United States, Sweden, the Netherlands and Belgium all had falls in the ratio of industrial to total employment in 1965-1975 of comparable size to Britain's. Germany and France just about maintained the same manufacturing ratio, while Japan and Italy were exceptional in increasing theirs.[6]

One aspect of a relatively slow growth rate has been the fall in the British share of world trade or world exports of manufactures. Repeated investigations have shown that this decline cannot be explained by any special features either of the commodity composition of British exports or of the market outlets for them. It is simply that if the United Kingdom has a lower growth rate than competitor countries, one would expect, other things being equal, a declining share of world exports relative to those countries' share. It is thus a consequence rather than a cause.

There is a more specific doctrine relating Britain's slow growth to trading performance. This is that the country has a special difficulty in earning enough overseas to support a full-employment level of activity. The doctrine is the theme song of the annual reviews of the Cambridge Economic Policy

Group. The essential argument is that even if exchange rates move so as to keep British money costs competitive with those of other countries, imports will be too high and exports too low to maintain full employment. This would imply that British products are not merely inferior in design, performance, or delivery, but are continually deteriorating in these respects. The Cambridge group's case rests on the very strong assumption that the annual fall in terms of trade required to stay in equilibrium would be so steep and meet such strong union resistance that it could not be brought about without an inflationary explosion.

The whole diagnosis of output being limited by a demand or balance-of-payments constraint is open to serious question. The rise in import penetration took place in a series of jumps during periods of boom or supply bottlenecks or during periods of sterling overvaluation. The increase in British exports, relative to any given increase in world real incomes, has been substantially less than that of exports of other countries; but it is disputable whether such ratios are a true measure of the income elasticity of demand for British exports. Failures on the supply side – even when the unemployment statistics have been high – have limited the response of British industry to increases in overseas demand.

Spending and taxes

The level of government spending is also often blamed for recent poor performance. We should, however, be very careful in citing figures of the ratio of public spending to the national product, as different definitions produce widely different figures. The United Kingdom is in the middle rather than at the top of the international league, despite an exceptional bulge in the early 1970s.

Was there a dangerous switch of workers from private manufacturing to public services? Up to 1971 the shifts closely paralleled trends in other countries. The shift into public-service employment after 1971 up to 1975 seemed more worrying, but we should, however, note that of the 850,000 workers who entered public-service employment between 1971 and 1975, nearly 650,000 were females, over half part-time. It is stretching credulity to suppose that these women and girls would otherwise have been employed in factories at

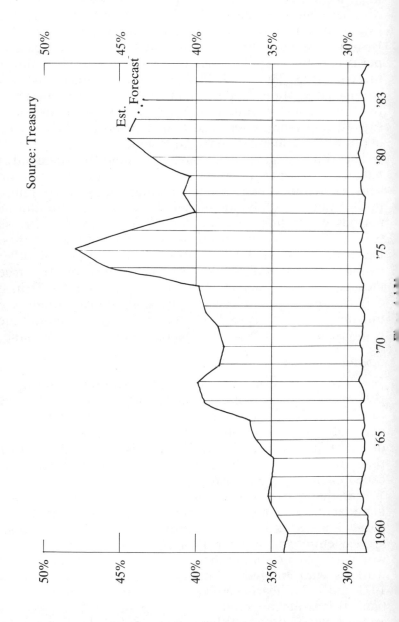

Chart 11: UK public expenditure as percentage of GDP at market prices

Source: Treasury

a conventionally acceptable wage. The rise in public employment has in any case been subsequently reversed.

Let me not be misunderstood. Large parts of public expenditure are not devoted to genuinely public goods and do little to transfer resources to the poor. These expenditures take place only because of the imperfections of the political market. But there is no need to claim that public spending is (a) out of control, (b) higher than in other countries, or (c) in itself a likely cause of economic breakdown or political collapse.

Not surprisingly, international tax comparisons lead to a similar picture. On comparable definitions, the United Kingdom has a tax burden of about 42 per cent of GNP, half-way down the list just below France and Germany, higher than that of the United States, but a good deal less than the Scandinavian countries. In these comparisons, social security levies are included with taxation, where they properly belong.

Table 9: Taxes and social security contributions as a percentage of gross national product at factor cost

	1970		1975		1980	
	Percentage	Rank	Percentage	Rank	Percentage	Rank
Norway	48	1	54	1	59	1
Sweden	46	2	49	2	55	2
Netherlands	42	5	49	3	52	3
Austria	43	4	46	4	49	4
France	41	6	42	6	48	5
Belgium	39	8	45	5	48	6
German Fed. Rep. .	39	7	42	7	44	7
United Kingdom ...	43	3	41	8	42	8
Finland	36	10	40	9	39	9
Italy	30	12	31	13	38	10
Canada	37	9	37	10	36	11
Australia	28	13	33	11	35	12
United States	33	11	32	12	33	13
Switzerland	25	14	30	14	31	14
Japan	21	15	24	15	28	15

Source: Economic Trends, London, HMSO, December 1982

Table 10: Impact of UK personal tax

Year	Effective rate of income tax plus national insurance contributions (married man with two children on average earnings) (%)
1964-65	9.7
1970-71	21.3
1973-74	21.6
1976-77	26.3
1977-78	24.1
1982-83	30.2*

Source: Hansard

* Family also received 8.8% in child benefits in that year.

We come nearer to the source of complaint if we notice that the United Kingdom raises a relatively high proportion of revenue from taxes on households; and the *personal* tax burden did rise sharply in the middle 1970s. Most of the increase in the personal tax *burden* was due not to any increase in tax *rates*, but to the failure to index the tax starting points and higher rate brackets against inflation until the very late 1970s.

For most of the postwar period the real trouble was, however, not the average tax rates, but the very high marginal rates, both at the top and at the bottom of the income scale. The top marginal rates were not only higher until 1979 than in other industrial countries, but were reached at a much lower level of income. They were entirely political taxes. The revenue collected at the top was trivial in statistical terms; and the real effect was likely to lower revenue, thus reducing what was available for redistribution. As important, from the point of view of the British growth rate, was the diversion of scarce energy and talent into trying to convert income into capital or into benefits in kind not taxable at these rates.

What proportion of the lag in Britain's growth rate do these tax rates explain? We can only guess, but two facts are worth pondering. One is that the confiscatory marginal tax rates of the mid-1970s cannot explain any of the lag before World War

II. Secondly, the western country which most nearly approached the United Kingdom in the severity of its tax progression, Sweden, has been much higher in the growth league for most of the postwar period. Despite a recent setback, Sweden has a level of GNP per head which is comparable to that of the United States.

State intervention

Nor can we really ascribe the UK growth lag to any generalised fault known as state intervention. For the greater part of the postwar period, there is no evidence that there was more state intervention in the marketplace in the United Kingdom than in other western countries. During the 1950s and most of the 1960s – even during the Labour governments of 1964-70 – most industrial decisions were made in the marketplace. Moreover, among industrial economies there is little connection between growth rates and the degree of state involvement in the economy. Germany has prospered under free-market doctrines, while Japan and France have often prospered under a sort of right-wing *dirigisme* – a common front between government and industrial organisations designed to bypass the market wherever possible. At the level of specific industries, agriculture has been subject to more government intervention than almost any other industry in most western countries. Yet it has been characterised by a high rate of productivity growth.

A generalisation worth venturing is that a country can get away either with a great deal of state intervention or with a great deal of egalitarian social policy, but not with the two together. Sweden, for instance, had a high level of social services and fiscal redistribution but, until well into the 1970s, was a model market economy. Industrial policy was geared to encouraging workers to shift as quickly as possible to the most profitable industries, and investment was guided by world markets rather than by government planning. In France and Japan, on the other hand, 'planning' was combined with a highly unequal distribution of income and the bulk of taxation tended to come from sales and turnover levies.

One further tentative generalisation may be suggested. The more democratic a country's institutions, the more likely is government economic intervention to hold back rather than

encourage growth. Growth depends on change; and change
can be disturbing. The general citizen has a dispersed stake in
change and efficiency spread over thousands of different
decisions. Particular industries and interest groups have a
much more concentrated interest in stopping change or in
securing inefficient decisions for their own narrow benefit. In
a highly democratic society, geographically or professionally
concentrated groups have much more influence than do
general citizen interests. A concrete example of what I have in
mind was the decision of Conservative Premier Harold
Macmillan in a conflict over the location of a steel mill
between Scotland and Wales at the beginning of the 1960s.
The resolution was to have two smaller, suboptimal mills, one
in each area.

In its time the steel-mill decision was untypical. Most such
decisions would then have been taken in the marketplace.
After 1972 there was a notable increase in the quantity of
government intervention in the United Kingdom and a
deterioration in quality. We have had a multiplication of
discretionary subsidies to individual concerns with no realistic
prospects of paying their own way and with no genuine
spillover benefits to justify subsidy. The standard of living of
UK consumers was reduced and the development of poorer
countries impeded by putting barriers on low-cost imports. In
these respects the Thatcher Government made much less
difference than commonly supposed. It was, if anything, even
firmer than its predecessors on Japanese and Third World
imports. It did however start reversing the union legislation of
the mid-1970s, which seemed almost deliberately designed to
make worse the pricing out of work of the less skilled, the less
able, the victims of prejudice, the young, the old, women, and
coloured immigrants – all in the name of high-sounding
principles such as 'the rate for the job'.

Incomes policy and inflation

Perverse regulation, especially in the labour market, has
increased in most European countries. If it has at times been
worse in the United Kingdom, it has been from a desire to
keep the unions sweet for pay controls. Indeed many of the
occasional perversities of British economic policy have
stemmed from the belief that inflation must be fought by

regulation of specific pay settlements. To create a climate in which the unions will tolerate such intervention has been the object of much government activity, when an incomes policy has been in operation, which it was during most of the 1960s and 1970s. The UK seemed to be experiencing a respite from attempted pay controls in the 1980s, although it would be unwise to make firm predictions about its duration. To obtain support for pay restraint in 'incomes policy' phases, governments have introduced (often against their better judgment) price control and high marginal tax rates, and have expressed a special sensitivity to union leaders' views on many aspects of policy. The 1972-79 period of especially perverse intervention began, not with a change of government, but with the conversion of the Heath Conservative government to pay and price controls.

This conversion, and the emphasis of subsequent governments on pay restraint, can itself be explained by the fact that the United Kingdom had a much larger jump in inflation rates than most other countries in the great inflation which hit the western world in the 1970s. Sudden and severe inflation nearly always increases the pressure for direct pay or price controls, however questionable their economic logic.

The exceptionally severe and explosive British inflation was, however, both a superficial and an ephemeral aspect of the British disease. It lasted, as already mentioned, for only a decade, and its passing may lessen the temptation to some policy perversities. The main enduring temptation to misguided intervention which arrived with the 1970s arose of course from an understandable preoccupation with soaring unemployment. Severe recession or stagnation, whether or not combined with inflation, increases pressure for make-work policies. The vogue of ideas such as the National Enterprise Board and 'Planning Agreements', or the ability of politicians to dress up make-work policies as industrial regeneration, together with the recurrent bouts of pessimism about the future of capitalism, are all characteristic of severe inflation or slump, and still more of the combination of both.

Unemployment has much intensified since the 1960s, but inflation in Britain fell back to the OECD average or less in the late 1970s and remained there apart from a temporary resurgence in 1979-80. Some of the improvement was due to the effect of North Sea oil on sterling, but much the greater part reflects the monetary and fiscal guidelines eventually adopted by the British governments – both Labour and Conservative.

More important is the fact that the lesson has been learned from the inflationary period. By this I do not mean that inflation has been conquered or that some ideal monetary rule will be followed, but simply that the British authorities have now had irrefutable evidence that beyond a very limited point creating money to finance budgetary deficits leads to an inflationary crisis rather than the much-desired real growth.

The great temptation to monetary overexpansion comes from the temporarily benign effect of such expansion on output and employment, and the delayed effect on prices. Even this temporary gain to output is very much smaller than it used to be in the United Kingdom, if indeed it exists at all. This is partly because the foreign exchange and other financial markets are now fully alert to monetary indicators. An expansion of the money stock, or mere *fear* of a future budget deficit likely to be financed in this way, has a much more immediate effect than it used to have on the exchange rate and on inflationary expectations, and little if any of the stimulus affects output. A temporary trade-off between inflation and employment is nowadays more likely to exist in a continental economy with little experience of rapid inflation than in an open economy with such experience.

The argument so far

Let me summarise so far. The lag in the British growth rate goes back at least a century, although it took on a new dimension in about 1960 when the level as well as the growth rate of British real income began to fall behind similarly placed European states. In addition the United Kingdom has shared in the poor output and employment performance of the post-1973 economic cycles. But I have suggested that British inflationary excesses were ephemeral and therefore not fundamental aspects of the British disease. Many other much-criticised British policies are also followed to a comparable degree by other governments, working under similar political pressures. Moreover, these errors are too recent or temporary to explain the longer-term weaknesses. The tax rates of the 1970s hardly shed light on weaknesses of British management which worried Lord Haldane before World War I.

Can anything be said, then, of the deep-seated lag in British growth rates? And does British experience throw any light on the stagflation problem, which still remains serious, even if it is likely henceforth to show itself in Britain more in stagnant output and employment than in runaway inflation?

These broader questions bring us to two subjects which are always raised in any discussion of long-run British economic performance. These are the class system and the trade unions.

The class system

Contrary to travellers' tales, the United Kingdom is *not* more stratified than other societies in any obvious statistical sense. Income disparities, even before tax, are less in the United Kingdom than in the United States, Japan, France, or Germany. Rates of occupational mobility between father's and son's occupation are substantial – over 60 per cent of men in the top occupational classes have parents two or more classes below them. Indeed 40 per cent are the sons of manual workers or lower-grade technicians. There is at least as much upward mobility in the United Kingdom as in the United States; and a greater proportion of British university students have working-class backgrounds than is the case on the Continent of Europe. Nor are these overnight developments. Economic divisions in the society have been lessening since the turn of the century if not earlier.[7]

Yet, there is a sense in which Britain is more class-ridden than other capitalist or mixed economies. It is to be found in the features of British society furthest removed from pecuniary matters. It lies in such things as emphasis on the social pecking order, concern with subtle differences of speech and manner, and the educational segregation from an early age of a so-called elite in fee-paying and often unpleasant residential institutions, strangely known as public schools. These features have given us the British novel; and they are a boon to the travel industry. If anyone doubts that they add to the bitterness as well as the gaiety of British life, he should take the first opportunity to see – or at least read –

John Osborne's play of the 1950s, *Look Back in Anger*.

One important feature of this type of class division is that it cuts right across the higher echelons of society. Most British managers have not had the traditional upper-class education; and a captain of industry can feel socially inferior over a glass of sherry with a country parson or a retired army major. The old school conservative and the socialist reformer come together in a common dislike of merely commercial values. In all societies people care about their status in the eyes of their fellowmen. In Britain, however, social status has less to do with merely making money than in almost any other western society.*

Union power

The other old-established British institution, which needs to be mentioned, is the trade-union movement. But here again we must be careful of misdiagnosis. The number of days lost in British industry through strikes, even in the troublesome period of the early 1970s, was less than in the United States or Canada (although more than in Germany or France). The quantities involved are insignificant – just over one day per man-year on average. Strikes are overwhelmingly in large concerns. Well over 90 per cent of workers in establishments employing less than 500 do not have any experience of strikes from one year to the next.[8]

Monopolistic union practices are a different matter. Their effect on productivity is difficult to quantify, although the

---

* The low status attached to pecuniary success in industry in Britain is the theme of Martin Wiener's *English Culture and the Decline of the Intellectual Spirit, 1850-1980* (Cambridge University Press, 1981). This volume became almost a cult book in management education circles in Britain. Professor Wiener traces several interrelated attitudes hostile to individual success: the contempt expressed for material success, 'getting on' and profit maximisation as individual motives; hostility towards capitalism and even more the market system; the low status accorded to industry, compared with finance and the professions (let alone the grander pursuits of the farmer or landed gentry); the exaltation of the country above the town in literature, essays and the musings of politicians across the political spectrum; the reverence for the past over the present and future; and boasting about the national dislike for progress and change.

These aspects of English life have been satirised and condemned in countless books and newspaper articles, which became a flood just before the advent of Sir Harold Wilson's first Government in 1964, which was pledged to the white heat of a technological revolution that never occurred.

Wiener's main contribution to this much-traversed territory is his detailed account of the gentrification of the industrial class, which reached its peak of influence at the time of the Great Exhibition of 1851, but two or three decades later was mainly concerned to merge with the traditional upper middle classes. In general, however, the book is good on description but short on analysis of the reasons for the syndromes depicted.

It also seems to me that the author misses the nature of the problem. If people dislike lives devoted to getting and spending, if they prefer the quiet of their gardens to the business or technological rat race, that is their affair. These preferences only become a political or economic 'malaise' when they are combined with material aspirations incompatible with them. It is this combination which Professor Wiener fails to explain or even highlight.

international productivity comparisons cited earlier may give a clue. A good analysis of the logic of unionism was provided in the 1940s by the American economist, Henry Simons. He shows that unions derive their influence over wages from the power to exclude and that the main losers are other workers. He cites severe restrictions on entry such as:

> . . . high initiation fees, excessive periods of apprenticeship and restrictions upon numbers of apprentices, barriers to movements between related trades, and, of course, make-work restrictions, cost-increasing working rules, and prohibition of cost-reducing innovations, not to mention racial and sex discrimination. . . .

> There is every prospect that opportunities for collective, collusive, monopolistic action in particular labour markets will increase indefinitely wherever organization is possible. This prospect alone suffices to explain the ominous decline of private investment and the virtual disappearance of venturesome new enterprise. . . .

> Investors now face nearly all the disagreeable uncertainties of investors in a free-market world plus the prospect that labor organizations will appropriate most or all of the earnings which would otherwise accrue if favorable contingencies materialized.[9]

Even this is not the worst of it. Partial unionism is 'a device by which the strong may raise themselves higher by pressing down the weak'. It makes 'high wages higher and low wages lower'. This works when 'everybody does not try it or when few have effective power. Attempts to apply it universally are incompatible with order.' Simons goes on:

> In an economy of intricate division of labor, every large organized group is in a position at any time to disrupt or to stop the whole flow of social income; and the system must soon break down if groups persist in exercising that power or if they must continuously be bribed to forgo its disastrous exercise. . . . The dilemma here is not peculiar to our present economic order, it must appear in any kind of system. This minority-monopoly problem would be quite as serious for a democratic socialism as it is for the mixed individualist-collectivist system of the present. It is

the rock on which our present system is most likely to crack up; and it is the rock on which democratic socialism would be destroyed if it could ever come into being at all.

He did not pretend to have a remedy but spoke about the possibility of 'an awful dilemma: democracy cannot live with tight occupational monopolies; and it cannot destroy them, once they attain great power, without destroying itself in the process.' His remarks can be regarded as an elaboration of Dicey's contrast at the beginning of the twentieth century between the effects of the individual pursuit of self-interest and its collective pursuit.[10] This is the distinction glossed over by British trade union leaders when they say with monotonous regularity: 'If there is to be a free-for-all, we are part of this all.'

Democracy and interest groups

Simons's forebodings were followed in the United States by over three decades of unparalleled prosperity in which the membership and influence of US trade unions declined. Unfortunately, a premature prediction is not necessarily a wrong one. We still do not know whether the gloomy forebodings of Dicey and Simons were averted or merely postponed.

The underlying question concerns the impact, not merely of unions, but of all producer and special-interest groups on the functioning of the economic system which has been a recurrent theme of this volume. The problem is not one of inflation, as so often wrongly supposed, but in part of unemployment. If the total effect of the monopolistic activities of producer groups is to price so many people out of work that the resulting unemployment rate is higher than the electorate will tolerate, then our system of political economy is doomed.[11] If the government in such a situation tries to spend its way into full employment, the result will be not just inflation, but accelerating inflation. Despite the apparent calm of Britain in the prolonged afterglow of the Falklands campaign, we do not know if the sustainable unemployment rate is too high for democratic stability or, if it is, what the role of union-type monopoly is in making it so. The fact that we cannot rule out the pessimistic hypothesis is itself important.

The Simons quotation also raises the question of the effects of uncertain property rights on investment. Investment can take place under state ownership, under workers' cooperatives, or under untrammelled private ownership. The private enterprise system can probably adapt to the capture by unions of a large proportion of the return on new investment – provided that proportion is predictable and stable. The main eventual effect might then be higher profit margins and higher gross returns. But a system of confused and unpredictable property rights under a nominally private enterprise system is highly discouraging to investment – and thereby also depressing to employment in the longer run.

It is difficult to pronounce on the breakdown hypothesis in general terms.[12] A great deal depends on things such as the proportion of the population unionised – which is much greater in the United Kingdom than in the United States – as well as on the degree of toleration of undercutting of union suppliers by others. Much also hangs on the electorate's toleration of higher unemployment in today's circumstances, on which premature judgments could easily turn out to be wrong.

Moreover, we should not conceive the producer-group threat too narrowly. Collective action to secure real wages incompatible with full employment may come not just through the strike threat alone, but also through political action – import price ceilings, minimum wage laws and farm support are only some of the more obvious areas. The uncertainty and insecurity of property rights which Simons feared can be the result of regulatory agencies or of legislative hyperactivity as well as of unions. The real danger is that the end result of action taken by people through collective activity will be unacceptable to the same people in their capacity of consumers and voters – a perverse invisible hand. The fact that Simons was premature in his forebodings in the case of the United States does not mean that they can be dismissed.

Why have restrictive policies, not only by unions, but by all producer groups, had more impact in the United Kingdom than in many other countries? Professor Mancur Olson[13] has an interesting hypothesis derived from his theory of comparative growth rates (summarised in the last chapter).

The central conclusion that Olson draws is that 'the longer the period in which a country has had a modern industrial pattern of common interest and at the same time democratic freedom of economic organization without upheaval and disorganization, the greater the extent to which its growth rate will be retarded by organized interests.' Thus it is not surprising that the British disease should have come first to the country which pioneered the industrial revolution and had the longest record of civic freedom and settled institutions.

But there is no need to end this chapter on a fatalistic note. As the output gap widens between a slowly growing country held back by restrictive interest groups and other countries employing best-practice techniques, the incentive to catch up also becomes larger. The more atrophied become a country's techniques and habits, the greater becomes the return to innovation. The gains can become so great that it may be possible to make agreements to share them with the restrictive interest groups. Moreover, restrictive practices are never of the same severity across the economy; and if innovation is blocked in traditional or well-organised sectors, talent and capital will drift to newer areas, where group loyalties have not yet 'solved' the free-rider problem. In the last resort, too, the returns to political entrepreneurship from trying to change the institutional or political rules in favour of better economic performance may become so great that the changes are made.

The conclusion to which I am leading is not that the United Kingdom is about to have an economic miracle, but that its problems are from now on likely to become typical of mixed advanced democratic economies in general. The British disease pertains not to a particular country but to a stage in political and economic development. The disease is that of collective action by special interest groups preventing a reasonably full use being made of our economic resources. There is some hope that this disease, like many others, may eventually produce its own cure.

11 Breaking the Mould

An early beginning; The post-1979 traumas; Monetary policy;
Sterling and pay; The political dimension; The main mistakes;
The medium term strategy; Ideology and policy; Supply-side
Thatcherism; 'The resolute approach'; Social market policies;
Political improvement.

An early beginning

The Government intends in the years ahead a continuing
and substantial reduction of the share of resources taken by
public expenditure. It is also part of this strategy to reduce
the public sector borrowing requirement so as to establish
monetary conditions which will help the growth of output
and the control of inflation. The Government sees this
strategy as the basis of a three-year programme that will
firmly establish the recovery of the nation's economy and
which will also allow the UK to make its proper
contribution to the stability and prosperity of the world.

This is a quotation from a statement which goes on to give
figures of how the government plans to reduce public
spending and the public sector borrowing requirement as
proportions of the national product, and details of the
expected decline in the growth of the monetary aggregates.
The statement goes on to say that reduction of personal
taxation will have high priority if any budget margin is
available as 'my own belief is that present levels have proved
discouraging to effort and efficacy'.

Is this a section of a British budget speech made after Mrs
Margaret Thatcher became Prime Minister in 1979 or in the
early 1980s when the reduction of inflation became a main
priority? Not at all. This piece of firm no-nonsense
Thatcherism with its doctrinaire hostages to fortune is a
quotation from a statement of Mr Denis Healey, Chancellor
of the previous Labour Government, in his Letter of Intent to
the IMF in December 1976.

Whenever I spoke to international or British gatherings on

'Thatcherism' in the first few years after 1979, the audiences were prepared for an attack or a defence. But they were taken aback by the contention that however much they were denounced by Labour in opposition, the most characteristic features of financial Thatcherism were also pursued by the last Labour Government from 1976 to 1979, with only modest backsliding in the period approaching the 1979 election.

The post-1979 traumas

It is far from my intention to deny that major changes took place during the Parliament that began in 1979 and that came to an end in 1983. The word 'Thatcherite' came into vogue as a description for a new style of policy, intended as a conscious break with the postwar era. At the very same time a new political grouping was formed by an 'Alliance' of Social Democrats, who had broken away from the Labour Party in 1981, together with the Liberals. Although the Thatcherites and Alliance supporters were often in bitter confrontation with each other, they shared a common desire to 'break the mould' (to use the Social Democrat slogan), in the one case in economic policy and in the other in the constitutional and political sphere.

The prospect of easing the politico-economic problems described in the previous chapter depended heavily on the interaction, and even mutual irritation, of the Thatcherites and the Alliance. A few members of the Alliance sensed this when they privately spoke of the need for 'Thatcherism with a human face and more intelligently applied'. But the majority of Alliance activists were so bemused by the left-right spectrum and ritual denunciation of 'monetarism' that they thought their natural bedfellows were in the Heath wing of the Conservative Party.

Monetary policy

But it would be a great mistake to link these wider issues too closely with the evolution of macroeconomic policy after the Conservative victory of May 1979. For by almost any of the best known indicators the policies followed by the new government were a continuation of those followed by the Callaghan-Healey regime from 1976 onwards. The incoming Conservative Government was frequently criticised for its

Table 11: UK economic indicators 1970-1983

	'70	'71	'72	'73	'74	'75	'76	'77	'78	'79	'80	'81	'82	'83†
	% change in annual average over previous year													
RPI*	6.4	9.4	7.1	9.2	16.1	24.2	16.5	15.8	8.3	13.4	18.1	11.9	8.6	5.0
GDP at current market prices	9.6	12.2	10.8	15.0	13.8	26.1	18.8	15.5	15.0	17.3	16.8	9.4	8.8	8.0
GDP at constant prices	2.0	1.5	2.6	7.2	−1.9	−0.9	2.6	2.4	3.8	1.9	−2.1	−2.2	0.8	2.5
Manufacturing production	0.4	−0.5	2.6	8.4	−1.7	−6.2	1.4	1.6	1.0	0.3	−8.5	−6.3	−1.2	3.0
Sterling M1	6.4	11.8	13.6	8.7	4.8	15.6	13.8	14.4	20.2	11.5	4.9	10.0	7.8	
Sterling M3	6.2	11.9	22.5	25.9	15.6	8.8	8.3	8.0	15.3	12.6	16.6	16.0	11.9	
OECD consumer prices	5.6	5.3	4.7	7.8	13.5	11.3	8.6	8.9	7.9	9.8	12.9	10.6	7.3	6.0
OECD real GDP	3.9	3.7	5.5	6.3	0.7	−0.5	5.3	3.7	3.8	3.4	1.3	1.2	−0.5	2.0
Annual Averages														
Interbank rate (3 month)	7½	6⁵/₁₆	6¹³/₁₆	11⅛	13½	10¾	11¾	8⅛	9½	14	16¾	14⅛	12³/₈	
UK unemployment exc. school leavers (000s)	N/A	774	826	591	591	902	1229	1313	1299	1227	1561	2420	2793‡	3060

* Retail Prices Index
† forecast
‡ new basis

Source: Third Report from the House of Commons Treasury Committee, 'Monetary Policy', updated by Financial Times Statistics Division

severe monetary policy. Yet in terms of the broadly based aggregate Sterling M3, under which targets were set by governments of both parties until 1982, the rate of increase was slower under Labour for the years 1975-78 than under the Conservatives' first years, 1979-82.

Various notorious distortions reduced these monetary aggregates under Labour and increased them under the Conservatives. The removal of controls over the growth of bank deposits (the 'corset'), the abolition of exchange controls, and innovations such as the move of the banks into the home loan market in the first Conservative years of office, were bound to affect the meaning of the monetary aggregates. So the correct argument is not that money became easier, merely that there was no sudden change towards greater severity.

A glance at interest rates might at first sight suggest that domestic monetary policy was very much tighter. The table shows interbank rate at nearly 17 per cent in 1980. It was, however, still lower than the rate of inflation. Real interest rates (gross of tax) did not become substantially positive until 1981-82.

A similar story is told by fiscal policy. The Public Sector Borrowing Requirement (PSBR), for all its imperfections, was used as a guide by both Labour and Conservative governments. Mr Healey had been looking forward to a continuing gradual reduction of the PSBR as a proportion of the Gross Domestic Product. Yet it was slightly higher in 1980-81, the second year of a Conservative chancellor, than in the last year of Mr Healey. Public expenditure also rose in the first three years of Conservative rule, before levelling off or dipping slightly (see Chart 11 in the previous chapter). There are indeed arguments that the PSBR should have been allowed to rise more in 1979-81, and subsequently come down more slowly, in view of the severe recession; but they could not have been supported from the practice of the previous Labour Government.

The budget of 1981 was seen by some as a climacteric, when taxes were raised in the face of severe recession and when policy became truly 'Thatcherite'. If so, it was by inadvertence. The intention was to resume the path of gradual reduction in the PSBR as proportion of the national

Chart 12: UK unemployment and vacancies (3-month moving average: seasonally adjusted)

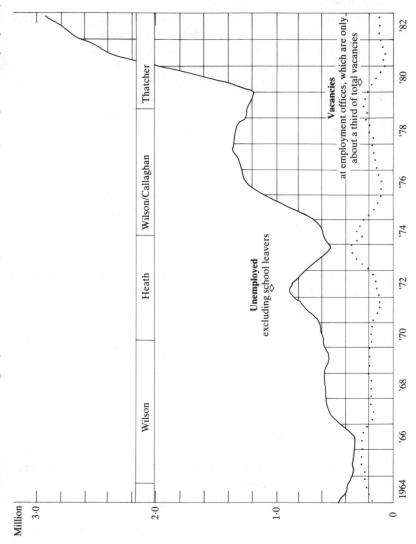

product. Treasury advisers thought they had made allowance for the recession in budgeting for a higher PSBR for 1981-82 than that set out in the Medium Term Financial Strategy (MTFS) formulated the previous year. But this was a subtlety that failed to penetrate outside the dusty yellow corridors of the New Public Offices which house the Treasury and did not even penetrate into every room there.

The impression of 'tightening up' was increased (a) by the abortive revolt of a group of Conservative ministers and MPs glorying in the name of 'wets', (b) the faster than predicted rise in unemployment (the Treasury's output forecasts were reached, but its productivity forecasts were much exceeded) and (c) the £2 billion undershooting of the PSBR behind its planned level in the 1981-82 financial year. The main aim of the government in tightening fiscal policy was not, however, to restrict further overall, but to shift the monetary-fiscal mix so that interest rates could fall. Similar advice had been showered on President Reagan (who took office in February 1981) but the American President's failure to take the advice and his long connivance at large budget deficits delayed the fall in interest rates in other countries too.

Sterling and pay

It is not however to the minutiae of domestic policy that we have to go for the main clue towards everything, both good and bad, that happened in the macroeconomic field in the first two or three years of the Thatcher Government. The responsibility lies with two events. First there was the wage explosion which began a little earlier than people suppose. Increases in average earnings, which had been at 9 per cent in 1977, start to rise to 13-15 per cent by 1978-9 as the Callaghan pay policy disintegrated, and then took off under the Tories to the dizzy heights of 20 per cent in 1980 before subsiding to an underlying rate which by 1983 was probably slightly over 7 per cent.

The 1979-80 pay explosion was due not only to the notorious pay awards of the Clegg Commission, set up to buy off the public sector strikes in the 1979 winter of discontent (before the election), which both main political parties pledged themselves to honour. It was due even more to the widespread belief, either that financial policy would turn 'accommodative' to finance Clegg-size awards throughout the economy and/or that a pay freeze was imminent. While in other countries unions accepted that wages could not keep pace with prices during the second oil price shock, no such restraint was shown in the UK until union leaders learned by bitter experience and millions of people had been priced out of work.

The second main event took place in the foreign exchange markets. At the very same time that labour costs were soaring above those of the UK's competitors', sterling took off into the stratosphere. In January 1981 the trade weighted average for sterling was 25 per cent higher than two years before. The rise of sterling was more an event than a policy, reflecting a variety of factors. There was the impact of North Sea oil, not only directly on trade but even more through the increased attractions of the currency of a country self-sufficient in oil. There was also the so-called 'Thatcher factor' (akin to the subsequent Reagan factor for the dollar).

The combination of the rise in sterling and the wage explosion in the early days of the Thatcher Government resulted in an exceptionally steep deterioration in British competitiveness. The real exchange rate – the exchange rate adjusted for cost changes – rose to a peak of 40 to 50 per cent (above 1975) in the winter of 1980-81. It fell back after the sterling slides of 1981 and 1982-83, but the legacy of the earlier wage explosion looked like affecting British competitiveness for a long time.

The steep rise in the real exchange rate brought down inflation more quickly than most observers expected and put great pressure on the profit margins of all producers exposed to international competition. It thus contributed to the doubling of adult unemployment (which had already doubled once before under Labour) to 3 million or 12 per cent of the employed labour force.

The profit and employment squeeze had a silver lining in that it brought about improvements in manning levels and a reduction in restrictive practices, something that employers had vainly striven for decades to achieve. The government received both blame for the rise in unemployment and occasional praise for its courageous strategy. Both were exaggerated. No government would have dared to embark on

Chart 13: Sterling

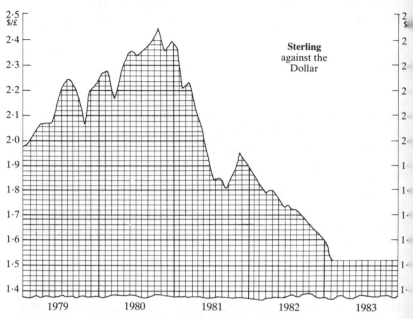

Sterling
against the
Dollar

1979   1980   1981   1982   1983

a deliberate policy of squeezing out surplus labour, which was an event neither planned nor foreseen.

In fact the role of policy was largely negative. The Thatcher Government in the crucial period of 1979-80 feared the effects on the money supply either of intervening in the foreign exchange market to hold sterling down or of reducing interest rates enough to have the same effect. Even if either move had been tried, it might well have been found difficult to execute in 1979-80, when sterling was still the international portfolio managers' favourite currency.*

As time went on, the original target measure, Sterling M3, gradually ceased to be the main guide to policy, long before its

* There would be pretty general agreement that the contractionary and disinflationary pressures on the British economy in 1979-81 were transmitted via the exchange rate. There is less agreement on why sterling rose so far. The direct trade effects of the displacement of normal exports by North Sea oil did not account for more than a fraction of the sterling rise, even on the calculations of those who stressed the oil factor. The hypothesis followed here is that British possession of North Sea oil was one of a number of factors which increased the portfolio attractions of sterling for overseas holders. This implies that the main change was in the *demand* for money, domestic and international. Those technical monetarists who stress the *supply* of money would point to the dip in the narrow monetary aggregate M1 shown in Table 11. But a more extensive glance at the table will show what a broken reed M1 is, taken on its own, as a guide. The inflationary explosion of 1974-75 was preceded by a very rapid *fall* in the growth of M1 in 1972-74. The drop in inflation from 24 per cent to 8 per cent in 1975-78 during the Healey period is utterly incomprehensible if one follows M1.

Chart 13: Sterling (*continued*)

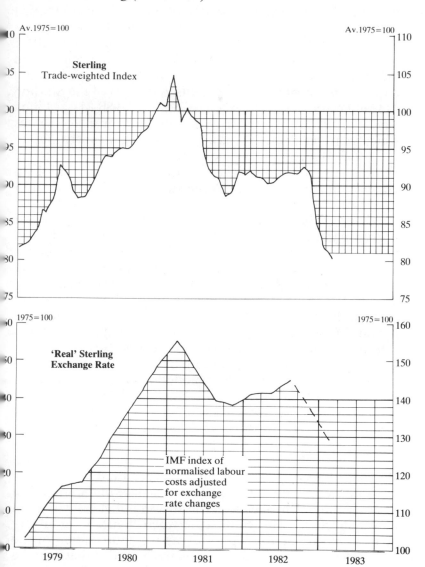

official dethronement. As early as the second half of 1980, a number of interest rate reductions were made, even though monetary growth, after all corrections and allowances, was well above target. These reductions were partly a result of pressure from industry, but even more were they due to the fact that the economy was showing all the signs, good and bad, of tight money; and this aroused distrust of the Sterling M3 indicator. Around the winter of 1980-81 a lobby developed in Downing Street for the narrower aggregates which were, as Table 11 shows, growing very slowly; and in the 1982 Budget, three monetary targets were installed without any indication of their relative weight, or the role to be given either to them or to the state of sterling in interest rate decisions.

While these changes were occurring, public sector borrowing was coming under better control and indeed undershot the target for 1981-82. The chancellor's emphasis naturally shifted from the obscurity of the monetary aggregates to the objective which was being achieved. Thus, by 1982, British financial policy could not be regarded as 'monetarist' in any technical sense; it was a combination of a medium term fiscal strategy with some attempt to prevent sterling from falling too quickly. There was also a hope – not much more than that – that the pursuit of these aims would prevent the movement of *three* monetary aggregates (in place of Sterling M3 alone) from straying too far outside the projected band which was itself raised by 3 per cent above that originally planned for the 1982-83 financial year.

The political dimension

Would a Labour Government have persisted with even a moderately tight monetary policy in the face of the sharp rise in the sterling exchange rate? The answer is that it did so when it was in office. The conflict between domestic monetary control and trying to stop an excessive appreciation of the currency first emerged in 1977, and by the end of that year the Labour Government 'unplugged' sterling and allowed it to rise in the market. Sterling fell back in 1978, but by the first few months of 1979 it was rising merrily again, well before the government changed or anyone even knew that there was going to be an election on 3 May (which resulted from an unexpected parliamentary defeat on devolution).

Behind the facts and figures, there was, of course, a contrast between the Callaghan and the Thatcher philosophies. The outgoing Labour Government adopted 'sound finance' reluctantly, because it could not see any other option, while the Thatcherite element in the Conservative Government did so out of conviction, amounting in the Prime Minister's personal case to moral certainty. A Labour Government would have been subject to some, if not all the pressures which pushed the party leftwards in Opposition; and at some stage it almost certainly would have loosened the financial reins.

Even if a Labour Government had managed to continue the Callaghan-Healey strategy, it would certainly have become much more agitated about unemployment than its Conservative successors and would have intervened much more at a micro-level to keep down the jobless figures. The palliatives would have been a mixture of good and bad. More imagination would have been shown in marginal labour subsidies to try to price particular groups into work and to forestall redundancies. On the other hand, the contraction of manpower in certain industries, needed for long-term structural reasons, might have been delayed further, thus aggravating the underlying problems.

Nevertheless, if one looks at broad strategy and at actions and statistics rather than political rhetoric, it is clear that the fundamental change in policy took place not after the election but in 1976, less than half way through the term of the Labour Government. For it was then that traditional demand-boosting full employment policies were abandoned. Unemployment rose remorsely from 600,000 or 2½ per cent of the employed labour force in 1974, when the Labour government took office, to reach 1·3 million in 1977 and 1978 (excluding school-leavers) − a sensational and shocking increase by postwar standards. Yet fiscal and monetary policy was actually tightened in the face of these events, as fiscal policy was to be again during the subsequent unemployment rises under the Conservatives.

The main mistakes

The particular severity of the British unemployment problem

was due to a combination of severe structural change and an ossified labour market. The British economy has had to adjust to (a) sharp fluctuations in energy prices which have made many processes and products obsolescent; (b) the drift in the most efficient location of many traditional manufacturing industries towards the newly industrialising countries; (c) the rapid reduction in inflation; (d) the effects of North Sea oil in crowding-out non-oil exports; and (e) the long delayed attack on overmanning. The first three were common to other industrial countries in varying degrees, the last two unique to Britain. They combined to produce very heavy manpower losses in manufacturing industry.

These forces would have been at work whoever had been in power, but it is possible to find some specific Thatcher mistakes, within the broad framework of the post-1976 policies, which unnecessarily aggravated the recession:

1   The decision to give priority in the first budget to a reduction from 33 to 30 per cent in the basic rate of income tax. Without it, VAT would have had to rise to only 11 per cent instead of 15 per cent. The steep rise in VAT contributed to the severity of the 1979-80 wage explosion.

2   The failure to realise that the deteriorating world economic situation (which most British political leaders were too insular to take on board in the opening months of 1979) would have been ample justification for trimming the election commitment to Clegg and taking a much tougher line on public pay settlements from the beginning.

3   The obsession with the Sterling M3 monetary aggregate. A more critical approach to it within the context of a counter-inflationary policy might have avoided the rise from 14 to 17 per cent in Minimum Lending Rate in November 1979. (The rate remained at 16 or 17 per cent until twelve months later.)

4   An insular approach to money. The Bank of England should have been allowed to do more *as a profit-maximising speculator* to cut off the extreme peak in sterling in the winter of 1980-81. A recognition that the international as well as the domestic demand for a currency needs to be taken into account in setting monetary targets (the case for which is outlined in Chapters 7 and 9) would

have enabled the monetary consequences of such intervention to be borne with a better conscience.*

In contrast to other commentators, I would not put the 1981 fiscal judgment among the main errors. Indeed, as experience of other countries shows, fiscal laxity has proved the wrong way to adjust for recession in the early 1980s, and some commitment to the PSBR goals was a necessary condition for the monetary relaxation belatedly made.

Nor would I give much weight to the Thatcher Government's lack of interest in 'pay policies'. Quite apart from the general merits and demerits of such policies, they would not have been feasible in the crucial 1979-80 period. Because of 'Clegg' a new pay policy initiative could not have been taken until 1980; and its main effects would, if even temporarily successful, not have been seen until 1981. By then the earnings increase had already halved under market pressures.

How much difference did these mistakes or new elements make to the rising unemployment trend? A number of different studies from radically different intellectual standpoints have reached a remarkably similar estimate that without them adult unemployment in 1982 might have been 2½ million rather than three million. These studies are empirical, based on comparison with other countries or projections made before the change of government, and are thus compatible with very different views on how the increase might have been avoided.[1]

The effect on unemployment was far too high for the Thatcher government to deserve an easy conscience; on the other hand it also suggests, in conformity with common sense, that the greater part of the rise in unemployment has had comparatively little to do with government actions, good or bad. Britain's unemployment, over and above the general stagflation of the west, was due to a more deep-seated industrial malaise. The exchange rate squeeze merely precipitated a shakeout which would in any case have

---

* For the record: the first two criticisms are not hindsight and were made by me in the *Financial Times* at the time. The third and fourth criticisms were unfortunately not. Even in retrospect I think that lower interest rates and exchange rate intervention would have had to be accompanied by a much greater commitment to a medium-term financial strategy and a much greater willingness to adopt a profit-maximising attitude to foreign exchange operations than was evident at any time in the Bank of England. Otherwise short-term tactical adjustments could have looked like – and might well have turned into – wholesale retreat on the financial front.

happened over a somewhat longer period. Organised workers – and in many cases managers as well – too long refused to adapt to a world in which many of their existing products and processes were obsolete or could be undertaken far more cheaply in the new industrialised countries. Nor were they willing to accept the level of real earnings that would have priced them into work in their existing occupations.*

The medium term strategy

The one important innovation of the Conservative Government was its Medium Term Financial Strategy (MTFS) inaugurated in 1980, which gave monetary and fiscal projections for three or four years ahead. There was a precedent even for this in the two-to-three-year programme presented by Mr Healey to the IMF; but the Thatcher Government did take it further. The MTFS was disliked by the left and by establishment economists because of its financial emphasis and by many Conservatives (including some Thatcherite ministers) because of its element of planning and forward projection. Nevertheless, it was the only innovation for which the Thatcher government stood a chance of being remembered in the macroeconomic field.

It is hardly surprising that mistakes were initially made in a pioneering venture. The MTFS did not succeed in its key task of discouraging unions and employers from pricing workers out of jobs until it was already too late, with unemployment approaching 3 million. Indeed, the MTFS was not published until the government's second budget in 1980, by which time a round of pay rises averaging over 20 per cent had already been negotiated and much of the damage had been done.

One mistake was to state the MTFS originally in terms of one particular definition of money, namely Sterling M3 – roughly notes and coin plus deposits. When Sterling M3 exploded in the summer of 1980 (rising at an annualised rate of over 20 per cent, compared to the target of 7 to 11 per cent), a body-blow was dealt to the strategy's credibility – even though many of those who sneered the most inconsistently blamed excessively 'tight' government policy for the rise in unemployment.

---

* More than one wit has remarked that Britain had always had many millions of unemployed; the difference was that previously they were unemployed 'on the job'.

Table 12: UK medium-term financial strategy

Year	Money GDP Projection (1)	Money GDP Outturn (2)	Inflation^ø Actual (3)	Real GDP Actual (4)	Money Supply Target* (5)	£M3 Outturn (6)	M1 Outturn (7)
1980	11	14	18	−3½	7-11	20	9
1981	10	9	11	−2	6-10	14½	8½
1982	10	8	7	1	8-12 (5-9)	10	11
1983	9½				7-11 (4-8)		
1984	9½				6-10		
1985	9				5-9		

N.B. The projections for Money GDP for 1980 and 1981 are based on the current Treasury estimates of velocity trends. The projections for 1982 onwards are based on the 1982 MTFS, not the 1983 one for reasons given in the text.

Columns 1, 2, 3 and 4 represent financial years. Columns 5, 6 and 7 represent target years, usually from February to February. GDP figures refer to Gross Domestic Product at market prices ('average' estimate).

^{ø}Measured by 'Market price GDP deflator'.

*For 1980 and 1981 the target was expressed in terms of £M3; for 1982 and subsequent years it was in terms of three aggregates, £M3, M1 and 'PSL2' (not shown). The figures in brackets represent the original 1980 targets, raised in the 1982 Budget.

As repeatedly argued in Part II, the correct way to restate the strategy was not to search for other intermediate monetary objectives alternative or additional to Sterling M3. Instead it should have been restated in terms of Money GDP which was logically its final objective.

Indeed it was possible to translate the original MTFS targets into Money GDP by means of the Treasury's stated assumption of a 1 to 2 per cent trend annual rise in velocity, and this has been done in the accompanying table. In the 1982 Financial Statement figures were at last provided of the growth of Money GDP; but as projections not objectives. Looking at the figures in the table, there can be some argument about whether the speed of decline in GDP growth between 1980 and 1981 was excessive, starting from a year of combined inflation and recession. But once inflation had begun to come down into single figures a growth rate of 10 per cent left reasonable room for a recovery of output, provided that inflation stayed low.

Unfortunately, when Money GDP began to slip below projections in 1982, the Chancellor, Sir Geoffrey Howe, did not accept the need for a correction and went out of his way to disown any Money GDP objective. The Money GDP projections were accordingly revised downwards in the 1983 Budget. Under the influence of falling oil prices and election fears, the exchange market produced its own partial corrective in the shape of the depreciation which the British government insisted could do no good and the Money GDP figures in the table are based on the original 1982 estimate. But the lack of any coherent official attitude to the exchange rate, and the risk that euphoria following a Conservative victory would drive sterling up again, reduced the potential benefit to exports and import-substitutes.

Ideology and policy

Demand management under both the Callaghan and Thatcher governments – for all the mistakes and missed opportunities – had in common a modesty of aim. The modesty followed from what I called earlier the post-Keynesian counter-revolution – accepted openly by the Conservative leadership and tacitly by Labour in 1976-79. In essence this denies the ability of the postwar type of demand management to achieve chosen levels of full employment. If it is true, it is equally true for a socialist fundamentalist, a social democrat, a liberal Republican and a *laissez-faire* enthusiast. If untrue, it is untrue for all. The same applies to the relationship between the quantity of spending power and the price level.

Moreover, contrary to what is often supposed, there is nothing inherently 'right wing' or conservative even in the *policies* advocated by 'monetarists', whether stated 'narrowly' or in terms of the broader counter-revolution. If policies for stable prices involve an attack on budget deficits (a connection, incidentally, strenuously denied by Friedman), they can be achieved by raising taxes as well as cutting government spending (indeed they were partly so achieved under Mrs Thatcher in 1981). 'Monetarism' as such has nothing to say about the level of public spending as distinct from how it should be financed.*

In Britain the pioneering moves towards a more 'monetarist' orientation had been undertaken, even before Denis Healey, by Roy Jenkins, who looked after Britain's finances in the Labour Administration of the late 1960s. Further east, the 'hard money' (if not always sound money) attitude of communist governments is proverbial, while true Marxists have always been scornful of the long-term effectiveness of budget deficits and cheap money to overcome capitalist unemployment.

The ideological element has entered in response to the policy vacuum created by the collapse of postwar full employment policies. If unemployment and other malfunctioning are to be tackled, structural and even constitutional reforms are required. The nature of these reforms is highly divisive politically, in a way that postwar 'demand management' never was.

Many Keynesian economists, for instance, reacted to the failure of their earlier medicine by adding more and more

---

* To demonstrate how such issues cut across normal political allegiances, it is worth pointing out that the main pioneer among Chicago economists in the 1930s of the constant money supply growth rule was Paul Douglas, a Democrat who accepted nearly all the left-wing platform of his time – such as a 'planned economy', public housing and the encouragement of unions. Douglas became a hero, a US Senator, and a hawk on Cold War issues; but he never abandoned his advocacy of interventionist and egalitarian domestic policies. He also continued to champion the monetarist rule, and was a moving force behind the Treasury/Federal Reserve Accord of 1951 which abandoned the pegging of interest rates and opened the way to Fed regulation of the money supply.

ingredients – such as detailed (and not merely broad-brush) wage and price controls, import controls, and state intervention in industry – which injected a note of hostility to market forces wholly at variance with the original Keynesian approach. There is no guarantee or even suggestive evidence that the interventionist reaction to the failure of mainstream Keynesianism will provide an escape from stagflation – at least, not without thoroughgoing state direction of what people buy, where they work and how much they are paid.

'Monetarists', by contrast, have tended to fill the vacuum in employment policy by a critique of union privileges and state intervention, which is no part of 'monetarism', however defined, but is based on a desire to unshackle market forces rather than fetter them further. Behind the smokescreen of the 'monetarist' controversy, therefore, lies a much more serious argument between rival views of human society (neither wholly pleasant) which was papered over by several decades of good fortune and money illusion.

Supply-side Thatcherism

It was not until 1982 or 1983 that the Thatcher Government really began to think of what it wanted to do on the 'supply side' of the British economy. At the time of writing, the proposals are still too much at the drawing board stage for any attempt at full description.

In the early years of the government its most important structural innovations were financial. The first was the long-overdue spread of indexed or inflation-proofed securities of all shapes and sizes, originally and mainly for government debt but spreading slowly into other spheres. Properly used, indexation can actually ease the path to lower inflation.[2]

The second and more important financial reform was the abolition of exchange control in 1979. It will take many years for the full effects to be felt. Although initially the main beneficiaries were the 'fat cats', the ultimate effect must be to bring the return on investment in the UK into line with other countries and prevent the UK from being an island of low returns. So far from reducing manufacturing investment, as was alleged, the natural effect of capital outflows was to reduce the real exchange rate and generate a current surplus to finance the outflow, a development favourable to manufacturing output and profitability.

On the other hand the Conservatives were pledged on Mrs Thatcher's word to retain the worst capital market distortions, the tax concessions for home purchase, and were unlikely to remove those for company pension funds. The result was to canalise the investment of personal savings into financial institutions that cannot be expected to make more than token investments in small local companies, and also to create an investment distortion in favour of bricks and mortar. These effects were aggravated by the loss of pension rights which people experience when changing jobs, which no one found a way of rectifying. The continuation of tax concessions on home mortgage payments made it politically more difficult to remove distortions from the rented sector.

Council houses were still heavily subsidised relative to market rents; and controls and threats of controls had long ago killed off any private enterprise investment in houses to let. The sale of council houses improved labour mobility only by transforming tenants into owners and depleting the supply of rented accommodation.

In its industrial and social policies, the government took far longer to generate its supply-side response. Acts were passed to make closed shops less easy to achieve and to restrict secondary picketing; but few litigants took advantage of the new laws, and the weakening of union power was mainly attributable to unemployment. Of far more fundamental impact was the government's onslaught on the nationalised industries. Some such as Britoil and British Telecom were due to be sold; others were subject to more competition or (like hospital laundry services) ordered to make more use of private contractors. But the impact of the campaign was limited (a) by the predominance of the desire to realise for cash, irrespective of whether monopoly was being broken up or not, and (b) by the lack of interest in extending ownership of 'privatised' industry to the non-share-owning classes.

More effective than privatisation in dealing with union monopoly would be a decentralisation of pay negotiations in the public services – the Health Service, local authorities, the Civil Service and so on – so that more account can be taken of local and occupational labour markets. A move away from centralised bargaining between monopoly employers and monopoly unions may do more to make labour markets responsive to supply and demand than the more ambitious plans for new-style incomes policies to ape the behaviour of competitive markets. But though such moves ought to be common ground between Thatcherites and social market Alliance supporters, progress here was at a snail's pace.

'The resolute approach'

The decisive turn-round in the Thatcher government's popularity in the country came as a result of its pursuit of the Falklands War in April to June 1982, in which a thousand people were killed and several times that many injured.

It cannot be entirely a coincidence that there was a concurrent coarsening of government economic policy, as has been remarked in relation to the lack of development of the Financial Strategy in the face of the unexpected further phase of recession in 1982. In the course of that year the strategy degenerated into a pursuit of a declining PSBR for its own sake and an ideological opposition to devaluation going way beyond anything justified by theory or experience and eventually flying in the face of what the foreign exchange market was in fact doing.

In the social field, as some documents leaked in February 1983 showed, a healthy desire to free the individual citizen from the power of professionals such as doctors, teachers, and social workers became mixed up with a desire to tell citizens how to use their independence. Peculiar features are bound to arise when the traditional party of authority tries to become the spokesman for individual freedom. It is all part of the tragic division between political and social liberalism, which has moved left of centre, and economic liberalism, which has moved to the right.

Social market policies

Moves towards a more competitive and decentralised economy *need* not, however, depend on the Conservatives retaining power in every election. Indeed there are some obstacles to the functioning of markets and some kinds of decentralisation where Social Democrats and Liberals might be more inclined to be reformers. Their ideas will be important, whether they have direct political leverage or whether, because of the distortions of the electoral system, they serve for a time mainly as a source of ideas for the general political debate.

It is a weakness of 'New Right' literature in Britain that it has been so preoccupied with frontier raids on state provision of social services that it has not paid sufficient attention to the growing threat to market principles in their former heartlands in industry and commerce. A government led by Mrs Thatcher was every bit as anxious as Wilsonian and Heathite Administrations to set European steel production quotas or to limit imports from the Third World to whose welfare such lip service is paid.

The excessive influence of producer groups in extracting subsidies and (more sinister because more indirect) support of other kinds reduces the state's ability to make an effective response to the problems of poverty. It is possible to be in favour of redistribution without either being an egalitarian or believing that there is such a thing as a 'just reward' for particular occupations which a body of wise men can ascertain.

The biggest obstacle to an effective social market economy is the epidemic of recessions, slow growth and rising unemployment from which the world has suffered since 1973. This gives the protectionists and special interest groups their chance. The problems of the industrial world have not been brought about by unions; but the existence of union and other institutional obstacles to the market pricing of labour has made adjustment to a harder world environment a thousand times more difficult.

A return to reasonably full employment will require a large rise in the very depressed return on capital and in the share of profits in the national income. It will require a fall – or much slower increase – in real pre-tax earnings per hour of effort. The shift is required not merely to provide the wherewithal for, and a return to, investment. More important, but hardly recognised in the public debate, it is required to ensure that investment is sufficiently labour-using, so that we do not have the employment-less prosperity which is the most that businessmen now seem to expect.

The art of policy will be to allow and encourage the shift to profits to take place, while minimising the adverse effects on the distribution of wealth and income. Labour is instinctively hostile to the shift from wages to profits, and the Conservatives are not sensitive to the adverse social and distributional implications of such a shift if it is left entirely unguided. The vacuum provides Social Democrats with a golden opportunity to step in, which they show little sign of taking.

The first way of reconciling a shift from wages to profits with protection of the least well off is through the fiscal system – child allowances, the raising of tax thresholds, income supplements to those with low pay at work, eventually building up to a negative income tax. These fiscal shifts cannot be financed entirely from taxation of the higher dividends which will accompany any return to full employment. Most middle-ranking taxpayers will have to pay more in taxes if they are sincere in their compassionate utterances.

Secondly, and ultimately more important, there will need to be a big shift in the ownership of productive property. The mistake of socialists and collectivists is that they attack the existence or size of profits rather than the ownership of profitable assets. If most wage earners were also capitalists, the social arguments against a shift to profits would disappear. This is partly happening through the pension funds, but adding further power to these funds has well-known drawbacks. A reform of Capital Transfer Tax to make it into an inheritance or accession tax, levied on the *recipient*, would be an encouragement to the dispersion of hereditary property.

But more direct measures to give ordinary citizens a stake in the ownership of productive assets are also required. Workers' co-ops have certainly a role here, but I can see no case for making these the sole form of business enterprise and I can see disadvantages in workers having all their eggs – their equity property as well as their wage – in one basket. A good deal could be done by the 'giving away' (at a sacrifice in Treasury revenue) of state-owned industries on the lines of a scheme by Barry Riley and myself for 'A People's Stake in North Sea Oil' in which state revenue would be paid out directly to citizens, whose entitlements could be sold on the market.[3] Going beyond that there is a case for public unit trusts, whose shares would be distributed to all citizens, to whom a growing proportion of the equity of each major company would be transferred.

Support for a social market economy is not the same as support for conventional capitalism. It is compatible with the welfare state, both in the sense of cash transfers to the poor and the non-monopolistic collective provision of services such as education and health. It is also compatible with quite sweeping changes in the distribution of property ownership.

The wrong way to emphasise the 'social' part of 'social market economy' is to water down the emphasis on the market. On the contrary a radical policy ought to attack all the market distortions such as agricultural protection, and tax concessions for pension funds and owner occupiers, to which conservative interests are strongly attached (and alas not only conservative ones).

The right way to emphasise the 'social' part is to insist on a more widely dispersed ownership of property so that the benefits of 'unearned income' and the degree of personal independence which it makes possible become widely available, instead of being confined to the few. So far from these matters being a digression from 'economic management' they provide the groundwork and framework required for such management to have any chance.

Political improvement

The Economic Consequences of Democracy, the predecessor to the present volume, published in 1977, concluded with a plea for a 'new constitutional settlement'. The United Kingdom has long suffered from a winner-takes-all two-party system. Under it people have had no alternative but to vote for almost any Labour or Conservative leadership, irrespective of qualities or programme, if they have been sufficiently frustrated to want to dismiss the existing government – which they very often have been. This gives party activists and interest groups a disproportionate influence, relative to normal voters, because their leaders can afford to indulge them.

The significance of the Alliance is that it has a chance of ending this state of affairs and the series of contrived revolutions and counter-revolutions which make long-term

business planning so frustrating. Alliance economic policy
has been characterised as 'Forward to the 1960s' and there is
indeed too great a preoccupation with 'incomes policy',
'industrial strategy' and 'reflation'. But far more important is
the fact that whatever its parliamentary strength at any one
particular time, the new group, by providing an alternative
opposition, makes far less likely the arrival of a Labour
Government completely opposed to – or having to make a
show of being opposed to – the profit motive and the market
system. The Labour Party itself will no longer be able to run
on such policies just to please its activists and count on
arriving in office on the basis of disillusionment with the
Conservatives.

The need to appeal to a wider public should also have a
beneficial impact on the Conservatives. Indeed, one reason
why Thatcherite policies ran into such heavy political weather
is that they were the result of a takeover of the Conservative
leadership to which the old guard were quite unreconciled.
Ministers were unable to reach out to a broader political
spectrum. Arguments about policies were bogged down in
theological disputes about the nature of Conservatism, just as
arguments about nationalisation or nuclear arms were once
conducted in terms of 'the meaning of socialism'.

Thus there is a chance of seeing, not necessarily
immediately but after one or two more elections, an end of
the notorious policy switches between and within every
Parliament which makes the British political environment so
much a curse to the business community. Changes may be
slower but will in the end have broader support, and be less
likely to be reversed, than under our present system of
elective dictatorship.

A conclusion in terms of political and constitutional reform
may disappoint any readers who expect something like a
twelve-point programme for economic resurgence. After
several decades of intensive and almost obsessive
concentration by British public figures (and their advisers and
critics) on the problems of economic management, it would
be astonishing if there were a brand new programme waiting
in the wings which all political leaders had rejected out of
stupidity or wickedness. The message of the preceding
chapters surely is that the entrenched position of industrial,

economic and political interest groups will limit what can be achieved by any form of economic management, new or old.

In Part I of this book I queried the legitimacy of the interest-group interpretation of democracy, and in the remaining parts I have tried to show its results in practice. If the role of interest groups is to be lessened and that of the individual citizen to be increased, the main hope lies in constitutional and political reform. The most important aspect of such reform may not be Acts of Parliament, or new-found procedures, but the evolution of attitudes, assumptions and unwritten rules which govern the affairs of nations no less than those of the individual human beings of which nations are composed.

References

Preface

1 See my contribution to *The Political Economy of Inflation* (ed. Hirsch and Goldthorpe), Martin Robertson and Harvard University Press, 1978.

1 The Wenceslas Myth

1 Michael Oakeshott, *On Human Conduct*, Oxford University Press, 1975.

2 Lester Thurow, *The Zero Sum Society*, Basic Books, New York, 1980.

2 Two Cheers for Utilitarianism

1 1st edition published 1789, revised edition, 1822. Quotation from Chapter 1, paragraphs 2-4. (Blackwell Edition, edited W. Harrison, 1948, p.126)

2 *Dei Delitti e delle Penne*, quoted by Anthony Quinton in: *Utilitarian Ethics*, Macmillan, 1973.

3 *Economic Nationalism in Old and New States*, Allen & Unwin, 1968.

4 This decomposition is based on the introductory chapter of Amartya Sen, *Choice, Welfare and Measurement*, Oxford University Press, 1982. See also the introduction by Sen and Bernard Williams to *Utilitarianism and Beyond* (ed. Sen and Williams), Cambridge University Press, 1982.

5 *Moral Thinking*, R.M. Hare, Clarendon Press, 1981.

6 'Morality and Foreign Policy', reprinted as Chapter 11 of *Capitalism and the Permissive Society*, Macmillan 1973.

7 For a fuller discussion see *Capitalism and the Permissive Society*, Chapter 2.

8 Armen Alchian, 'The Meaning of Utility Measurement', in *Price Theory* (ed. Harry E. Townsend), Penguin, 1971.

9 In *Utilitarianism and Beyond* (cited above).

10 Some of the key papers are to be found in *Choice, Welfare and Measurement*.

11 John Harsanyi in *Utilitarianism and Beyond*.

12 Sen and Williams in *Utilitarianism and Beyond*.

13 John Elster in *Utilitarianism and Beyond*.

14 T. Scanlon in *Utilitarianism and Beyond*.

15 *Anarchy, State and Utopia*, Blackwell, 1979.

16 See chapters by T. Scanlon and J. Nagel in *Reading Nozick* (ed. Jeffrey Paul), Blackwell, 1981. There is a short discussion in Chapter 7 of Brittan and Lilley, *The Delusion of Incomes Policy*, Temple Smith, 1977.

17 *A Theory of Justice*, Oxford University Press, 1972; Harvard University Press, 1971.

18 In *Utilitarianism and Beyond*.

19 'Two Concepts of Liberty'. reprinted in *Four Essays on Liberty*, Oxford University Press, 1969.

3   Hayek, Freedom and Interest Groups

1 Macmillan, 1973.

2 Routledge, 1960.

3 Routledge, 1973-79.

4 Routledge, 1948.

5 David Friedman, *The Machinery of Freedom*, 1973.

6 Reprinted in F.A. Hayek, *Studies in Philosophy, Politics*

and Economics, Routledge, 1967.

7   Lord Hailsham, *The Dilemma of Democracy* 1978.

8   For a much fuller discussion see *Capitalism and the Permissive Society*, pp. 90 *et seq.*

9   Irving Kristol and Daniel Bell (eds.), *Capitalism Today*, Mentor, 1971.

10   *The Economic Prerequisite to Democracy*, Blackwell, Oxford, 1981.

11   A.B. Atkinson, *Journal of Economic Theory*, No. 2, 1970.

12   *The Denationalisation of Money*, Institute of Economic Affairs, 1979.

13   Michael Oakeshott, *On Human Conduct*.

4   The Argument Summarised

1   For an account of postwar demand management in the UK see S. Brittan, *Steering the Economy*, Penguin, 1971.

2   The origin in my mind of the term 'counter-revolution' is Milton Friedman's Wincott Memorial Lecture, *The Counter-Revolution in Monetary Theory*, Occasional Paper 33, Institute of Economic Affairs, 1970, and Harry Johnson's riposte, 'The Keynesian Revolution and the Monetarist Counter-Revolution', reprinted in *On Economics and Society*, University of Chicago Press, 1975.

3   Nigel Lawson, *The New Conservatism*, Centre for Policy Studies, 1980.

4   This four-point summary is derived from a review of my work by David Hale, 'Reaganism Before and After', *Policy Review*, Fall 1982.

5   For a fuller, but simple, explanation see Rod Cross, *Economic Theory and Policy in the UK*, Martin Robertson, 1982.

5 Jobs, Output and Prices

1 'The Relationship between Unemployment and the Rate of Change of Money Wages in the UK, 1861-1957', *Economica*, 1958, pp.783-91; reprinted in R.J. Ball and P. Doyle (eds.), *Inflation*, Penguin, 1969.

2 An early still relevant explanation of these effects is to be found in Milton Friedman, *Essays in Positive Economy*, Chicago University Press, 1953, Chapter 4.

3 A. Okun, *Prices and Employment*, Blackwell, 1981.

4 The quotation from Thomas Sargent is taken from a transcribed discussion in *Manhattan Report*, New York, 1982. For fuller accounts see *Rational Expectations and Econometric Practice* (ed. R. Lucas and T. Sargent), London, Allen and Unwin, 1981 and R. Lucas, *Studies in Business Cycle Theory*, Blackwell, 1981.

5 For a good account of the credibility hypothesis see William Fellner, *Towards a Reconstruction of Macroeconomics*, American Enterprise Institute, Washington DC, 1976.

6 The Case for Money GDP

1 Henry Wallich, *Changes in Monetary Policy*, Speech to City Institute, Washington DC, 21 January 1983.

2 Examples include Fellner, Meade, Tobin and the US Council of Economic Advisers under Martin Feldstein.

3 *How to End the Monetarist Controversy*, London, Institute of Economic Affairs, Second Edition, 1982.

4 *Economic Report of the President*, US Government Printing Office, Washington DC, 1983.

5 See for instance M. Beenstock and T.A. Longbottom, 'Money, Debt and Prices in the UK', *Economica*, 49, London, November 1982.

6 James Meade (with David Vines) *Stagflation*, Volumes 1 and 2, Allen and Unwin, 1981 and 1983.

7 Organisation for Economic Co-Operation and

Development (OECD), *Towards Full Employment and Price Stability* (McCracken Report), HMSO, 1977.

7   Money in Longer Perspective

1   *Monetary Trends in the US and the UK*, M. Friedman and A.J. Schwartz, Chicago University Press, 1982, 68-72.

2   F.A. Hayek, *Denationalisation of Money*, 2nd Edition, London, Institute of Economic Affairs, 1978.

3   R. McKinnon, 'Exchange Rate and Macroeconomic Policy', *Journal of Economic Literature*, Vol XIX, June 1981.

4   Morgan Guaranty, *World Financial Markets*, December 1980. David Lomax, *National Westminster Bank International Supplement*, 9 June 1980.

5   R. Cameron, *Banking in the Early Stages of Industrialisation*, Oxford University Press, 1967.

8   Unemployment and Pay

1   *Capitalism and the Permissive Society*, Chapter 3.

2   'Youth Unemployment', *OECD Observer*, HMSO, March 1981.

3   *The Battle for Jobs*, Trades Union Congress, London, 1983.

4   A good, relatively unmathematical summary of 'disequilibrium' and other relevant theories is to be found in Rod Cross, *Economic Theories and Policy in the UK*, Martin Robertson, 1982.

5   P.J. Forsyth and J.A. Kay, 'The Economic Implications of North Sea Oil', *Fiscal Studies*, July 1980.

6   Commission of the European Communities, *Annual Economic Review*, 1982-83, Brussels, 1982, Chapter 7.

7   R. Layard *et al.*, *Wages, Unemployment and Incomes Policy*, Working Paper No. 479, Centre for Labour Economics, London School of Economics, 1982.

8   R. Layard, *More Jobs, Less Inflation*, Grant McIntyre, 1982.

9   R. Layard, *More Jobs, Less Inflation*.

10   *Unemployment Causes and Cure*, Patrick Minford and Associates, Martin Robertson, 1983.

11   For an account of such schemes see the *Report from the Select Committee of the House of Lords on Unemployment*, HL 142, London, HMSO, 1982.

12   S. Brittan and P. Lilley, *The Delusion of Incomes Policy*, Temple Smith, 1977. This is updated in my chapter in R.E. J. Chater, A. Dean, R.F. Elliott (eds.), *Incomes Policies*, Oxford University Press, 1981.

13   Mancur Olson, *The Rise and Decline of Nations*, Yale University Press, 1982.

9   Economic Stresses in the West

1   Cited in the *Memoirs of Lord Chandos*, Bodley Head, 1962.

2   Published in *International Financial Markets*, Morgan Guaranty, New York, monthly.

3   *International Trade, 1981-1982*, GATT, Geneva, 1982.

4   Irving Fisher, *100 per cent Money*, New Haven-City Printing Co., 1945.

5   F.A. Hayek, *1980s Unemployment and the Unions*, Institute of Economic Affairs, 1980.

6   As advocated by Professor Ronald McKinnon of Stanford in testimony before Congress in 1982.

7   See Herbert Giersch and Frank Waller, 'Towards an Explanation of the Productivity Slowdown in Advanced Economies' *Economic Journal*, March 1983.

8   Michael Beenstock, *The World Economy in Transition*, Allen and Unwin, 1983.

9   *The State of the World Economy*, Report by the French Institute for International Relations, Macmillan, 1981.

10   *The Rise and Decline of Nations*.

10 How British is the British Sickness?

1 Alfred Marshall, 'Memorandum on Fiscal Policy of International Trade' (1903), reprinted in *Official Papers 404-06*, 1926.

2 Angus Maddison, 'Phases of Capitalist Development', 1977, *Banca Nazionale Del Lavoro Quarterly Review*, 103.

3 Daniel T. Jones, 'Output, Employment, and Labour Productivity in Europe Since 1955', *National Institute Economic Review 72*, 1976.

4 Clifford F. Pratten, *Labour Productivity Differentials Within International Companies*, 1976.

5 For instance, National Economic Development Office, *Cyclical Fluctuations in the UK*, 1976.

6 C.J.F. Brown & T.D. Sheriff, *Deindustrialization in the UK*, National Institute of Economic and Social Research, 1978.

7 See *Royal Commission on Distribution*, Reports Nos. 3 & 5, HMSO 1976 and 1977. See also Sir Henry Phelps Brown, 'What is the British Predicament?' *Three Banks Review*, December 1977.

8 See Phelps Brown, 'What is the British Predicament?' and 'Concentration of Industrial Stoppages in Great Britain: 1971-75,' *Department of Employment Gazette*, 9, 1978.

9 Henry C. Simons, 'Some Reflections on Syndicalism', in *Economic Policy for a Free Society*, Chicago University Press, 1948.

10 A.V. Dicey, *Law and Public Opinion in England* (new edition), Macmillan, 1963.

11 This proposition is known as the Jay Hypothesis. Peter Jay, *Employment, Inflation and Politics*, Institute of Economic Affairs, 1976.

12 The impact of union power on unemployment, inflation and democratic stability is discussed further in Brittan, *The Economic Consequences of Democracy*, pp. 185-222.

13 *The Rise and Decline of Nations.*

11 Breaking the Mould

1 These are (a) C.F. Pratten, 'Mrs Thatcher's Economic Experiment', *Lloyds Bank Review*, January 1982; (b) estimates contained in an article by Dr Tony Barker of Cambridge Econometrics in the same issue; and (c) Roy Batchelor, *A Natural Interpretation of the Present Unemployment*, City University Banking Centre, 1982. The implications of these studies are discussed in S. Brittan, 'The Thatcher Effect Revealed', *Financial Times*, 14 January 1982.

2 S. Brittan and P. Lilley 'Living with Inflation', in *A Management Guide to Company Survival* (ed. C.J. Wood), Associated Business Programmes, 1976.

3 S. Brittan and B. Riley, *A People's Stake in North Sea Oil*, Liberal Publications Department, 1980.

Index